P9-EES-218

ERNEST HEMINGWAY:
THE MAN AND HIS WORK

ERNEST HEMINGWAY: THE MAN AND HIS WORK

Edited by John K. M. McCaffery

COOPER SQUARE PUBLISHERS, INC.
NEW YORK
1969

Published by Cooper Square Publishers, Inc.
59 Fourth Avenue, New York, N. Y. 10003
Library of Congress Catalog Card No. 69-17516

Printed in the United States of America

Acknowledgment

Grateful acknowledgment is made to Charles Scribner's Sons for courteous permission to publish the quotations included in the various essays in this volume. Thanks are also due the authors, agents, publishers, editors and periodicals from whom reprint permission was secured. Individual acknowledgment and copyright notice appears at the foot of the first page of each article.

CONTENTS

Introduction

The picture of Ernest Hemingway by John Groth which leads off this volume serves several good purposes: It introduces Hemingway, as a man; it places him in a familiar milieu—"War and rumors of war" is Hemingway's constant background—and Groth's notes are written with the proper measure of respect, admiration and curiosity which should govern the reaction of a young artist to an older man, to the Titan. Both Hemingway and Groth were war reporters, and although the younger man's tools were sketchbook and pencil as against typewriter and copypaper, Groth realizes that his reactions to this war were strongly conditioned by Hemingway's reports of World War I. (It is worthy of ironic note that John Groth began his career as a discovery of *Esquire Magazine* during that period when *Esquire* published so many of those Hemingway pieces which draw critical fire from the critics gathered in this volume.)

Several things about the Groth portrait, however, are worthy of further note. First, the naturalness with which Hemingway fits into the background of a battlefield—it is almost as if this battlefield, as indeed all battlefields, had been lifted whole from a Hemingway novel. It is important, too, that, although some of the GIs whom we meet in this sketch were aware of Hemingway's importance and reputation, many of them were not. Obviously, Hemingway achieved the same ease and warmth with all of them.

It is this picture of Hemingway as a man among men—warm, companionable and, with that compassion which all men who have seen war must have for those who are experiencing it for the first time—which is most consonant with my own concept of Hemingway, coming as it does from casual conversations and contacts in the publishing world, the yarns of sportswriters and the impressions of professional athletes. John Groth's account reminds me of the enthusiasm and help which Hemingway has given to young writers and how much of himself he has expended in that help and enthusiasm. It is this Hemingway which must have produced his widely publicized nickname "Papa."

Malcolm Cowley's article reprinted here from *Life* also presents to us an attractive man—a man secure in warm, long-lasting friendships, but also a man who naturally expresses friendliness and warmth to the casual acquaintances who make up his daily living.

But it is the "Papa" Hemingway which is conspicuously missing in the reports from the critics included in this volume. And this, despite the fact that Hemingway, the man, is at least as important to many of these critics as Hemingway, the writer. For, if there is one common denominator of this collection, it is the striking fact that, with only a few exceptions, the personality of the subject has made a profound impact on the critic and has, in almost every case, affected the tone of the criticism.

It is impossible for the critic to disregard Hemingway's importance. The extraordinary range and stature of the writers included in this volume attest to that. Moreover, his continued productivity belies the oft repeated dictum that American novelists lack stamina, that they burn themselves out in their youth. The attitudes expressed by the critics in this volume would indicate that Hemingway's work has never been found irrelevant to our times and that almost all of it has retained an extraordinary freshness and immediacy, a freshness and immediacy which the intervention of time and catastrophe has not dulled. A testament to the quality of importance and expectation which any of Hemingway's work has is the subterranean excitement which infected all publishing circles before the publication of his last novel. Publishers' row manifested all the anxious expectancy of a prospective father waiting outside the delivery room.

It should be noted, too, that rarely has a living writer been accorded such important criticism, over a period of years, by critics of such high competence and reputation.

If, then, Hemingway is granted importance, relevance and stamina, if he is accorded virtuosity and full stature as an artist, and if—as I have said—the personality of the man is an obtrusive factor in his career, why does this collection reflect none of the affection which marked the John Groth and Cowley portraits? After all, this volume reflects the opinions of Hemingway's intimates as well as it does those of objective reviewers.

The reader will notice that the period in Hemingway's life which marked the appearance of *To Have and Have Not*, *The Green Hills of Africa* and the *Esquire* pieces was the period marked by critical attacks of the most notable savagery. *To Have and Have Not* was the particular object of critical excoriation. Many reviewers felt that Hemingway had "lost his touch," that the brutal chaos and decayed order, the futility of his characters and the formlessness of his structure indicated a collapse as complete as that of our stock market social order in 1929. Both *Death in the Afternoon* and *The Green Hills of Africa* were regarded as an impotent retreat in the face of the problems of a new world whose limits had been defined by Marx. As one reads the passages which concern these years, we are reminded of one of Hemingway's own bulls, pierced by the bandilleras, blood streaming down its flank, sullen, at bay, but still dangerous, still capable of hooking wickedly with a polished horn-tip.

We cannot disregard the fact that these were the years of Stork Club affrays, arguments about "hair on the chest," fights with Max Eastman. Hemingway was the gossip columnist's delight. But the intense malice with which some of the critics have unconsciously exploited the acts of these years would suggest that the acts had the sensational value of Wordsworth's illegitimate child, Byron's love for his sister, and Frank Harris's imagined copulations with almost anyone. But I suspect that Hemingway's peccadillos served merely as an excuse to reflect feelings about Hemingway which, in many cases, must have smoldered beneath the surface and which could not be released by the subconscious until convention had provided a convenient excuse. Excellence always excites envy and public excellence excites gossip which is a public expression of envy.

Perhaps we must remember that this man is a magnificent artist who combines the sensitivity, perception and craftsmanship which are the concomitants of his art, with highly developed skills in such "manly" fields as hunting, fishing, boxing and sailing. (Harry Sylvester, who used to box with Hemingway frequently, once told me that Hemingway was the strongest man he had ever known.) Is it too much to suggest that some of this critical feeling may spring from the fact that most reviewers are not notable for their quickness with a double-barreled shotgun, their strength against a hooked marlin, or indeed, their skill as fighters? (I don't say this in derogation. I neither hunt nor fish myself and I haven't thrown a punch at anybody in a long time.)

But, if any criticism is to be significant, as far as Hemingway is concerned, it must concern itself with the central fact that Hemingway is first and above all an artist. William McFee once said of Joseph Conrad that, though he was perhaps not the greatest novelist, he was "incomparably the greatest artist who ever wrote a novel." The distinction which McFee rightly makes here is equally illuminating for Ernest Hemingway, because such a distinction points out the outstanding quality of an artist—that he is, by the fact of his artistry, unique.

The unique quality of the artist stems from the primary artistic function which is to *see* and it is the individuality, the originality, perhaps even the personality of his perceptions which give to Hemingway, as to every artist, his quality. But to see an object, a place, a time or a person, requires a formed image, a whole whose parts are integrated with a central concept. To see is to impart form to inchoate material. But to see thus, in a unique, formed whole, requires an extraordinary discipline on the part of the craftsman for he must rigidly exclude the didactic, the accidental and the irrelevant.

If the artist excludes the didactic, the accidental and the irrelevant as Hemingway does, the artist becomes difficult, if not impossible, to pigeonhole and to predict. Thus, James T. Farrell will criticize Hemingway for nihilism and immaturity since Hemingway in his novels does not express, didactically, a particular type of social thinking. Thus too, Leo Gurko withdraws from Hemingway because of his (Gurko's) distaste for cosmic bloodshed and violence.

To maintain the position that he must express an "accepted" attitude seems to me to be as futile as to damn Goya for not taking sides in the war which he presents with such horror, revulsion and obsessive violence in that series of sketches known as *Desastres*. It is obvious that Hemingway, in the steady progression of his work, resists pigeonholing quite as successfully as does Goya.

As far as Hemingway's predictability is concerned, few of the critics, who in these pages rip and slash at *To Have and Have Not* and the social attitudes which produced it, could conceivably have predicted *For Whom the Bell Tolls*. Yet, in retrospect, *For Whom the Bell Tolls* seems a logical and inevitable development on Hemingway's part. In retrospect too, it must seem to us that Hemingway has been more sensitive to the dynamics and tempo of our time than many novelists who wrote with less artistry but with a closer orientation to specific social and political attitudes.

There is so little favorable comment in this volume of criticism on *To Have and Have Not* that I am constrained to return to it as it illustrates succinctly, it seems to me, some of the attitudes which I have expressed in the preceding paragraph. Here is a novel widely condemned as formless, compulsive, nihilistic—the inevitable effect of an immaturity which exile had concealed. But here again, it seems to me, we have an example of Hemingway, the artist, for we realize that, in form, content and attitude, this novel is an extraordinary recreation of the chaos, brutality and fear of a society on the edge of an abyss. Somewhere in the *Summa*, Aquinas speaks of art as being "the right disposition toward a true end." "The right disposition"—the form—for 1932 was formlessness and who is to say what is the right true end?

It would be inaccurate and ungenerous, however, if these paragraphs gave the impression that the critics represented here concentrated their efforts on the negative aspects of Hemingway's writing or that this collection does not represent a wealth of information about Hemingway and many sensitive as well as robust perceptions of his quality as a writer. It is obvious that Hemingway has stimulated critical thinking of a very high order—that his work, paradoxically, has brought out the best in the critics. I suppose that if each critic represented in this book should issue a selection of his best criticism, he would inevitably choose his piece on Hemingway for inclusion.

We can account for some of this excellence by the fact that Hemingway has been and is contemporary. His novels have so crystallized the circumstances of our times that the critic is given material which enormously simplifies his own task of interpretation and analysis. It is, for instance, very helpful to comment on the Twenties if we use *The Sun Also Rises* as our point of reference and the same thing can be said for most of Hemingway's other works.

But when we say that Hemingway has stimulated the best in the critics, perhaps we have not said enough. For it should be pointed out that the nature and brilliance of most of the critical writing collected here partake of the same qualities of excitement and interest which we derive from Hemingway's work.

It seems to me that no one who reads this collection could possibly come away from it unenriched. One comes away from these writings with a better knowledge of Hemingway and a powerful stimulus to read him and to reread him in the light of these critical attitudes.

John K. M. McCaffery

THE MAN

JOHN GROTH

A Note on Ernest Hemingway

1946

The first time I saw Ernest Hemingway was in early September, 1944. The First Army had edged into Germany. I reached the Fourth Division Headquarters in late afternoon. The Public Relations Officer told me that Hemingway was staying in a farmhouse in the Siegfried Line. He would take me there if I liked. I liked it very much—a chance to see Hemingway at war.

It was night; raining. There was shelling when we arrived at the farmhouse, which was only a darker shape in the surrounding blackness. A quickly opened and shut door, and we were in what seemed for the moment a brightly lighted room, though the only light came from an oil lamp on a table at the far end of the room. Behind the lamp, Hemingway was seated: big, and centered in a group of GIs. Of course, I'd never met him before, but his appearance was as familiar to me as that of Jack Dempsey

---

From The Living Library edition of *Men Without Women* by Ernest Hemingway. Copyright 1946 by The World Publishing Company.

or Babe Ruth. He looked like I'd remembered him in pictures, and as I had imagined he would be: with grenades and cognac on the table before him.

Who I was didn't matter to him. I was somebody in combat clothes. I was welcome, as any similarly clad man would have been. He didn't note my correspondent insignia; he never noted rank. Wouldn't I join them? What was my pleasure? Cognac, kümmel, wine?

There was plenty of cognac. A demijohn three feet high bulged in the corner of the room. It had been "liberated" the day before. It was half gone already. Hemingway and his "irregulars," as the GIs and Frenchmen in GI clothes who stayed with him were called, had paid a visit to the gauleiter—grocer in nearby Bleialf. While Hemingway kept the frightened German frying eggs, Red Pelkie and Kimbrough (he indicated them as he talked) removed the ten gallon demijohn from the friendly cellar.

As Hemingway talked, I sketched him. He asked me if I wasn't the John Groth who had illustrated his stories in *Esquire* years before. He told me that he had liked the drawings: the bayonets sticking, and the hand-to-hand struggle—but that they were hardly true of war as it really has been fought since 1918. He would take me up front in the morning, and I would see war as it is.

On the situation map back at division headquarters, the farmhouse was indicated as "Task Force Hemingway." There were no American soldiers between it and the Germans, fifteen hundred yards away in their pill-boxes. Our army was short on infantry in September, 1944, and there were wide stretches between units. The left flank of one outfit ended one thousand yards to the right, and the right flank of another outfit ended one thousand yards to the left. At night, German patrols would sometimes feel their way in the valley below Schloss Hemingway. Each night, the schloss was put into a state of defense. The Germans who lived there—the farmer, his wife, and daughter—had already been locked in the cellar before I arrived. "Papa," as Hemingway was called by the "irregulars," outlined the plan of defense for that night. He would stay on guard all night. He would awaken us if a patrol came into the yard. The door was locked, and no one was to answer a knock or a summons. If an entry was attempted, Pelkie, at one upstairs window, and Jean, one of the French boys, from another window on the same level, were to lay down a cross-fire. Meanwhile, he, Kimbrough, and Marcel, the other French boy, would fire from the lower windows. All this was exciting and a little unbelievable. But Hemingway convinced me of its possible realism by dropping a couple of grenades into my lap, and thus making me a part of it. He instructed me to drop them in the road below my window should he give the alarm.

With some bewilderment, I went upstairs to bed. It was hard falling asleep in a dirty feather bed with all my clothes on. (I had been instructed to wear them in case we had to run for it.) Grenades were on the night-table next to my head, a crucifix on the wall, and the Hemingway I'd read so much about downstairs on guard with a tommy gun, and with grenades hanging from his belt. Finally, I fell asleep. I was bounced awake by heavy artillery fire from a battery on the hill behind us. In a space of quiet, I could hear the pop-corn crackle of small arms fire in the valley below us. Being absolutely sleepless now, I got up. I looked down the stairs and into the living-room. There, as he had said he would be, was Hemingway, awake, on guard, reading a pocket-size magazine, with a tommy gun on his lap. It was four a.m. Later, he told me that one patrol had been in the pasture to the left of the house.

That morning, he showed me war. We jeeped past men and machinery moving up. Not comfortably, for jeep seats are not wide, and Hemingway is. (And there were canteens of cognac on each hip.) When we reached pill-boxes that had been captured the day before, he set up his canteens on the bank of a depression behind one of the boxes, making an impromptu bar.

Infantry men stopped with him for a drink. They all knew him, but not as Ernest Hemingway the writer. They knew him as "Pop." He'd been with them in their drive across France. He'd been everywhere they had been. He didn't need any qualification.

The cognac finished, he took me to the edge of a small forest. We lay in the underbrush with an artillery observer, and looked toward inner Germany. He told me the yellow field before us would erupt in flame if anything moved there. Beyond the yellow field were enemy pill-boxes, and beyond them was the town of Brandscheid. Our artillery was shrouding Brandscheid with smoke. While we watched, a German staff car crested a hill, and disappeared in flame. The inevitable counter battery fire began, so we returned to the comparative safety of the pill-boxes. This was war—long distance, and not as I had imagined it would be. No bayonets sticking men, no charges of shouting infantry.

On the way back to the farmhouse, we stopped at a regimental command post. The colonel was briefing his officers at dinner. With more men and matériel coming up, the outlook was good. There was warm food; they had been on K rations. It was pleasant inside. Pictures—taken by Kimbrough, and showing men of the Fourth Division entering the Siegfried Line—had been brought by Hemingway, and they were being passed around when an explosion batted through the window, breaking it, and cutting loose the lamp from the ceiling. Eighty-eights were coming in. When candles were lighted, we were all—officers and correspondent—on the floor, making ourselves small, and groping for helmets. All, that is, except one: Hemingway was still seated at the table, his broad back to the window, helmetless, eating.

Schloss Hemingway was the social center in that part of the line. Generals and correspondents and many others who knew of Hemingway came to visit. Many stopped by who didn't know who he was. They liked him.

One rainy afternoon, I was sitting at an open window drawing. Two ragged, bearded GIs, wet from rain, came into the yard and began poking about, exploring, looking for a chicken, an egg—anything that might break the boring monotony of stalemated war. One of our GIs caught them up short with: "What the hell you guys doin' here?"

They came back with: "What's it to you?" And there were "sez yous" and "Oh yeahs" until our GI climaxed it with: "You can't hang around here. This is Mr. Hemingway's home."

They returned with: "Who the —— is he?" At that moment, "he," framed in the doorway, said, "Come in, fellows. Have a drink."

Nobody refuses a drink at war. They went in. I could hear the three of them as they talked of girls and guys, baseball and football, of cards and craps, boxing and wrestling, and of the things of war: the weapons, the booby traps, the way a guy feels —everything that guys at war talk about when they are together. Hemingway dropped his conjunctives, and talked better GI than they did. After an hour, he said goodbye, and went upstairs to work on a piece he was doing for a magazine. The two boys joined the GI who had first hailed them in the yard.

One of them said: "Who is this guy? He's an okay joe."

Our GI said: "Ernest Hemingway."

"Who's he?"

"He's a big shot. I don't know exactly what he does, but he's really a big shot." (Even Hemingway's jeep driver knew him as Hemingway the guy, rather than Hemingway the famous writer.)

I could hear the two GIs, as they went up the road, repeating: "Ernest Hemingway . . . Ernest Hemingway . . ." as if to remember.

An hour later, with the noise of a lynch mob, several dozen GIs and officers came into the yard. An intellectual back at the battery had recognized the name, and they had come to see him and to have their short snorters autographed. A sergeant drew a copy of *To Have and Have Not* from his musette bag. He had carried it all the way from the beachhead. He had the unique experience of having Hemingway autograph his copy in the Siegfried Line in Germany. Hemingway asked him if he'd read it. He said he would—now.

The first drawings I made for *Men Without Women* were elaborate ones. The publisher liked them, but I reread the stories and realized that while the drawings were good enough as drawings go, they were not right for Hemingway stories. A terse, emotional, shorthand kind of sketch is best.

Anyway, I feel these stories deeply, and I am privileged to have had the chance to illustrate them.

GERTRUDE STEIN

Hemingway in Paris

1933

The first thing that happened when we were back in Paris was Hemingway with a letter of introduction from Sherwood Anderson.

I remember very well the impression I had of Hemingway that first afternoon. He was an extraordinarily good-looking young man, twenty-three years old. It was not long after that that everybody was twenty-six. It became the period of being twenty-six. During the next two or three years all the young men were twenty-six years old. It was the right age apparently for that time and place. There were one or two under twenty, for example George Lynes but they did not count as Gertrude Stein carefully explained to them. If they were young men they were twenty-six. Later on, much later on they were twenty-one and twenty-two.

So Hemingway was twenty-three, rather foreign looking, with

---

passionately interested, rather than interesting eyes. He sat in front of Gertrude Stein and listened and looked.

They talked then, and more and more, a great deal together. He asked her to come and spend an evening in their apartment and look at his work. Hemingway had then and has always a very good instinct for finding apartments in strange but pleasing localities and good femmes de ménage and good food. This his first apartment was just off the place du Tertre. We spent the evening there and he and Gertrude Stein went over all the writing he had done up to that time. He had begun the novel that it was inevitable he would begin and there were the little poems afterwards printed by McAlmon in the Contact Edition. Gertrude Stein rather liked the poems, they were direct, Kiplingesque, but the novel she found wanting. There is a great deal of description in this, she said, and not particularly good description. Begin over again and concentrate, she said.

Hemingway was at this time Paris correspondent for a canadian newspaper. He was obliged there to express what he called the canadian viewpoint.

He and Gertrude Stein used to walk together and talk together a great deal. One day she said to him, look here, you say you and your wife have a little money between you. Is it enough to live on if you live quietly. Yes, he said. Well, she said, then do it. If you keep on doing newspaper work you will never see things, you will only see words and that will not do, that is of course if you intend to be a writer. Hemingway said he undoubtedly intended to be a writer. He and his wife went away on a trip and shortly after Hemingway turned up alone. He came to the house about ten o'clock in the morning and he stayed, he stayed for lunch, he stayed all afternoon, he stayed for dinner and he stayed until about ten o'clock at night and then all of a sudden he announced that his wife was enceinte and then with great bitterness, and I, I am too young to be a father. We consoled him as best we could and sent him on his way.

When they came back Hemingway said that he had made up

his mind. They would go back to America and he would work hard for a year and with what he would earn and what they had they would settle down and he would give up newspaper work and make himself a writer. They went away and well within the prescribed year they came back with a new born baby. Newspaper work was over.

The first thing to do when they came back was as they thought to get the baby baptised. They wanted Gertrude Stein and myself to be god-mothers and an english war comrade of Hemingway was to be god-father. We were all born of different religions and most of us were not practising any, so it was rather difficult to know in what church the baby could be baptised. We spent a great deal of time that winter, all of us, discussing the matter. Finally it was decided that it should be baptised episcopalian and episcopalian it was. Just how it was managed with the assortment of god-parents I am sure I do not know, but it was baptised in the episcopalian chapel.

Writer or painter god-parents are notoriously unreliable. That is, there is certain before long to be a cooling of friendship. I know several cases of this, poor Paulot Picasso's god-parents have wandered out of sight and just as naturally it is a long time since any of us have seen or heard of our Hemingway god-child.

However in the beginning we were active god-parents, I particularly. I embroidered a little chair and I knitted a gay coloured garment for the god-child. In the meantime the god-child's father was very earnestly at work making himself a writer.

Gertrude Stein never corrects any detail of anybody's writing, she sticks strictly to general principles, the way of seeing what the writer chooses to see, and the relation between that vision and the way it gets down. When the vision is not complete the words are flat, it is very simple, there can be no mistake about it, so she insists. It was at this time that Hemingway began the short things that afterwards were printed in a volume called In Our Time.

One day Hemingway came in very excited about Ford Madox

Ford and the Transatlantic. Ford Madox Ford had started the Transatlantic some months before. A good many years before, indeed before the war, we had met Ford Madox Ford who was at that time Ford Madox Hueffer. He was married to Violet Hunt and Violet Hunt and Gertrude Stein were next to each other at the tea table and talked a great deal together. I was next to Ford Madox Hueffer and I liked him very much and I liked his stories of Mistral and Tarascon and I liked his having been followed about in that land of the French royalist, on account of his resemblance to the Bourbon claimant. I had never seen the Bourbon claimant but Ford at that time undoubtedly might have been a Bourbon.

We had heard that Ford was in Paris, but we had not happened to meet. Gertrude Stein had however seen copies of the Transatlantic and found it interesting but had thought nothing further about it.

Hemingway came in then very excited and said that Ford wanted something of Gertrude Stein's for the next number and he, Hemingway, wanted The Making of Americans to be run in it as a serial and he had to have the first fifty pages at once. Gertrude Stein was of course quite overcome with her excitement at this idea, but there was no copy of the manuscript except the one that we had had bound. That makes no difference, said Hemingway, I will copy it. And he and I between us did copy it and it was printed in the next number of the Transatlantic. So for the first time a piece of the monumental work which was the beginning, really the beginning of modern writing, was printed, and we were very happy. Later on when things were difficult between Gertrude Stein and Hemingway, she always remembered with gratitude that after all it was Hemingway who first caused to be printed a piece of The Making of Americans. She always says, yes sure I have a weakness for Hemingway. After all he was the first of the young men to knock at my door and he did make Ford print the first piece of The Making of Americans.

I myself have not so much confidence that Hemingway did do this. I have never known what the story is but I have always been certain that there was some other story behind it all. That is the way I feel about it.

Gertrude Stein and Sherwood Anderson are very funny on the subject of Hemingway. The last time that Sherwood was in Paris they often talked about him. Hemingway had been formed by the two of them and they were both a little proud and a little ashamed of the work of their minds. Hemingway had at one moment, when he had repudiated Sherwood Anderson and all his works, written him a letter in the name of american literature which he, Hemingway, in company with his contemporaries was about to save, telling Sherwood just what he, Hemingway thought about Sherwood's work, and, that thinking, was in no sense complimentary. When Sherwood came to Paris Hemingway naturally was afraid. Sherwood as naturally was not.

As I say he and Gertrude Stein were endlessly amusing on the subject. They admitted that Hemingway was yellow, he is, Gertrude Stein insisted, just like the flat-boat men on the Mississippi river as described by Mark Twain. But what a book, they both agreed, would be the real story of Hemingway, not those he writes but the confessions of the real Ernest Hemingway. It would be for another audience than the audience Hemingway now has but it would be very wonderful. And then they both agreed that they have a weakness for Hemingway because he is such a good pupil. He is a rotten pupil, I protested. You don't understand, they both said, it is so flattering to have a pupil who does it without understanding it, in other words he takes training and anybody who takes training is a favourite pupil. They both admit it to be a weakness. Gertrude Stein added further, you see he is like Derain. You remember Monsieur de Tuille said, when I did not understand why Derain was having the success he was having that it was because he looks like a modern and he smells of the museums. And that is Hemingway, he looks like a modern and he smells of the museums. But what a story that of the real Hem, and one he should tell himself but alas he never will. After all, as he himself once murmured, there is the career, the career.

But to come back to the events that were happening.

Hemingway did it all. He copied the manuscript and corrected the proof. Correcting proofs is, as I said before, like dusting, you learn the values of the thing as no reading suffices to teach it to you. In correcting these proofs Hemingway learned a great deal and he admired all that he learned. It was at this time that he wrote to Gertrude Stein saying that it was she who had done the work in writing The Making of Americans and he and all his had but to devote their lives to seeing that it was published.

He had hopes of being able to accomplish this. Some one, I think by the name of Sterne, said that he could place it with a publisher. Gertrude Stein and Hemingway believed that he could, but soon Hemingway reported that Sterne had entered into his period of unreliability. That was the end of that.

In the meantime and sometime before this Mina Loy had brought McAlmon to the house and he came from time to time and he brought his wife and brought William Carlos Williams. And finally he wanted to print The Making of Americans in the Contact Edition and finally he did. I will come to that.

In the meantime McAlmon had printed the three poems and ten stories of Hemingway and William Bird had printed In Our Time and Hemingway was getting to be known. He was coming to know Dos Passos and Fitzgerald and Bromfield and George Antheil and everybody else and Harold Loeb was once more in Paris. Hemingway had become a writer. He was also a shadow-boxer, thanks to Sherwood, and he heard about bull-fighting from me. I have always loved Spanish dancing and Spanish bull-fighting and I loved to show the photographs of bull-fighters and bull-fighting. I also loved to show the photograph where Gertrude Stein and I were in the front row and had our picture taken there accidentally. In these days Hemingway was teaching some young chap how to box. The boy did not know how, but by accident he knocked Hemingway out. I believe this sometimes happens. At any rate in these days Hemingway although a sportsman was easily tired. He used to get quite worn out walking from his house to ours. But then he had been worn by the war. Even now he is, as Hélène says all men are, fragile. Recently a robust friend of his said to Gertrude Stein, Ernest is very fragile, whenever he does anything sporting something breaks, his arm, his leg, or his head.

In those early days Hemingway liked all his contemporaries except Cummings. He accused Cummings of having copied everything, not from anybody but from somebody. Gertrude Stein who had been much impressed by The Enormous Room said that Cummings did not copy, he was the natural heir of the New England tradition with its aridity and its sterility but also with its individuality. They disagreed about this. They also disagreed about Sherwood Anderson. Gertrude Stein contended that Sherwood Anderson had a genius for using the sentence to convey a direct emotion, this was in the great American tradition, and that really except Sherwood there was no one in America who could write a clear and passionate sentence. Hemingway did not believe this, he did not like Sherwood's taste. Taste has nothing to do with sentences, contended Gertrude Stein. She also added that Fitzgerald was the only one of the younger writers who wrote naturally in sentences.

Gertrude Stein and Fitzgerald are very peculiar in their relation to each other. Gertrude Stein had been very much impressed by This Side of Paradise. She read it when it came out and before she knew any of the young american writers. She said of it that it was this book that really created for the public the new generation. She has never changed her opinion about this. She thinks this equally true of The Great Gatsby. She thinks Fitzgerald will be read when many of his well known contemporaries are forgotten. Fitzgerald always says that he thinks Gertrude Stein says these things just to annoy him by making him think that she means them, and he adds in his favourite way, and her doing it is the cruellest thing I ever heard. They always however have a very good time when they meet. And the last time they met they had a good time with themselves and Hemingway.

Then there was McAlmon. McAlmon had one quality that appealed to Gertrude Stein, abundance, he could go on writing, but she complained that it was dull.

There was also Glenway Wescott but Glenway Wescott at no time interested Gertrude Stein. He has a certain syrup but it does not pour.

So then Hemingway's career was begun. For a little while we saw less of him and then he began to come again. He used to recount to Gertrude Stein the conversations that he afterwards used in The Sun Also Rises and they talked endlessly about the character of Harold Loeb. At this time Hemingway was preparing his volume of short stories to submit to publishers in America. One evening after we had not seen him for a while he turned up with Shipman. Shipman was an amusing boy who was to inherit a few thousand dollars when he came of age. He was not of age. He was to buy the Transatlantic Review when he came of age, so Hemingway said. He was to support a surrealist review when he came of age, André Masson said. He was to buy a house in the country when he came of age, Josette Gris said. As a matter of fact when he came of age nobody who had known him then seemed to know what he did do with his inheritance. Hemingway brought him with him to the house to talk about buying the Transatlantic and incidentally he brought the manuscript he intended sending to America. He handed it to Gertrude Stein. He had added to his stories a little story of meditations and in these he said that The Enormous Room was the greatest book he had ever read. It was then that Gertrude Stein said, Hemingway, remarks are not literature.

After this we did not see Hemingway for quite a while and then we went to see some one, just after The Making of Americans was printed, and Hemingway who was there came up to Gertrude Stein and began to explain why he would not be able to write a review of the book. Just then a heavy hand fell on his shoulder and Ford Madox Ford said, young man it is I who wish to speak to Gertrude Stein. Ford then said to her, I wish to ask your permission to dedicate my new book to you. May I. Gertrude Stein and I were both awfully pleased and touched.

For some years after this Gertrude Stein and Hemingway did not meet. And then we heard that he was back in Paris and telling a number of people how much he wanted to see her. Don't you come home with Hemingway on your arm, I used to say when she went out for a walk. Sure enough one day she did come back bringing him with her.

They sat and talked a long time. Finally I heard her say, Hemingway, after all you are ninety percent Rotarian. Can't you, he said, make it eighty percent? No, said she regretfully, I can't. After all, as she always says, he did, and I may say, he does have moments of disinterestedness.

After that they met quite often. Gertrude Stein always says she likes to see him, he is so wonderful. And if he could only tell his own story. In their last conversation she accused him of having killed a great many of his rivals and put them under the sod. I never, said Hemingway, seriously killed anybody but one man and he was a bad man and, he deserved it, but if I killed anybody else I did it unknowingly, and so I am not responsible.

It was Ford who once said of Hemingway, he comes and sits at my feet and praises me. It makes me nervous. Hemingway also said once, I turned my flame which is a small one down and down and then suddenly there is a big explosion. If there were nothing but explosions my work would be so exciting nobody could bear it.

However, whatever I say, Gertrude Stein always says, yes I know but I have a weakness for Hemingway.

MALCOLM COWLEY

A Portrait of Mister Papa

1949

When I told Hemingway that I was writing an article about him—which of course he hadn't seen—he asked me to state that he is not responsible for any inaccuracies or legendary accomplishments of any sort which may have been attributed to him. Material for the article was gathered from persons who know the subject. Hemingway has stated to me that he would be delighted if it should be proved that none of the events in the article ever happened and that the events he would be most delighted to have disproved would be his hitting his head in London against a static water tank, and his ever having worked for in any capacity, or ever been associated with, a nickel-priced (maybe it is a dime now) weekly which is definitely repeat definitely not repeat not the Saturday Evening Post.*—M.C.*

It is twenty years since Ernest Hemingway wrote *A Farewell to Arms*, which has come to be almost universally regarded as the best American novel of World War I. What novel will be the best of World War II is likely to remain for some time an open and argued question.

So far there have been several good ones, including *The Gallery*, with its warmth of feeling, *The Naked and the Dead*, with

From *Life* Magazine, January 10, 1949. Copyright by Time, Inc. Reprinted by permission of the author and publisher. Slightly revised by the author.

its furious realism, and more recently *The Young Lions*, with its panorama of the American army in Europe. Most of the new war novels have been more skillfully written than those of the other war, always excepting *A Farewell to Arms*. Almost all of them have shown Hemingway's influence to some degree, but without equaling his patient workmanship or his mere zest for living. The chances are that when the smoke has cleared it will be found that Hemingway, now grizzled and paternal, has written the best novel of this war, too.

He started it long ago, before Pearl Harbor, and he is taking his time to finish it. By now he has more than a thousand pages of manuscript and he thinks that some of them are good, but he wants them all to be wonderful. That is as much as he will say about the novel, even to his publisher and members of his family.* The late Maxwell Perkins, his editor at Scribner's, used to be bothered by people telephoning to ask what the book was about. Max let his secretary answer the calls, even if they came from important persons. "Tell them," he instructed her, "that it's about land, sea and air." Perhaps the description will prove to be as good as any. Hemingway could write a wartime novel of service by sea, air and land that was based on nothing but his own adventures.

His service by sea was for Naval Intelligence in his 40-foot cabin cruiser, the *Pilar*, which had been transformed into a Q-boat. Disguised in various fashions it cruised for nearly two years, 1942-44, off the north coast of Cuba. The *Pilar* carried a crew of nine, besides radio equipment, machine gun, bazooka and high explosives. Its aim was to be hailed and ordered alongside by a German submarine, in which case Hemingway was prepared to carry out a scheme that would lead to the destruction of the U-boat and possibly to that of the Q-boat as well.

It was just as well for the life expectancy of the skipper and his crew that no U-boat came within hailing distance. At various

* This portrait was published in January 1949, when Hemingway was in Italy. After a serious illness that winter he decided to interrupt the long novel and write a shorter one, *Across the River and Into the Trees*. He plans to resume work on the big manuscript.—M.C.

times, however, the *Pilar* helped to discover the location of submarines which were later reported by the Navy as "presumed sunk." Spruille Braden, then United States ambassador to Cuba, had authorized the mission and procured the necessary armament. He said in a letter about Hemingway's Cuban service:

> The mission was extremely dangerous, as certainly a fishing boat under normal circumstances would be no match for a heavily armed submarine. However, Ernest had worked out the plan intelligently and, I believe, would have won the battle had he been able to make the contact. In fact, he would have made the contact had not my naval attaché called him into Havana one day when he was on a location he himself had picked, where a submarine did show up within twenty-four hours. Even so he obtained valuable information on the location of German subs on various occasions. So worthwhile was Ernest's contribution that I have strongly recommended him for a decoration.

The service by air followed his service by sea. After the last two German submarines had appeared off Cuba in the spring of 1944, Hemingway was flown to England by the RAF, to which he was accredited as a correspondent. He liked the English pilots and they flew him on a respectable number of operational missions, before and after D-day.

The service by land began on July 20 and continued until the early spring of 1945. Officially Hemingway was a correspondent for *Collier's Weekly* accredited to the Third Army; but he didn't enjoy being an observer and wrote only enough articles (six in eleven months) to keep from being sent home. He also stayed away from the Third Army, not liking General Patton. At first he holed up with an American pursuit squadron in Normandy; then, after the breakthrough at St. Lo, he attached himself to the Fourth Infantry Division of the First Army, where he found good friends and a satisfactory amount of fighting.

The best of his friends was Colonel (now Brigadier General) C. T. Lanham of the 22nd Regiment. The fighting was almost continuous, but it reached a climax in Huertgen Forest, just across the German frontier. There, in a November battle that lasted for eighteen days, Buck Lanham's regiment of 3,200 men suffered more than 2,600 casualties. Four battalion commanders were lost within thirty-six hours. Hemingway stayed with the regiment until the end of the battle, sharing all its dangers and hardships except deprivation of alcohol. To prevent that final misfortune he carried two canteens on the Gott-mit-Uns belt he had taken from a dead German. One canteen was filled with gin, the other with dry vermouth, and he poured them together to make lukewarm but powerful martinis.

Back in August, when the Fourth Division was sweeping eastward from Normandy, Hemingway ranged ahead of it in his jeep and began making contact with the French irregulars. He was an imposing figure with his broad shoulders and barrel chest, the head that he said was too big for a U. S. Army helmet, the deep scar on his skull—from colliding with a stationary water tank in the London blackout—and the immense fan-shaped beard he grew in wartime. The French were convinced that he must be a general, but Hemingway told them he was only a captain.

A guerilla asked him, "How is it that a man so old and wise as you and bearing the scars of honorable service is still a captain?"

"Young man," Hemingway answered on this occasion, and on many others, "the reason is simple and it is a painful one. I never learned to read and write."

His driver, "Red" Pelkey, thought that the French irregulars were the best outfit he had ever been with. "Nobody gives a damn if they get killed or not," he said. Hemingway's jeep kept appearing in unexpected places. "I always keep a pin in the map for old Ernie Hemingway," said the commander of the Fourth Division, Major General R. O. Barton, when he was briefing the other correspondents. A few days later the division reached the Seine above Paris, with Germans in front and on both flanks. "Old Ernie Hemingway is out there 60 miles ahead of everything in the First Army," General Barton told his staff. "He's been sending back information. But now what do you think he says? He says that if he's going to hold out where he is, he'll need tanks."

That was at the beginning of the week he spent in Rambouillet, thirty miles southwest of Paris. Hemingway had driven into the little town on August 19, just behind a roving detachment of mechanized cavalry. Allied flags had blossomed from every window, but soon the detachment was ordered elsewhere and the flags disappeared. The Rambolitains, as the inhabitants are called, knew that there were heavy German tanks in the neighborhood and they had a well-grounded fear of being massacred if the Germans reoccupied the undefended town. Hemingway determined to hold it, with a truckload of French irregulars and the moral support of Colonel David Bruce of OSS, who had picked on Rambouillet as a likely spot for carrying on his counterintelligence work.

"Ernest's bedroom at the Hotel du Grand Veneur was the nerve center of all operations," said Colonel Bruce in a letter. "There, in his shirtsleeves, he gave audience to intelligence couriers, to refugees from Paris, to deserters from the German army, to local officials and to all comers. A fierce-looking Frenchman with a machine gun at the ready stood guard at the door. Within, Ernest, looking like a jolly dark Bacchus, dispensed the high, low and middle justice in English, French and broken German." Two fancy ladies accused of commerce with the enemy were brought to him for judgment. Instead of ordering their heads to be shaved, as their captors demanded, he read them a stern moral lecture and set them to washing dishes. A Polish deserter from the Wehrmacht was cross-examined and then put to work peeling potatoes; an Austrian sergeant washed the jeeps.

After posting guards on all the roads, Hemingway's chief concern was to locate the German defenses south of Paris. He sent out armed patrols to attract German fire and civilian volunteers on bicycles to penetrate the German lines; some of them pedaled all the way into Paris and came back to Hemingway with sketches, reports and hatfuls of fresh eggs. He had the help and advice of a French secret agent famous under his pseudonym of "Mr. Sheep"—M. Mouton. Soon General Leclerc arrived in Rambouillet with the French armored division that had been chosen to liberate Paris. General Leclerc didn't like American correspondents or French irregulars, but Hemingway and M. Mouton had dinner with his chief of staff and gave him a detailed summary, with sketches, of the German defenses on all the roads between Paris and Rambouillet. "I believe," says Colonel Bruce, "that this information had a determining effect on the successful accomplishment of Leclerc's march to Paris."

On the early morning of August 25, Hemingway followed one of the French armored columns as far as the village of Buc, near Versailles, where he knew that it would be halted briefly by German resistance. Then, at the head of his irregulars—who by now formed a motorized detachment of more than 200 men—he made his way into the city by back roads. Task Force Hemingway was fighting a skirmish at the Arc de Triomphe when the main Leclerc column was still on the south bank of the Seine. That evening Robert Capa, the photographer, came into Paris with other correspondents who had been held back by Leclerc's strict orders. Capa went straight to the Ritz, where he recognized Hemingway's driver standing guard outside the door. Said Pelkey, speaking in Hemingway's style, "Papa took good hotel. Plenty stuff in cellar. You go up quick."

After the Rambouillet affair there was an argument in army circles whether Hemingway should be decorated for an outstandingly good example of intelligence reporting, or whether he should be summarily courtmartialed for having violated the Geneva Convention, which governs the conduct of war correspondents. The decoration came much later in the form of a Bronze Star; but first the Inspector General of the Third Army submitted his activities to a formal investigation. It began on September 2, 1944 and occupied the better part of eight weeks. In October Hemingway was called back from the Siegfried Line to be interrogated. Other correspondents testified like gentlemen that they had never seen him with weapons on his person. Finally he was advised that the investigation—to quote the Adjutant General—"disclosed no violation by him of the existing regulations for war correspondents." He hurried back to the Fourth

Division, which was then preparing for the battle of Huertgen Forest. "In the next war," he told Buck Lanham, "I'm going to have the Geneva Convention tattooed on my backside in reverse, so I can read it with a mirror."

If Hemingway's novel about the last war is based on his own service by land, it is certain to contain more first-hand accounts of combat than any of the war novels that have so far appeared. His passion for adventure will go into the book, together with the feeling of comradeship that he found among American soldiers at the front. The novel may be tragic, but it won't be niggling. "Most of this last war made sense," he says, "while the first one made little sense to me. Also I had such good companionship. I had never known such fine people and it was the first time I ever had a chance to fight in my own language."

Hemingway was enthusiastic about the officers and men who fought beside him and they returned warmth for warmth. "There is absolutely no question," Buck Lanham says, "but that Ernie was one of the most admired and best beloved people who ever associated with the 22nd Regiment. When the veterans of the regiment formed an association, he was one of only two non-military men elected to honorary membership." Most of them didn't suspect that he was a famous author. "Hey, who is this guy Hemingway? He's a good Joe," one of them said to the driver who had temporarily replaced Red Pelkey. "I don't know," the driver answered. "He's some kind of big shot. I been driving him around for a month and I still don't know what he does." One correspondent described in conversation a ride that he took with Hemingway, when they started before dawn for Lanham's post of command in Huertgen Forest. "Everybody knew his jeep," the correspondent said. "Out of the dark woods you could hear hundreds of voices saying, one after another, 'Good morning, Mr. Hemingway.' It was like a royal progress."

The officers of the Fourth Division had an affectionate variety of nicknames for him. They called him Ernie, a name which he tolerates only from close friends, or the Kraut Hunter, or Old Dr. Hemingstein—when he argued with the psychiatrist about combat fatigue—or they repeated his own description of himself as Ernie Hemorrhoid, the poor man's Pyle; but mostly they called him Papa or Pop. Those were the names he liked best and they have followed him back to Cuba, where the household servants, the villagers in San Francisco de Paula, the fishermen at Cojímar and the waiters in his favorite Havana cafés all address his as *Papá*. You order a daiquiri, trying to explain how you want it made, and the waiter at the Café Florida says brightly, "*Como Papá?*" If you answer, "Yes, like Papa," a double daiquiri without sugar appears in a shaker brimful of shaved ice.

"Papa, you write that we may drink," said a Cuban lawyer in the Ambos Mundos, while Hemingway reached for the check as always and beamed as if from the head of a family table. Sometimes his friends describe him as having a papa complex, which, they explain, is exactly the opposite of a father complex. Instead of seeking for a substitute father to support and protect him, he keeps trying to protect and lay plans for others. Younger men and women come to him for advice about their literary problems and their love affairs, while he talks to them as if he were ninety years wise instead of only forty-nine. "I was lucky enough," he says, "to associate with older people when I was young and with young people now that I'm older."

Mr. Papa, as he often signs his letters, is a big man with an erect carriage that makes him seem taller than his six feet. He grew a sizable paunch after the war, but has now trained himself down to 208¾ pounds, or not much more than his former boxing weight of 198. He is built like a boxer, with small ankles, big calves, narrow hips, broad shoulders and muscular arms that measure 17 inches around the biceps. His head is big and leonine, with wavy hair, now gray at the temples, a bristly mustache and usually a quarter-inch of stubble on the cheeks, for he has a tender skin and hates shaving. When he puts on his steel-rimmed army-issue spectacles, Mr. Papa looks like a scholar poring over a Greek manuscript. When he grins, he looks like a schoolboy masquerading in an iron-gray wig.

At home in Cuba he often kicks off his strollers and goes barefoot like a schoolboy. His feet are large and well-shaped; his broad hands have the very long, square-cut fingers of a skilled mechanic or a surgeon. He doesn't smoke, partly to preserve his extremely keen sense of smell; sometimes he sniffs the wind like an apprehensive bear. He doesn't enjoy big parties. Usually he talks to one person at a time in a low, confidential voice, while keeping his dark-brown eyes fixed on his guest. Gertrude Stein was trying to be malicious when she said that his eyes were "passionately interested, rather than interesting," but in fact she was paying him a compliment. Mr. Papa looks and listens and remembers. "When people talk, listen completely," he said in a letter of advice to a young writer. "Most people never listen."

He lives on a patriarchal scale, surrounded by his family, his friends and his retainers. There are no flocks or herds on his Cuban estate, but there are cats—twenty-two by a recent count—and half a dozen dogs that wander in and out of the big Spanish-style farmhouse. Finca Vigia (or Lookout Farm) is the name of the property and it consists of fifteen acres with gardens, a tennis court, a swimming pool and a white tower at the top of which is Hemingway's study. Outside the farmhouse door is a ceiba tree, sacred in voodoo rites, with its smooth bark the color of an elephant's hide.

The living room, sixty feet long, has its walls lined with the heads of beasts that Hemingway shot in Africa. In the late afternoon the room is often noisy with guests and the Chinese cook seldom knows how many to expect for dinner. Finca Vigia needs a staff of servants; besides the cook there are two houseboys, two or three gardeners and a chauffeur for the two big cars and the station wagon, not to mention an engineer for the fishing boat anchored in the little harbor at Cojímar.

Mr. Papa's expenses are high, but so are his earnings, and this in spite of the fact that he hasn't published a novel since 1940. His books have a continued sale in the United States. Abroad they are always appearing in new translations, though he is having the usual difficulties in collecting his foreign royalties without traveling to all the countries where they are impounded.

Ever since *For Whom the Bell Tolls* was sold to Paramount for $150,000 most of his income has come from Hollywood. Three of his four novels have now been filmed and the late Mark Hellinger, encouraged by the success of *The Killers*, had undertaken to produce a whole series of his short stories. Hellinger's death last year put an end to that profitable arrangement, but recently 20th Century-Fox bought *The Snows of Kilimanjaro* for $125,000, a record price for a short story.

Mrs. Papa—also known as "Kitner" and "Miss Mary"—runs the household efficiently and makes out the income-tax returns. Before she became Hemingway's fourth wife she was Mary Welsh, the daughter of a prosperous lumberman in Bemidji, Minn. She graduated from Northwestern, worked on the Chicago *Daily News*, then on the London *Express*; and she was in the London bureau of *Time* when Hemingway met her in 1944. Years earlier he had described Maria, the heroine of *The Bell*, as having high cheekbones, a straight mouth with full lips and golden-brown hair cut short all over her head, so that it was little longer than the fur on a beaver pelt. All those phrases apply to Miss Mary.

At Finca Vigia there is a separate house for Hemingway's three sons, who worship their father and visit him at every opportunity. John (or Bumby) is the only son of the first marriage and is now twenty-five. He has a distinguished war record as a captain in the OSS assigned to missions behind the German lines. Patrick (or Mousie) is twenty and a student at Stanford University. Gregory (or Gigi) is seventeen and in the senior class at Canterbury School. Like Patrick he is good in his studies, but his father complains that his growing interest in books is likely to be the ruin of a superb wing shot. Gigi was only eleven when he came within one bird of winning the pigeon-shooting championship of Cuba, against four past champions of the island, two past champions of Spain and the gunnery instructors of a United States air squadron.

Mr. Papa also shot that afternoon and finished five birds behind Gigi. "Ernest is a strong contender in tournament shoots, but not usually a winner," says his friend Winston Guest, who has held several championships. "In the field he is quite simply the best shot I ever saw." The testimony is confirmed by others, who say that Hemingway not only has exceptionally fast reflexes but also seems to read a bird's mind, so that he knows just how it will act in the wind. These friends report that his hunting trips in Cuba and in the Sun Valley region are organized like military campaigns.

Hemingway's friends are a curiously assorted company. Among them are wealthy sportsmen of the international set, West Point generals (he often says that generals are good people), priests, prizefighters, jockeys, matadors, movie stars (Gary Cooper, Ingrid Bergman, Marlene Dietrich) and convicts lately escaped from Devil's Island. One of the convicts thanked him for money and explained that he had spent happy years in the French penal colony. "I shall never regret," he said, "the little misunderstanding that sent me there."

Hemingway is also fond of Loyalist exiles, especially the Basques, whom he regards as the best people on earth. His other friends include—or have included, for many of them are dead—Spanish grandees, Cuban politicians of several parties, saloonkeepers of all grades and nations, ski instructors, hardware clerks, Chicago gangsters, prostitutes, rummies, gossip columnists, a Russian correspondent executed in the purge, Max Perkins, Gertrude Stein and the Duke and Duchess of Windsor.

Whatever their social or financial level, most of the friends have achieved excellence in some particular activity that engages Hemingway's passionate interest. They also have another quality in common: physical or moral courage combined with the habit of being dependable in a crisis. They are men and women who have taken risks, and that is one reason why the mortality among them has been high. Hemingway has taken risks and survived, but he carries scars—literally from the crown of his head to the sole of his right foot.

The scar on his foot is like an embossed Christmas tree and goes back thirty years to the time when he was wounded by a trench mortar burst near Fossalte di Piave. There are several scars on his scalp, but the largest is the souvenir of a party at the Dorchester, in London. On the night of May 25, 1944, he was being driven home through the blackout when the jeep collided with a stationary water tank in Lowndes Square. His wound had to be closed with fifty-seven stitches, but he pulled the stitches out on the boat that carried him to Fox Green Beach on D-day. On his forehead, his shoulders, his right arm and both legs are other scars recording different events, so that the story of his life is engraved on his body.

He was born July 21, 1899, in Oak Park, a Chicago suburb sometimes described as the middle-class capital of the world. He was the second child and first son of a family in which there would be two boys and four girls. His father, Clarence Edmonds Hemingway, was a brawny, bearded doctor whose two passions in life were hunting and fishing. His mother, born Grace Hall, had been a soloist at the First Congregational Church, where the Hemingways worshiped. She was devoted to music and the distinguishing feature of the big stuccoed Hemingway house was a music room thirty feet square with a concert stage where she sometimes sang to invited audiences. Both parents tried to model the son after themselves. The father gave him his first fishing rod when Ernest was not yet three years old and his first shotgun when he was ten; the mother gave him a cello. Instead of practicing the cello he often tried to sneak off and go fishing.

That was at Walloon Lake, in Michigan, where the Hemingways spent their summers. Ernest went barefoot there and felt more at home than among his well-dressed schoolmates in Oak Park. Sometimes his father took him along when making professional visits to an Indian camp far back in the woods. Dr. Hemingway had a small head for his huge body and very small piercing black eyes under bushy eyebrows. It was said that on a bright summer day he could count potato bugs across a mile-wide lake. He was famous as a wing shot, in and out of season, and once a neighbor protested that he was breaking the law. "Never mind the law, madam," he shouted. "Shoot the birds!"

When Ernest was fourteen and big for his age, he persuaded

his father to pay for a course of boxing lessons advertised by a Chicago gymnasium. The first lesson might have been the last. Ernest was invited to spar with Young A'Hearn, a crack middleweight training for his next bout. "I'll take it easy," A'Hearn promised him; but soon they were trading punches and then Ernest was lying on the floor with a broken nose.

"I knew he was going to give me the works the minute I saw his eyes," Ernest told a friend.

"Were you scared?"

"Sure, he could hit like hell."

"Why did you go in there with him?"

"I wasn't that scared."

Ernest was back at the gymnasium next day, to everyone's surprise. It seems that other students had been given the same treatment and that very few of them appeared for a second lesson. Ernest was one who finished the course and he continued to practice boxing. Two years later his left eye was injured in a sparring match and the doctors thought for a time that the other eye might be affected. He had grown too rapidly and was always getting injured in those days. In his last year at Oak Park High School he played right guard on the famous football team that lost the scholastic championship to Evanston, but later won an intersectional game with Toledo. Hemingway had to be retired from both games because of injuries.

At high school he went out for everything, according to the testimony of others in the class of '17. He was an editor of *Trapeze*, the school weekly, for which he wrote a news-and-gossip column. He contributed stories to the school quarterly and one of the stories, called "Sepi Jingan," was early but authentic Hemingway, with a halfbreed for hero, lots of dialogue and two killings in four pages. He played in the school orchestra. He belonged to the debating club, to the Hanna Club, which heard lectures by prominent citizens, and to the Boys' Rifle Club. Besides making the football team, in his senior year he was on the swimming team, managed the track team and wrote the class prophecy. Yet he wasn't happy at high school and twice he ran away from home. His classmates describe him as a lonely boy, sometimes the butt of jokes, who didn't go to dances until his last year. To judge from his high-school record he had a strong competitive spirit and a burning wish to excel. He wasn't a born sportsman who somehow learned to write; on the contrary he was a born writer and student.

The country went to war in the April before his graduation and Hemingway tried to enlist, but the medical examiners rejected him because of his injured eye. He decided not to go to college; instead he made his way to Kansas City and talked himself into a job on the *Star*, where he proved to be a better-than-average cub reporter. His chance to go abroad came in the spring of 1918, when he heard that the Red Cross was recruiting ambulance units for service on the Italian front.

The front was quiet on the night of July 8. Hemingway, then stationed at Fossalte di Piave, went forward to a listening post on the river bank, a hundred yards beyond the Italian trenches. A big Austrian trench-mortar bomb, of the type that used to be called ash cans, exploded in the darkness. "I died then," Hemingway told his friend Guy Hickok. "I felt my soul or something coming right out of my body, like you'd pull a silk handkerchief out of a pocket by one corner. It flew around and then came back and went in again and I wasn't dead any more."

The ash can had been filled with quarter- and half-inch pieces of sawed-off steel rods and the surgeons later found that there were 237 of the pieces in his legs. The three Italians in the listening post all had their legs blown off. When Hemingway recovered consciousness two of them were dead and the other was screaming. Hemingway carried him back toward the trenches. Two Austrian searchlights caught him in their beams and a machine gun followed him. He was hit again in the knee and the ankle, but reached a dugout before he collapsed with his burden. The soldier on his back was dead.

In the hospital Hemingway was awarded the Croce de Guerra with three citations and the Medaglia d'Argento al Valore Militare, which was the second highest Italian military decoration and carried with it a pension from the government of about $50 a year. He went back to Oak Park in the spring of 1919 with the medals and other souvenirs, including a new aluminum kneecap, a grafted bone in his foot and various pieces of scrap metal that the surgeons had been unable to remove; one of them is now working out of his knee, after thirty years. For a long time he was afraid to sleep except by daylight, because he had been blown up at night. He thought that if he ever again closed his eyes in the darkness the soul would go out of his body and not come back. Much later, in Spain and China, he would learn to suspend the functioning of his imagination and would become as indifferent to danger as it is possible for an old soldier to be. In the early years, however, he forced himself to walk forward into danger because of his competitive spirit and because he was proving to himself that he was not that scared.

Before seeking new dangers he had to look for a job. In 1920 he went to work in Chicago editing a house organ for the Cooperative Society of America. He lived at Y. K. Smith's apartment on the Near North Side, where he met Sherwood Anderson and other writers and artists of the Chicago group. There too he fell in love with Hadley Richardson, of St. Louis, a family friend of the Smiths; they were married in September, 1921. After a short honeymoon in the Michigan woods they went to Toronto, where Hemingway again talked himself into a newspaper job. Soon his stories were being published under a byline and in December of that same year he sailed for Europe as a roving correspondent of the Toronto *Star*.

Anderson had given him a letter of introduction to Gertrude Stein, which he hastened to present. He also met Ezra Pound and tried teaching him to box. In a letter to Anderson he reported that Pound habitually led with his chin and had the grace of a crayfish or crawfish; but still he thought it was pretty sporting of Pound to risk his dignity. "We love Gertrude Stein," was a penciled note at the end of the same letter. Already Hemingway had shown her his poems and the novel he was writing. She liked the poems, which she thought were direct and Kiplingesque, but the novel she found wanting. She said, "There is a great deal of description in this and not particularly good description. Begin over again and concentrate."

For the *Star* he had been reporting the Greco-Turkish War. He thinks that he really learned about war from watching the battles in Asia Minor; and he learned about horror, too, from watching the evacuation of Smyrna when the Greeks broke the forelegs of their baggage animals and left them to die by the hundreds in the shallow water. In November, 1922, he went to Lausanne for the conference that discussed a peace settlement between Greece and Turkey. Hadley came there to meet him, carrying his manuscripts in a suitcase. At Lyon she left the compartment for a moment to get a glass of water and the suitcase was stolen. It contained everything he had written and saved until that time, the completed novel, eighteen stories and thirty poems—all of them irretrievably gone except one story, *My Old Man*, which was making the rounds of the magazines.

At twenty-three it is not a real disaster to lose one's manuscripts and it was even a stroke of good fortune for Hemingway, since the loss enabled him to begin over again and concentrate, as Gertrude Stein had advised. He studied writing as if he were studying geometry without a textbook and inventing theorems as he went along. Ezra and Gertrude were his two teachers. Ezra read his stories and sent them back blue-penciled, with most of the adjectives gone. Gertrude confined herself to general comments, but they were searching and sometimes merciless. Later Hemingway said of his apprentice years, "Ezra was right half the time, and when he was wrong he was so wrong you were never in any doubt about it. Gertrude was always right."

In 1923 his first booklet appeared in France; it was *Three Stories and Ten Poems*, printed in a very small edition by the Contact Publishing Company. A few copies got back to Oak Park and caused a scandal there. The poems were outspoken and neighbors who read them looked at the Hemingways as if that rather straitlaced family had given birth to a criminal. Oak Park has produced three famous men and today it is as proud of Hemingway as of the architect Frank Lloyd Wright. There was a time, however, when their names were treated as gingerly by *Oak Leaves,* the local weekly, as was that of Charles J. Guiteau, also from Oak Park, the disappointed office seeker who shot President Garfield.

In 1924 Hemingway had a second booklet called *in our time,* of which 170 copies were printed by the Three Mountains Press in Paris. It shouldn't be confused with *In Our Time,* capitalized, the book of stories published in New York the following year, for it contained no stories at all, but only the brief and diamond-sharp vignettes of postwar life that would be printed between the stories in the later volume.

In Our Time, capitalized, was a financial failure. Only 1,335 copies were printed and only a few hundred of these were sold in 1925, the year of publication. His second American book was *The Torrents of Spring,* whose sales in 1926 were only a spring trickle. His third American book was a novel, *The Sun Also Rises,* published that same fall. It was an immediate but not a sensational success, with 26,000 copies sold in the first year. Then, gradually, people began to notice what a widespread effect it was having on the new generation, the one that came of age after World War I. Hemingway, as Lord Byron had done a century before, gave the young people attitudes to strike and patterns of conduct to follow. They not only wrote like him, if they wrote, and walked with his rolling slouch if they had seen him, but also drank like his heroes and heroines, cultivated a hard-boiled melancholy and talked in page after page of Hemingway dialogue.

Meanwhile the new Byron was living modestly in Paris, with winter excursions to Tyrol for the skiing and summers in Spain for the bull fights. Magazine editors had started besieging him, but he didn't accept their offers unless they were willing to publish what he wrote exactly as he wrote it. "He could not be bought," said his friend the late John Peale Bishop. "I happened to be with him on the day he turned down an offer from one of Mr. Hearst's editors, which, had he accepted it, would have supported him handsomely for years. He was at the time living back of the Montparnasse cemetery, over the studio of a friend, in a room small and bare except for a bed and a table, and buying his midday meal for five sous from the street vendors of fried potatoes."

If he was then living alone it was because his first marriage had been breaking up and by March, 1927, had ended in a divorce. Later in the year he married Pauline Pfeiffer, a dark-haired fashion writer who worked in the Paris office of *Vogue* and who, like Hadley, had spent her girlhood in St. Louis. With his new wife Hemingway went back to the States, where he continued working on *A Farewell to Arms*, the war novel he had waited ten years to write. The book was finished at the end of 1928, after the Hemingways had established themselves in Key West, our southernmost city.

It was during the Key West years, 1928-38, that he earned his reputation as a fisherman, a big-game hunter and an all-around sportsman. For a long time after the war he had been troubled by his wounds and had tired easily. A robust friend of his had said to Gertrude Stein, "Ernest is very fragile. Whenever he does anything sporting something breaks, his arm, his leg or his head." But he kept on overcoming and sometimes overcompensating for his handicaps and by the Key West years he had developed endurance as well as strength. "He was a tough fisherman," said fishing captain Jakie Key, who often went out with him. "He'd fish all day, then lie down in his clothes and sleep on the deck while the boat drifted, and go back to fishing in the morning."

In 1933 he caught his first giant, a marlin weighing 468 pounds, which he brought to gaff in 65 minutes without using a harness. "It jumped like in the Apocalypse," he said. He became known for fighting his fish and boating them fast, before the sharks had time to mutilate them. After his return from Africa in 1934 —with a fine collection of mounted heads and with material for his least satisfactory book, *Green Hills of Africa*—he had a fishing boat, the *Pilar*, built to his design at a Brooklyn shipyard. He had taught himself navigation and soon was taking the *Pilar* on cruises through the Bahamas. At Bimini he boated the first unmutilated tuna—a 310 pounder—ever caught in those waters on rod and reel.

That was in the summer of 1935, the big season at Bimini when he caught so many marlin and won the fishing tournament. There was ill-feeling that year between the islanders and the visiting fishermen, and Hemingway tried to pacify the locals by giving them a chance to fight. He offered $200 to anyone who could stay four rounds in the ring with him and several of the locals tried it, but none lasted four rounds. Tom Heeney, the English heavyweight champion, was in Bimini early that summer before the ring was built and he boxed with Hemingway on the beach. The whole island was watching and at last Tom said, "Let's cut this out. We're doing this for nothing and we ought to be paid for it."

Hemingway was back at Bimini the following year when civil war broke out in Spain, the country he loved best after his own. The war aroused his social conscience, which had seemed dormant or dead. Soon he raised $40,000 on his personal notes to buy ambulances for the Loyalist armies. To pay off the notes he made several trips to Spain as correspondent for the North American Newspaper Alliance. During long visits to the front, he became a friend of the military leaders. He was taking a postgraduate course in war, after his freshman studies in Italy and his field work with the Greeks in Asia Minor.

Martha Gellhorn was also in Spain, reporting the war for *Collier's*; she was another St. Louis girl and she had met Hemingway in Key West when she came down with her mother to interview him. In Spain Hemingway read her stories, gave her advice and fell in love with her. He is a romantic by nature and he falls in love like a big hemlock tree crashing down through the underbrush; also he has a puritanical streak that keeps him from being a cocktail-party flirt. When he falls in love he wants to get married and stay married, and he regards the end of a marriage as a personal defeat. Nevertheless, divorce was in the air when he came back from Spain for the last time and set to work on *For Whom the Bell Tolls.*

He had been planning to write a novel about the Spanish civil war ever since the first of his wartime visits to Madrid. He had talked to André Malraux, who was then flying for the Loyalists, and they had agreed half-seriously to divide the war between them; Malraux was to take everything up to the Italian defeat at Brihuega in April, 1937. Malraux worked fast—too fast, Hemingway thinks—and his long novel *l'Espoir*, later translated as *Man's Hope*, was off the press in December of that same year. Hemingway was slower and Madrid had fallen, early in 1939, before the book was under way.

Even so he thinks that perhaps he wrote *The Bell* too soon. "But it wasn't just the civil war I put into it," he explains; "it was everything I had learned about Spain for eighteen years." *The Bell* is Hemingway's favorite among his novels. Two passages he likes to reread are the killing of the Franco cavalryman in the snow and El Sordo's fight on the hilltop, of which he says, "It is every guerilla action that was ever fought." During World War II the novel was used in both the American and the Russian armies as a textbook of guerilla fighting.

Much of *The Bell* was written in a fifth-story corner room of the Hotel Ambos Mundos, in Havana. When he carried the manuscript north in the summer of 1940, after seventeen months of steady work, there were still revisions to be made, so he took a drawing-room on the train from Miami. The air-conditioning system was out of order and the temperature in the room was 128, but he worked straight through to New York and had the manuscript ready for the printer. When the galley proofs came back he carried them to the Hotel Barclay and worked over them for ninety-six hours without leaving his room. Then he relaxed with a succession of companions. Said Damon Runyon, who was one of them, "Few men can stand the strain of relaxing with him over an extended period."

On November 4, 1940, a few days after *The Bell* was published, Pauline obtained her divorce in Key West on the ground of desertion. On November 21, Ernest married Martha Gellhorn in Cheyenne, Wyoming. Their honeymoon trip was a visit to China as war correspondents. Soon after their return to Havana, Hemingway started work on a new novel and, with interruptions caused by the war, he has been at work on it ever since.

Obviously it wasn't a war novel in the beginning, but he writes a book like an exploring expedition setting out into unknown territory. He knows his approximate goal, but the goal can change. He knows his direction, but he doesn't know how far he will travel or what he will find on a given day's journey. Rising early, he tries to be at his desk by eight o'clock; in the Key West days he often started work at six-thirty. Before starting to write he reads what he has written already—the whole novel, until he is halfway through writing it, and two or three chapters in any case. They give him his bearings and he is ready to march ahead.

He writes his novels with a pencil and Pauline used to say that he thought with his fingers. After an automobile accident in 1930, when the doctors told him that he might lose the use of his arm, he was afraid that he mightn't be able to write novels again. Another reason for writing in pencil is that, as he says, "You get three different sights at it to see if the reader is getting what you want him to. First when you read it over; then when it is typed you get another chance to improve it, and again in the proof. Writing it first in pencil gives you one-third more chance to improve it."

"The best way to stop," he says, "is when you are going good and when you know what will happen next. If you do that every day when you are writing a novel, you will never be stuck." Thus, if the day's writing carries him to the end of a chapter, he always writes at least the first sentence of the next chapter, so as not to be left on dead center. Usually he is through with the day's stint at twelve-thirty, though sometimes he works for two hours more. He thinks it is a mistake to do so much in one day that one is too weary to continue the following morning. When he stops he counts over what he has written, word for word, then he calls Rene, the houseboy, who brings him a tall glass of gin-and-tonic.

He keeps a record of his daily achievement. In a week last March he wrote 485 words on Monday, 516 on Tuesday, 638 on Wednesday, 912 on Thursday and 276 on Friday, making a total of 2,827 for the week. Saturday he went fishing on the *Pilar* and Sunday he made an expedition to Matanzas with Bumby. He makes his low daily records—like the 276 for Friday—when he is working on the expository passages of a novel. Dialogue goes faster, and he says that if he can get four people talking together everything goes like a dream.

Hemingway works hard when he is working; then guests come for luncheon and he stops thinking about his work. "Don't worry about it until you start to write the next day," he advised a younger writer. "That way your subconscious will work on it all the time. But if you think about it consciously or worry about it you will kill it and your brain will be tired before you start." He was talking about writing a novel, where the work has to continue from day to day. For short stories he has a different system. He thinks about them for a long time, perhaps for years, until they are clear in his mind; then when the right mood comes he sits down at the typewriter and hammers them out, perhaps with a few corrections on the first page and none afterwards. He once wrote three stories in a day, including "Hills Like White Elephants," which is one of his best.

After he has finished the first draft of a novel, he goes over the typed copy, "cutting out the crap," as he says. He is merciless to any of his own writing that seems to him false or overblown. He believes that if a writer once publishes something false, it spoils everything else he does, like the one bad apple in a barrel. Partly because he keeps setting higher standards for himself, he has worked longer on each successive novel. *The Torrents of Spring* wasn't really a novel, but at least it told a story of novel length and he wrote it in seven days. He spent six weeks on the first draft of *The Sun Also Rises*, then five months in making revisions. *A Farewell to Arms* took twelve months to finish and *For Whom the Bell Tolls* took seventeen. His new novel will take five or six years, after deducting his wartime service by sea, air and land.

"Papa hates to work," Miss Mary says; but he also loves to work and he loves taking his time. When he interrupts the writing of a novel he feels like a fugitive simultaneously from Paradise and from the chain gang. He thinks of writing as a trade that he is still learning and says that he is apprenticed out at it until he dies. Because he is always learning he thinks that he can teach others; it helps to clarify his own ideas, he says. "I love teaching," he adds, "and love a young ball team. I just like to see them work and teach what is teachable."

"Don't underestimate your Hemingway," said Arthur Koestler on a recent visit. "It is banal, but he is still the greatest living writer." Hemingway himself often speaks of others whom he admires for having greater natural talent. Faulkner, he thinks, has the most talent of anybody—"but he goes on writing after he is tired and it seems as though he never threw away the worthless. I would have been happy just to have managed him." Hemingway thinks he has managed his own talent by dint of discipline and patience, and by rejecting everything he wrote that seemed below his standard. He objects to being discussed as a sectional or a national writer, on the ground that any writer worth reading is just a writer.

"That's the hard league to play in," he says. "The ball is standard, the ball parks vary somewhat, but they are all good. There are no bad bounces. Alibis don't count. Go out and do your stuff. You can't do it? Then don't take refuge in the fact that you are a local boy or a rummy, or pant to crawl back into somebody's womb, or have the con or the old rale. You can do it or can't do it in that league I am speaking of. And you only have to do it once to get remembered by some people. But if you can do it year after year after year quite a lot of people remember and they tell their children and their children and their grandchildren remember, and if it's books they can read them. And if it's good enough it lasts forever."

HIS WORK

LINCOLN KIRSTEIN

The Canon of Death

1932

"The present volume, *Death in the Afternoon*, is not intended to be either historical or exhaustive. It is intended as an introduction to the modern Spanish bullfight and attempts to explain that spectacle both emotionally and practically." *Death in the Afternoon* is more than an introduction to bull-fighting. It is also a spiritual autobiography, a study of manners in the Iberian peninsula and a book, which though not fictional, concerns the craft of fiction. It also defines in a way which has perhaps never before been attempted, at least in the English language, the ecstasy in valor.

A book about bullfights, it is in more ways than one a book like a bullfight. Mr. Hemingway commences his apologia with a defense and a justification for the disembowelling of horses. To many of his readers *Death in the Afternoon* is a revolting book, not alone because of his descriptions of corporeal decay, nor from

From *Hound & Horn*, Volume VI, No. 2, Jan.-Mar., 1933. Reprinted by permission of the author.

his free speech. Indeed, there are qualities in the book which are so hateful that, like the horses, they are best suffered first.

Death in the Afternoon is, of all personal books, the most personal. The quality of its author's character is imprinted in the ink of the type on every page. The one thing Mr. Hemingway prizes above all others is that kind of valor which is the "strength of mind in resisting fear and braving danger; bravery; especially, courage and skill in fighting." There may be other kinds of courage but it is with physical courage alone he is occupied. His approach to physicality is immediate and tactile. He can only describe what he has seen with his eyes, touched with his hands. Not only does he distrust any other perception, he virtually denies its possibility. He divides most males, and this also is a book of "Men Without Women", into two classes, those with balls and those without. He allocates his maleness according to his prejudices and has always in mind his two categories. It is for them he does his writing, or at least for and in praise of those that have; in spite of and against those that haven't. Those that have balls are certain bull-fighters who are unimaginative enough to be incapable of fearing the intense danger to which they are constantly exposed, or those who imagining it, can transcend it, "Goya" and "William Faulkner." Those who have not are certain cowardly toreros who fake courage without achieving it, upper middle-class American snobs, "those who suck after intellectuals and marry money," magazine owners, well-fed, skull and bones-ed, porcellian-ed, beach-tanned, flannelled, Panama-hatted, sports-shod men, "Radiguet" and "El Greco."[1] This distinction may be infantile, naïve and limited, but it means a great deal to

[1] Hemingway accuses Meier-Graefe of going to Spain to see its paintings "in order to have publishable ecstasies about them." That he went to see bull-fights for the same reason would be as true. Hemingway's opinion of Greco is his own and will no doubt influence the same people who think *The Sun Also Rises* is a great work. From what we know of Greco, he did ***not*** "believe in the Holy Ghost, in the communion and fellowship of saints . . . and in fairies." He was had up by the Inquisition for heterodoxy, his library contained more classical than Christian writers, he was suspected of being an heretic; he was surely a supreme satirist, as anyone who looks at the Burial simply, knows. The documents of his domestic life would confuse Mr. Hemingway if he read them. There is no trace of viciousness at all.

Mr. Hemingway and it is the source of his limits. In the terms of his limits he can best be explained.

At the present, physical courage is scarcely a necessity, at least among people who are not professional sports-men, workers with treacherous machines, soldiers, steeplejacks, or the like. Chivalric valor lurks in the boy-scout manuals and is presupposed in sport, but one scarcely ever thinks of one's friends as brave or cowardly in terms of their bodies. Mr. Hemingway very much does. For him, valor is almost the ability to die well, and his contempt for his fellows who accept an unheroic end is close to the snobbish contempt of a bully, without kindness, sympathy or the profounder comprehension of the chemical roots of cowardice.

The presence of physical bravery, that is, on its most elemental plane, the plane of a child's courage, is a personal attribute not unlike physical beauty, as disparate, and for most purposes as irrelevant. Rank cowardice can be as sickening as a ghastly scar, when it is not psychopathic. The balance between action against odds and inaction may be a moral balance, but a nerveless bravery without thought of reverse possibility, however fair to see, is hardly the subject for praise or blame. Mr. Hemingway believes in the courage of immediate physical action above all other. It is an implicit belief in the innocence of animals, in the purity of uncorrupted flesh;—its god-like thoughtlessness. He is not busied with the courage of the mind, the energy of a moral activity resistless in its penetration to the heart of truth, unflinching at any self-imposed limits. He does not recognize that valor above the quickened pulse and caught breath, the valor necessary to ignore one's own hard erected categories, to exceed the limits that might endanger one's position as a finished technician on a certain plane of development. He does not admit the simple bravery of a man doomed to an exploitation of every possibility of human morality, for whom physical death, however superbly received, is no release.

Ernest Hemingway more deliberately and consciously than any American writer of fiction since Henry James has occupied himself with his education as a man of letters. Like every new artist of power he has the conviction that no one before him ever achieved the razor truth of indestructible accuracy in rendering emotion. So he went to Spain, where since the wars were over, such a simple thing as physical death could be anatomized down to its last ritualized detail. He occupied himself first with death, since it is less complex than life,—perhaps because the terrible unreality of war had rendered his perceptions anemic, and he could bear the simplicity of orderly death, the real limits of synthesized bloodletting, feeling here was life in its essential microcosm. One can hardly pass any judgment on this attitude in *Death in the Afternoon* until the appearance of its author's subsequent work. Then one can see whether or not an education in mortality has had the desired effect.

Death in the Afternoon has been called a classic of presentation. It commences with mentioning the unmentionable, the visceral comedies of a horse's ripped belly; take it or leave it. Shortly an old lady is introduced, a fiendish beldame of gracious cruelty and kindly spite, who speaks in the formal diction of an excellent translation of Cervantes. The old lady at first seems Hemingway's compacted adversaries,—those who are bored by bullfights, those who think he should stick to writing conversation, which he, at least, does well. She voices the reader's own unvoiced objections before he thinks of them, to allow the author to settle the score before he is sure it is this or that to which his enemy really objects. She is a device of genius, and in his dialogue with her it is at once apparent in its finished state what has been felt before in approximation—that Hemingway's talk is more dramatic than his situations, and he is admirably fitted as a writer of plays.

> "Old Lady: Well, sir, since we have stopped early today why do you not tell me a story?
>
> "About what, Madame?
>
> "Old Lady: Anything you like, sir, except I would not like another one about the dead. I am a little tired of the dead.
>
> "Ah, Madame, the dead are tired too."

One would think from this notice that the mention of bull fighting in *Death in the Afternoon* was secondary to various ideas of living and dying. But if Hemingway is forgotten as a novelist and as an influence, his book on bulls will be read always as the most complete definition of the decadence of that phenomenon. It gives one the very rare illusion, after having completed it, that one knows all about—that there is literally nothing more to learn of—a single segment at least, of human experience. His technical descriptions are also for laymen, and with the wonderful photographs a completely legible and absorbing guide. He has a visual memory which creates in one, his two kinds of Travel-Books, a true promise of Spain before you've been there, and a living reconstruction after you've come away.

Some artists have a superb overflow, an extra exuberance of creative energy which splashes all over the formal structure of their work. One thinks of Melville's chapter on the "Whiteness of the Whale", of Byron's bad rhymes. In Hemingway the overflow is there too, of a different sort, to be sure, but in the same relation. With him it is his personal sneers, his irritable cheapness, his disposal of men he dislikes as fairies with the same lazy bravado of Marxians dismissing the petty-bourgeoisie. It is his insistence on including private references to shock, and to give trouble to the collators of his posthumous editions. It is his bullying and his adolescent apology for the expression of any overt feeling, which fortunately by no means hinders him from its accurate and splendid analysis, and it is the other meanness and lack of grace which is only socially embarrassing, and which he so relentlessly scores in others.

But however irritating, this overflow is separate and meaningless. The sum of the book stands head and shoulders above his worst self; it is his best self. That it is as good as it is and no better is perhaps a severe judgment upon the whole nature of our literature. That the discipline to which its author subjected himself in order to write it was deliberate and possibly artificial, that the choice of the subject matter itself is remote from the majority of his countrymen's interest and of a decadent form of entertainment in a decadent period, is all true enough, and on account of that fact the book's importance is enormous as a definition of the state of affairs in which artists find themselves today. Hemingway, whether he likes it or not, is at once a reformer of literature and a violent reactionary. He has made it almost impossible for anyone to write loosely of a certain portion of physical experience again. His conviction that nothing is really like what most writers think it is, of the almost complete inexpressibility of the essence of anything, may cloud his own expression with a petulant impatience, but it is a sovereign warning for anyone who attempts less. *Death in the Afternoon* is an exhilarating, exhausting and thorough monument in spite of its author and its time, a tragic masterpiece whose tragedy is also implicit in the character of its author, of his time and of his work.

Hemingway's eloquence concerning the delights of dealing death is the climax and point to this book. Just as completely as he has shown us the minute shifts of wrist, sucked in belly and the profiled thrust, just as he has taken us to bull-testings, to the cafés where the hangers-on sit with the promoters over the food they eat, the talk they talk, just as he has smelled for us the exact taste of courage in the throat, "the smell of smoked leather or the smell of a frozen road", so has he unalterably demonstrated the transports of a matador, as he plays the whole crowd through the bull "and being moved as it responds in a growing ecstasy of ordered, formal, passionate, increasing disregard for death that leaves you, when it is over, and the death administered to the animal that has made it possible, as empty, as changed and as sad as any major emotion will leave you." Hemingway knows how separate and inert our contemporary existences are from the elements of living, from a more primitive and unconditional sensibility and he has almost erected a canon of death to restore to us the capacity for life. "Once you accept the rule of death Thou shalt not kill is an easily and a naturally obeyed commandment. But when a man is still in rebellion against death he has pleasure in taking to himself one of the god-like attributes; that of giving it."

He has penetrated further into the anatomy of a kind of bravery and cowardice than perhaps any living writer except T. E. Lawrence. The author of the *Seven Pillars of Wisdom* could afford to presuppose his courage, which Hemingway cannot, but he was writing about pure action engaging masses of men in actual carnage. "Blood was always on our hands: we were licensed to it." The bull-fighters are more priests than warriors. The blood on their hands is almost sacrificial and it was Hemingway's misfortune that the war failed to teach him how men died, so he had to investigate the artifice of how men have continued to kill and not be killed. Only the behavior of a man in the face of sure death seems to convince him of his ability to live. More insistent on a unique aspect of humanity than D. H. Lawrence, Conrad or Stephen Crane, he achieves by this concentration a greater intensity, if a slighter reference. Hemingway is an incomplete tragic artist whose wilful limits, as yet, exclude him from the company of creators of living character. He has, to be sure, given us characters, but they have the signature of his choice attached, and he has personally endowed them with their characteristics. They do not exist in their own air, independent of his approval, as do Anna Karenina, Starbuck, or Leopold Bloom. Convinced and a master of a physical world as he now is, can he dare to acquire a knowledge of the others? No one, at least in this country, knows how much there is to be known for the purpose which he has so far proudly professed.

MAX EASTMAN

Bull in the Afternoon

1934

There are gorgeous pages in Ernest Hemingway's book about bullfights—big humor and reckless straight talk of what things are, genuinely heavy ferocity against prattle of what they are not. Hemingway is a full-sized man hewing his way with flying strokes of the poet's broad axe which I greatly admire. Nevertheless, there is an unconscionable quantity of bull—to put it as decorously as possible—poured and plastered all over what he writes about bullfights. By bull I mean juvenile romantic gushing and sentimentalizing of simple facts.

For example, it is well known and fairly obvious that bulls do not run and gallop about the pasture; they stand solid "dominating the landscape with their confidence" as Hemingway brilliantly says. Therefore when they have dashed about the ring some minutes, tossed a few horses, repeatedly charged and attempted to gore a man and thrown their heads off because he turned out to be a rag, they soon get winded and their tongues hang out and they pant. Certain bulls, however, for reasons more or less accidental, go through the ordeal in a small area without much running and therefore get tired in the muscles before they get winded. These bulls do not hang their tongues out and pant. This plain fact, which would be obvious to anybody without smoke in his eyes, is romanticized by Hemingway to mean that some bulls are so "brave" that they will never let their tongues out, but hold their mouths "tight shut to keep the blood in" even after they are stabbed to death and until they drop. This is not juvenile romanticism, it is child's fairy-story writing. And yet Hemingway asks us to believe that what drew him to bullfights was the desire to learn to put down "what really happened in action; what the actual things were which produced the emotion that you experienced."

In pursuit of this rigorous aim he informs us that bullfights are "so well ordered and so strongly disciplined by ritual that a person feeling the whole tragedy cannot separate the minor comic-tragedy of the horse so as to feel it emotionally." And he generalizes: "The *aficionado*, or lover of the bullfight, may be said, broadly, then, to be one who has this sense of the tragedy and ritual of the fight so that the minor aspects are not important except as they relate to the whole." Which is just the kind of sentimental poppycock most habitually dished out by those art nannies and pale-eyed professors of poetry whom Hemingway above all men despises. Hemingway himself makes plain all through his book that the performance itself is not an artistic tragedy as often as one time out of a hundred. When it is, there is about one man out of a thousand in the grandstand who would know what you were talking about if you started in on "the whole tragedy" as opposed to the "minor comic-tragedy of the horse." The *aficionado*, or bullfight fan, is the Spanish equivalent of the American baseball fan. He reacts the same way to the same kind of things. If you could get the authorization to put on a bullfight in the Yankee Stadium, you would see approximately the same crowd there that you do now, and they would behave, after a little instruction from our star reporters and radio announcers, just about the way the Spanish crowd behaves. And they would not be—"broadly"—the kind of people, if there are such people, who can see an infuriated bull charge across a bull ring, ram his horns into the private end of a horse's belly and rip him clear up to the ribs, lifting and tossing his rider bodily in the air and over against the fence with the same motion, and keep their attention so occupied with the "whole tragedy" that they cannot "separate" this enough to "feel it emotionally." Bullfights are not wholly bad, but sentimentalizing over them in the name of art-form and ritual is.

Whatever art may be, the thing which exempts it from those rules of decent conduct which make life possible and civilization a hope, is that its representations are not real. A bullfight—foolishly so called by the English, since it does not except for a moment resemble a fight—is real life. It is men tormenting and killing a bull; it is a bull being tormented and killed.

And if it is not "art" in a sense to justify Hemingway's undiscriminating recourse to that notion, still less is it "tragedy" in a sense to sustain the elevated emotions which he hopes to erect over it with this portentous term.

Suppose that you attend a bullfight with your eyes and emotional receptors recklessly wide open, as a poet should. What do you see to admire and what to despise? Men moving in the risk of wounds and death with skill, grace, suavity and courage. That is something to admire—and the wild free fighting force of the animal as he charges into the arena, a sight so thrilling that words fail utterly. They fail Hemingway. Until Christians thought up the sickly idea of worshipping a lamb, this noble creature symbolized the beauty of divine power in a good half of the great religions of the earth.

Here, then, are two things to admire and they command admiration; they command sympathy. And then you see these admirable brave men begin to take down this noble creature and reduce him to a state where they can successfully run in and knife him, by a means which would be described in any other situation under the sun as a series of dirty tricks, these tricks being made possible by his well known and all too obvious stupidity—the limitations of his vision and rigidity of his instincts—this stupidity being further assured by breeding, by keeping him in a dim light before the running and by never giving him a second chance in the ring. You see this beautiful creature, whom you despise for his stupidity and admire because he is so gorgeously equipped with power for wild life, trapped in a ring where his power is nothing, and you see him put forth his utmost in vain to escape death at the hands of these spryer and more flexible monkeys, whose courage you admire and whose mean use of their wit you despise. You see him baffled, bewildered, insane with fright, fury and physical agony, jabbed, stabbed, haunted, hounded, steadily brought dreadfully down from his beauty of power, until he stands horribly torpid, sinking lead-like into his tracks, lacking the mere strength of muscle to lift his vast head, panting, gasping, gurgling, his mouth too little and the tiny black tongue hanging out too far to give him breath, and faint falsetto cries of anguish, altogether lost-baby-like now and not bull-like, coming out of him, and you see one of these triumphant monkeys strike a theatrical pose, and dash in swiftly and deftly—yes, while there is still danger, still a staggering thrust left in the too heavy horns—and they have invented statistics, moreover, and know exactly how much and how little danger there is—dash in swiftly and deftly and plunge a sword into the very point where they accurately know—for they have also invented anatomy, these wonderful monkeys—that they will end that powerful and noble thing forever.

That is what a bullfight is, and that is all it is. To drag in notions of honor and glory here, and take them seriously, is ungrown-up enough and rather sophomoric. But to pump words over it like tragedy and dramatic conflict is mere romantic nonsense and self-deception crying to heaven. It is not tragic to die in a trap because although beautiful you are stupid; it is not tragic to play mean tricks on a beautiful thing that is stupid, and stab it when its power is gone. It is the exact opposite of tragedy in every high meaning that has ever been given to that word. It is killing made meaner, death more ignoble, bloodshed more merely shocking than it has need to be.

Fortunately it is no great trick to close one's receptors in a certain direction, to deaden sympathies that are unfruitful. We all go through life with these emotional blinders on; we could not go through otherwise. You remember the anxious mother whose husband had taken their infant son into one of those sidewalk horror exhibitions—it was an illuminated view of a "famous painting of Nero throwing Christians to the lions."

"George, George, how could you subject Bobby's tender little growing mind to that shocking experience? What *did* he do? What *did* he say?"

"He said, 'Oh, Papa, there's one poor lion hasn't got any Christian!' "

This being the nature of the human infant, it is obvious that if you grow up in a society which does not extend sympathy to bulls in the bull ring, barring some heightened consciousness or gift of reflection in you amounting to an eccentricity, you will not do so either. For this reason the idea that bullfights prove Spaniards to be cruel, or as Havelock Ellis says, "indifferent to pain both in themselves and others," seems to me—with all respect to that eminent authority—the veriest nonsense. The appetites to which bullfighting appeals are a universal human inheritance, and if its survival in Spain must have some explanation other than cultural accident, I should associate it with the almost feminine gentleness of character to be felt in that country which seems to have need of this stoical over-protest of courage without mercy. At any rate, we expect an American poet who goes down there to see more and not less than a Spanish adolescent, whose one-sided obtundity in this matter is as inevitable as the misshapen callus on the bottom of any man's foot.

Why then does our iron advocate of straight talk about what things are, our full-sized man, our ferocious realist, go blind and wrap himself up in clouds of juvenile romanticism the moment he crosses the border on his way to a Spanish bullfight? It is of course a commonplace that anyone who too much protests his manhood lacks the serene confidence that he *is* made out of iron. Most of us too delicately organized babies who grow up to be artists suffer at times from that small inward doubt. But some circumstance seems to have laid upon Hemingway a continual sense of the obligation to put forth evidences of red-blooded masculinity. It must be made obvious not only in the swing of the big shoulders and the clothes he puts on, but in the stride of his prose style and the emotions he permits to come to the surface there. This trait of his character has been strong enough to form the nucleus of a new flavor in English literature, and it has moreover begotten a veritable school of fiction-writers —a literary style, you might say, of wearing false hair on the chest. Nevertheless I think it is inadequate to explain the ecstatic adulation with which Hemingway approaches everything connected with the killing of bulls in the bull ring.

He says that he went to see these spectacles because he was trying to learn how to write, and he wanted something "simple" to write about; violent death, he thought, was one of the simplest things; he had seen a great deal of violent death in the War, but the War being over and he still learning to write, it seemed necessary to see some more. I do not think you can call it psychoanalysis to remark that the only simple thing here is Ernest Hemingway. A man writes about—and travels over the earth to see—what he likes to dwell on. Moreover, it is not death Hemingway writes about or travels to see, but killing. Nobody above fourteen years old will contend that he has got into his book that "feeling of life and death" which he says he was working for. He has got into it an enthusiasm for killing—for courage and dominating and killing. Hemingway cannot feel—he cannot even see—the hero of his "tragedy" staggering toward death in blood loss and bewilderment. He withdraws automatically from any participation in that central fact. He did once feel, he tells us, the surprise of pain which makes the animal toss awkwardly like a great inflexible box when the banderillas are jabbed into his withers, but this live feeling vanished instantly and by an extraordinary magic the moment he learned that the bull is more and not less dangerous after he has been "slowed" in this way, and will now make better aimed, because more desperate, efforts to defend his life. After learning this, Hemingway felt no more sympathy for the bull "than for a canvas or the marble a sculptor cuts or the dry powder snow your skis cut through." Which is a clear statement—is it not?—of indifference to "the feeling of life and death," and total preoccupation with the art of courageous killing.

A like numbness of imagination afflicts this poet when the life and death of the matador is in question. The climax of his enterprise of learning how to write, at least the last mention of it, occurs on page 20, where after seeing a matador gored by a bull, he wakes in the night and tries to remember "what it was that seemed just out of my remembering and that was the thing that I had really seen and, finally, remembering all around it, I got it. When he stood up, his face white and dirty and the silk of his breeches opened from waist to knee, it was the dirtiness of the rented breeches, the dirtiness of his slit underwear and the clean, clean, unbearably clean whiteness of the thigh bone that I had seen, and it was that which was important." Is the clean whiteness of a man's thigh bone the "important" thing to a poet working for the feeling of life and death, or is it merely the most shocking thing, and therefore the most sought after by an ecstatic in the rapture of killing?

"Do you know the sin it would be," he says, "to ruffle the arrangement of the feathers on a hawk's neck if they could never be replaced as they were? Well, that would be the sin it would be to kill El Gallo." And we turn the page with a shudder for El Gallo.

It seems, then, that our ferocious realist is so romantic about bullfights, and so blind to much of what they "actually are," because he is enraptured with courageous killing. He is athirst after this quality of act and emotion with that high-fevered thirst of the saint after the blood of the living God, so that little else can open its way into his eyes or down to his heartstrings. He is himself, moreover, courageous enough—and with a courage rarer than that of toreros—to state plainly that he loves killing, and try to state why. It is because killing makes him feel triumphant over death.

"Killing cleanly and in a way which gives you esthetic pride and pleasure," he says, "has always been one of the greatest enjoyments of a part of the human race. . . . One of its greatest pleasures . . . is the feeling of rebellion against death which comes from its administering. Once you accept the rule of death thou shalt not kill is an easily and a naturally obeyed commandment. But when a man is still in rebellion against death he has pleasure in taking to himself one of the godlike attributes; that of giving it. This is one of the most profound feelings in those men who enjoy killing."

Hemingway is quite right about the pleasure derived by a part of our race, and in imagination, indeed, by all of it, from killing. One need only read the Old Testament to see how easy it was for our most pious ancestors in morality to cut a whole people out of the tiny circle of their tribal sympathy like the ring of light round a campfire, and enjoy with free hearts the delight of slaughtering them "so that there was none left in that city, man, woman or child." And one need only remark the popularity of murder stories—or of Hemingway's own book so gorgeously full of horses' blood and bulls' blood, and matadors' blood, and carpenters' blood, and even the blood of "six carefully selected Christs" crucified in his riotous imagination to make a holiday for his readers, in order to see that this little-satisfied thirst is wellnigh universal.

Had men not enjoyed killing, they would not be here, and the bulls would be doing it all. That is a significant fact. But nevertheless the important part of the killing has been done, and the present tendency is to suppress, to sublimate in representative art, even in some measure to breed out, this dangerous taste. For this we have the authority of Gene Tunney, a writer who stands at the opposite pole from Hemingway, having abundantly established his prowess in action, and in literature therefore being somewhat concerned, strangely enough, to establish his sensibility. Speaking in his biography of the "killer-instinct boys," he remarks that "the higher in human development one goes, the more controlled one finds this reaction." And if that is true in the prize ring, it is more certainly true among poets and artists and sensitive young men generally.

It is so true that the nervous horror of these young men, and their mental and moral sickness, after forcing themselves through the insensate butchery of the World War, may be said almost to have created an epoch in our literature. One by one they have recovered their tongues and stood up during these fifteen years, those stricken poets, and confessed that they were devastated and quite utterly shattered by that forced discipline in the art of wholesale killing—those have, that is, who were not too shattered to speak. And their speech, with the silence of the others, is the true aftermath in poetry of the Great War—not the priggish trivialities of the Cult of Unintelligibility, not the cheap moral of decorum (that shallow cult so admirably exterminated root and branch by Ernest Hemingway in a paragraph of this book), not the new Bohemianism of the synthetic-gin period, not the poetry of the new scientific hope in Russia, for it has had no poetry—but the confession in language of blood and tears of the horror unendurable to vividly living nerves of the combination of civilized life with barbaric slaughter.

Will it be too much like a clinic if I point out that Ernest

Hemingway is one of the most sensitive and keen-feeling of these poets, one of the most passionately intolerant, too, of priggery and parlor triviality and old maids' morals and empty skulls hiding in unintelligibility? I am not strong for literary psycho-analysis, but I must record a guess rising toward the middle of his book and growing to conviction in the end, that *Death in the Afternoon* belongs also among those confessions of horror which are the true poetry or the weightiest poetry of this generation. It does not matter much whether Ernest Hemingway knows this fact or not. We may hope he will find out, for a man cannot grow to his height without self-knowledge. But the important thing is for us to know.

We took this young man with his sensitive genius for experience, for living all the qualities of life and finding a balance among them—and with that too obvious fear in him of proving inadequate—and we shoved him into our pit of slaughter, and told him to be courageous about killing. And we thought he would come out weeping and jittering. Well, he came out roaring for blood, shouting to the skies the joy of killing, the "religious ecstasy" of killing—and most pathetic, most pitiable, killing as a protest against death.

J. KASHKEEN

Ernest Hemingway: A Tragedy of Craftsmanship

1935

1

We have never seen Hemingway. In his wanderings over the world he has never visited our country and in order to imagine what he is like we have to rely, though not without reservation, on what others say. And from what they say there arises a legendary figure: Hemingway—the hero and favorite of the young literary crowd in Paris and New York, "one of the gang," a boon companion at the Dingo Café in Paris or at Greenwich Village bars. Here is the evidence of his English friend, the well-known Ford Madox Ford:

> "Into the animated din would drift Hemingway, balancing on the point of his toes, feinting at my head with

Reprinted from *International Literature*, No. 5, 1935. (U.S.S.R.)

Editorial Note: Hemingway is so perfect and evident a representative of his time and milieu lately dealt with in a number of articles and books on the "Lost Generation" that for considerations of space we have found it possible to omit from the original Russian version of this article its introductory part treating of the post-war American scene and to confine ourselves to an analysis of Hemingway's work.

> hands as large as hams . . . At last Hemingway extended an enormous seeming ham under my nose. He shouted. What he shouted I could not hear: under the shadow of that vast and menacing object."

Other witnesses recall Hemingway taking part in Spanish bullfights and the memorable fiesta when he had the good luck of rescuing that clumsy amateur-torero John Dos Passos from a "sudden violent death."

They recall skiing parties in Switzerland, the sensational knockout at the *Salle Wagram* Hemingway gave a boxer for foul play. And while reading such testimonies you fancy a strong, fullblooded athlete, an excellent tennis-player, a first rate boxer, an inveterate skier, hunter and fisherman, a fearless torero, a distinguished front line soldier, an arrogant bully, and in addition to all that—on second thought as it were—a world famous writer. And under this impression of the legendary hero, the famous "Hem the Great" of a "lost generation," you open his books.

You read the joyless tale of Hemingway's favorite hero—ever the same under his changing names—and you begin to realize that what had seemed the writer's face is but a mask, and by degrees you begin to discern a different face, that of Nick Adams, Tenente Henry, Jake Barnes, Mr. Johnson, Mr. Frazer.

Then you think of another testimony of Ford Madox Ford's:

> "When, in those old days, Hemingway used to tell stories of his Paris landlords he used to be hesitant, to pause between words and then to speak gently but with great decision. His mind selecting the words to employ. The impression was one of a person using restraint at the biddings of discipline. It was the right impression to have had."

And you imagine the man, morbidly reticent, always restrained and discreet, very intent, very tired, driven to utter despair, painfully bearing the too heavy burden of life's intricacies. This conception of "Hem the Tragic" may be legendary as well, but such we see him in his books and one-sided as this conception may be it affords the possibility of a different sidelight on Hemingway and his writings. We accept it merely as a working hypothesis that might help us make out what he is actually like.

Hemingway shows us how complicated he is by his very attempts to be simple. A tangle of conflicting strains and inconsistencies, a subtle clumsiness, a feeling of doubt and unrest are to be seen even in Hemingway's earlier books as early as his presentation of Nick Adams's cloudless young days, but as he proceeds on the way of artistic development these features show increasingly clear and the split between Hemingway and reality widens.

Closely following the evolution of his main hero you can see how at first Nick Adams is but a photo film fixing the whole of life in its simplest tangible details. Then you begin to discern Nick's ever growing instinct of blind protest, at which the manifestations of his will practically stop.

Home with its bible, a copy of *Science and Health* on the table, Indians wrangling with Doc about logs he is supposed to have stolen, his mother's sugary, "Are you going out, dear," and the stench of the fire in which during a fit of housecleaning she destroys the collections of snakes and other specimens treasured by Nick's puerile father. In a word—the stuffy, stale atmosphere of provincial existence.

And beyond home—the meeting with the prize-fighter, the trip to the Indian camp, the sight of that living corpse Ole Andreson and the consequent longing "to get out of this town" into another mysteriously alluring world of boxers, killers, soldiers. And soon we see Nick along with many boys of his age escaping to the front.

Of his youthful impressions there remain the memories of the time when "he felt sure that he would never die," a liking for sound, simple people (Indians, the battler's Negro companion, and later—Romero, wrestlers, toreros); there also remains the hunter's sharp eye and the firm grip of the future artist.

Tenente Henry—the next incarnation of the same hero is Nick Adams, grown into a man wearing a uniform. His relations with Cat are still youthfully fresh and spontaneous. When he recalls his past ("Now I Lay Me") it bears a striking likeness to the past of Nick Adams. At the front he is glad to find everything so simple. "It was simple and you were friends."

Tenente Henry enjoys the definite, clear-cut relations between people, the good comradeship "We felt held together by there being something that had happened, that they did not understand," and the feeling of risk while it lasts.

But soon along with the debâcle at Caporetto he finds himself faced by the cruelty of the rear, choked by its lies and filth, hurt by the hatred of the working people to *gli ufficiali.* And as his shellshock had lost him his sleep so does the stronger shock of war make him a different man. By the time the war is over he has learned to discern "liars that lie to nations" and to value their honeyed talk at what it is worth.

> "I was always embarrassed by the words sacred, glorious, and sacrifice and the expression in vain. We had heard them, sometimes standing in the rain almost out of earshot, so that only the shouted words came through, and had read them, on proclamations that were slapped up by billposters over other proclamations, now for a long time, and I had seen nothing sacred, and the things that were glorious had no glory and the sacrifices were like the stockyards at Chicago, if nothing was done with the meat except to bury it. . . . Abstract words such as glory, honor, courage, were obscene beside the concrete names of villages, the numbers of roads, the names of rivers, the numbers of regiments and the dates." (*A Farewell to Arms*).

His illusions about the war gone, Tenente Henry means to get through with the "glorious conflict."

Disgusted with the rôle of a mute in this infamous show, unwilling to be used as cannon fodder in the Caporetto slaughter, the man admittedly brave, now feels rising within him the instinct for self-preservation, and fiercely struggles to save life by every means possible down to desertion. Catherine's tragic death puts a sudden stop to the short lived idyll of life's simpler joys.

Nick's youthfully fresh outlook on life is now overcast by the ghastly shadow of a close acquaintance with death in its ugliest forms, his mind is laid waste. The man of the front has no hopes or faith left.

Such he comes back home only to be immersed once more in the old familiar but now hopelessly alien things. "Nothing was changed in the town. But the world they were in was not the world he was in." Everything was awfully mixed up and one had to keep lying, lying about the war, about heroism, about the German machine-gunners chained to their guns, and one had to kneel by mother's side and pray God to make him a good boy again. Was this then the way to keep the promise made in the trenches of Fossalta? Really things were awfully mixed up.

After a stay at home, Hemingway's contemporary flees to Europe again, to wander, to live a bohemian life. But there also life seems too complicated after the front and the new milieu is barren and revolting, Hemingway knows this milieu to perfection; he depicts "our boys abroad" with a pity alternating with lashing irony. Every line of Hemingway's poignantly reserved story about the Eliots is an insult flung at their bourgeois-aesthetic marriage and in his "A Canary for One" he mockingly offers the lonely and languishing Juliet a caged canary by way of substitute for a glimpsed Romeo. Hemingway's hero has no use for happiness, he is busy getting through his divorce-suit and when in 1933 Hemingway himself recalls this time in his triptych "Homage to Switzerland," he seems to see this philistine Eden as a sort of theatre stage with puppet-people acting in it, their dialogue adopted from Berlitz's *Spoken English*.

The grave bitterness of the middle panel of the triptych is further accentuated by the figure of Mr. Wheeler—that prudent bourgeois tourist,—and by the brutal practical joke played on that harmless crank, the geographer.

Hemingway knows the value of the *plaisirs et les jeux* of the rich, he tells about them with undisguised sarcasm. But as for making sure of his own position, as for drawing the necessary conclusions from his instinctive disgust at the world of the philistine—that he cannot do, it is all too complicated.

What is left him is to wander over the world, "look at things and try new drinks." What is left him is surely the wrong path —simplify things as much as possible, play a solitary game of hide and seek, "eat, drink, copulate, fight the bull, take the dope" —in a word—be just like everybody.

The well trained athletic body is full of strength, it seeks for moments of tension that would justify this sort of life and finds them in boxing and skiing, in bull fighting and lion hunting, in wine and women. He makes a fetish of action for action, he revels in "all that threatens to destroy." (Pushkin).

But the mind shocked by the war, undermined by doubt, exhausted by a squandered life, the poor cheated, hopelessly mixed up mind fails him. The satiated man with neither meaning nor purpose in life is no longer capable of a prolonged consecutive effort. "You oughtn't to ever do anything too long" and we see the anecdote of the lantern in the teeth of the frozen corpse ("An Alpine Idyll") grow into a tragedy of satiety when nothing is taken in earnest any longer, when "there is no fun anymore."

As the process of decomposition goes on, strength itself, unapplied and unnecessary, becomes a weakness and a burden.

Action turns into its reverse, into the passive pose of a stoic, into the courage of despair, into the capacity of keeping oneself in check at any cost, no longer to conquer, but to give away, and that smilingly. The figure of Jake mutilated in the war grows into a type. It is the type of a man who has lost the faculty of accepting all of life with the spontaneous ease of his earlier days. And taken from this point of view the otherwise normal characters of the story "Hills Like White Elephants" may be said to stand on the verge of a similar moral disaster. Every last bit of effort now goes into hiding their pain, into keeping the stiff upper lip, into being the "undefeated" as before, though secretly they know that their strength is not what it used to be. Sick old Belmonte puts into his toothed wolf-jawed lipless grin all his pain and hatred, all his contempt for the mob ever crying for blood and impossible victories—and then goes out to kill another bull.

This "grin and bear it" attitude towards danger and death calls to mind the conception of the heroes in ancient tragedies. We know from the very first that there is no hope for Oedipus, the chorus knows it, he himself comes to know it, we see how inexorably things rush to the destined doom.

Though doomed the heroes continue their fight, and attain a tragic beauty and repose, facing the unavoidable bravely and in full armour. But Hemingway has no pity, he leads us onto the next stage. "The undefeated" are followed by the "baited."

Like the mob around the arena, like the obliging friends—the killers—life has no mercy, life relentlessly and steadily drives the weak into an impasse, turning the pose of the stoic into the "lie down and have it" torpor of the giant Ole Andreson with his hopeless "There ain't anything to do now."

And then there are those whom life has ensnared, and those who shun it. Disbelieving their power to affect what is bound to happen the weaker ones commit a number of accidental, inconsistent acts.

What's the use—there's no escape anyway.

The incapacity to find his way through questions he cannot solve, his reticence the admission of his own weakness,—those familiar steps on the path of the individualist—bring Hemingway's contemporary to desertion on principle. The theme of desertion is not new to Hemingway. Long ago Nick Adams fled from his home town, then he fled to the front. But here too the brave arditti decorated with all sorts of medals is a potential deserter at heart.

The wounded Nick says to Rinaldi "You and me we've made a separate peace. We're not patriots." Tenente Henry kills the Italian sergeant when the latter, refusing to fulfill his order, renounces his part in the war, but inwardly he is a deserter as well and on the following day we actually see him desert. "In the fall the war was always there, but we did not go to it any more" ("In Another Country"). This theme of sanctioned treason, or desertion in every form, so typical of the extreme individualist, recurs throughout Hemingway's work.

The mental confusion and vacuum of Hemingway's contemporary, and his self absorption logically lead him down to the last form of desertion. The task of saving the world is either impossible, or else too much for him to shoulder. Then let it be saved by those who wish,—Hemingway's characters say,—as for us—let's have some lunch. And here is what Hemingway himself says:

> "Let those who want to save the world if you can get to see it clear and as a whole. Then any part you make will present the whole if it's made truly. The thing to do is work and learn to make it." (*Death in the Afternoon*).

But to learn to do it is no easy job, especially for one whose sight is limited by the blinders of sceptical individualism. Life is too complicated and full of deceit. The romance of war had been deceit, it is on deceit that the renown of most writers rests. The felicity of the Elliot couple is but self-deceit; Jake is cruelly deceived by life; for Mr. Frazer everything is deceit or self-deceit, everything is dope—religion, radio, patriotism, even bread. There is despair in the feeling of impending doom, and morbidity in the foretaste of the imminent loss of all that was dear.

> "Madame, all stories if continued far enough end in death, and he is no true-story teller who would keep that from you. Especially do all stories of monogamy end in death, and your man who is monogamous while he often lives most happily, dies in the most lonesome fashion. There is no lonelier man in death except the suicide, than that man who has lived many years with a good wife and then outlives her. If two people love each other there can be no happy end to it." (*Death in the Afternoon*).

The theme of the end recurs in Hemingway's works with a growing persistence, the obsession of death is there, not to be driven off.

> "Now Catherine would die. That was what you did. You died. You did not know what it was about. You never had time to learn. They threw you in and told you the rules and the first time they caught you off base they killed you. Or they killed you gratuitously like Aymo. Or gave you the syphilis like Rinaldo. But they killed you in the end. You could count on that. Stay around and they would kill you." . . . "The world breaks every one and afterward many are strong at the broken places. But those that will not break it kills. It kills the very good and the very gentle and the very brave impartially. If you are none of those you can be sure it will kill you too but there will be no special hurry." (*A Farewell to Arms*).

The best of them are gone and in his memories he is among them. This business of conversing with friends that are dead is a gruesome affair, and one can't live on it long. Unless death be welcome—and one still holds on to life by instinct—one has either to find some definite purpose that would make life worth living or else look for stable values, for firm ground to stand on. "If he is to lose everything . . . he should find things he cannot lose" ("In Another Country").

In pursuit of solace Hemingway's hero seeks support in Catholicism. "Technically" he is a Catholic, only he does not know what that really means. He regrets being such a rotten Catholic, he wishes he could feel religious, expects to become more devout as he grows older like Count Greffi does, or to become a tin saint, like his nun. But somehow it does not come. Somehow we put little faith in the faith of this sceptic. "With a disposition to wonder and adore can no branch of Natural History be studied without increasing the faith, love and hope," Hemingway quotes from Bishop Stanley and he shows us one of the branches—studying the dead—which has filled him with unbelief and scepticism. For Hemingway "One of the simplest things of all and the most fundamental is violent death," but in his "Natural History of the Dead" we see this last thing wickedly stripped of all halo.

Even a Harry Crosby could hardly lean on such a notion of

death. Love is another thing of value but for Hemingway it is of short duration and involves the inevitable loss of the beloved. And besides he is always prepared to question the feeling, however sincere or poetical, and seeks to degrade it in a way that verges on mania.

And so the ultimate value—"A clean well lighted place." There should be a place for a man to go to, mustn't there? And he pictures a neat and cleanly cage where he could hide from himself. But it appears that in that clean and well lighted cage things look dark and doubtful. Well, then every thing under the sun is nonsense or Nothing. Nada on earth. Nada in heaven as well. "Our Nada who art in Nada." Perhaps there is rest to be found here, the sort of rest that comes after despair and the frustration of all hopes, but you see that Hemingway's hero unlike the waiter of the just quoted story, doesn't rest here. He goes on. Mr. Frazer, and the characters of the story "Wine of Wyoming" show us glimpses of acknowledging their past mistakes, of regretting things they have spoiled and broken, things that are gone never to return again. All the long sought values lose their worth when we see included among them the cheap solace of the sovereign bottle, while the very search for values results in their successive degradation and denial, in the scepticism of the cynic.

Each of Hemingway's stories is a perfectly-finished work of art. But perfect as his stories are when taken separately, their full meaning and depth appear only when we take them in connection with all the rest of his work, and include them in the main stream of his artistic evolution. "A Very Short Story" acquires a new meaning after you have read *A Farewell to Arms.* The suite: "Hills Like White Elephants," "Cat in the Rain," "A Canary for One," "Homage to Switzerland" can be fully understood only when placed against the settings of *The Sun Also Rises*; the stories about Nick form a natural cycle, each of them being a self-sufficing sketch for an unwritten novel.

If on closing Hemingway's books you recall and assort the disjoined pieces of the biography of his main hero you will be able to trace the decisive points of his life. Nick—first a tabula rasa, then turning away from too cruel a reality; Henry struggling for his life and trying to assert its joys, Jake and Mr. Johnson—already more than half broken and Mr. Frazer—a martyr to reflection and growing passivity. So we witness both the awakening and the ossification of the hero whose psychology is so intimately known to Hemingway himself, and as opposed to it a file of brave and stoic people—the Negro in "Battler," the imposing figures of Belmonte and Manola, the broken giant Ole Andreson; in a word—those people for whom Hemingway's double has so strong an instinctive liking, first worshipped as heroes and then brought down to earth.

Those brave and simple people seem to be living only in so far as Hemingway's main hero retains his vitality, and although placed in a different higher plane, to walk the way he walks. A way from an assertion of life however elementary, to the pseudo-stoical scepticism of despair. And as you turn the last page of Hemingway's latest book, as you recall his "Natural History of the Dead," the thoughts of Mr. Frazer and Mr. Johnson, the prayer "Our nada," the talk between Nick Adams and his son in the story "Fathers and Sons"—you see the face of the hero stiffen into a horrible grimace. What had seemed to be prosperity in the case of Richard Cory and Henry Crosby turned out but a show. It will deceive no one any longer. When the mind is fatally injured, the body however strong it might seem turns into a well embalmed mummy, a walking corpse that needs but a slight push to fall to dust.

> "It was not the undertaker that had given him that last face. The undertaker had only made certain dashingly executed repairs of doubtful artistic merit. The face had been making itself and being made for a long time." ("Fathers and Sons")

Hemingway's hero wants to be simple and sane, but the sore trial to which he subjects himself doesn't pass unavenged.

The artist's power to see is perverted and broken by the obsession of death. His what-the-hell tone, his affected stoicism, his would be indifference—are nothing but a pose taken on to hide the weariness, the refined scepticism, the despair. It is by them that Hemingway is driven to mere craftsmanship, often aimless and to our mind following the wrong trend.

> "Pamplona is changed, of course, but not as much as we are older. I found that if you took a drink that it got very much the same as it was always. I know things change now and I do not care. It's all been changed for me. Let it all change. We'll all be gone before it's changed too much and if no deluge comes when we are gone it still will rain in summer in the north and hawks will nest in the Cathedral at Santiago and in La Granja, where we practised with the cape on the long gravelled path between the shadows; it makes no difference if the fountains play or not. . . . We've seen it all go and we'll watch it go again. The great thing is to last and get your work done and see and hear and learn and understand; and write when there is something that you know; and not before; and not too damned much after. . . . The thing to do is work and learn to make it." (*Death in the Afternoon*).

This is not the devil-may-care, the *après nous le déluge* attitude, whatever Hemingway himself may have said a few lines before; it is merely the statement of the fact that his powers are limited. And it is not the apology of quietism, but rather the familiar gesture of hopeless simplification. Not to save the world, but so see it and to remake at least a tiny part of it, that's what Hemingway wants and calls upon others to do. *Il faut cultiver notre jardin*, he seems to repeat after Candide and as his aim he selects the attainment of craftsmanship. In this he radically differs from his idle heroes, but nevertheless for an artist of Hemingway's scope, for the head of a literary school to turn his back on really important themes and problems may only be qualified as an escape into seclusion, as desertion.

Still it is a good sign that in working for the sake of work, in fulfilling the prisoner's task he set himself, he remains the ever scrupulous professional. And it is this honest attitude towards his work, blind though it may appear to us, that has earned Hemingway the right to be classed among the masters.

2

In the best of his works Hemingway attains the simplicity of a great master. You believe in the simplicity of the pathetic Negro, in the imposing and genuine simplicity with which Belmonte, Manola and the entire fiesta is presented. You even believe in the ultimate primitiveness of the youthful memories of Nick Adams. We are all in favor of simplicity; we have been, for a long time.

> "My straw hat was almost filled with nuts, when I suddenly heard a noise. I looked round: Indians! An old man and a young one took hold of me and dragged me away. One of them threw the nuts out of my hat and stuck it on my head. After that I remember nothing. I probably swooned, for I came to under a tall tree. The old man was gone. Some people were arguing animatedly. My protector shouted. The old man and four other Indians came running. The old chief seemed to be talking very severely to the one that had threatened to kill me."

Who is it all about? Hemingway's Indians? No, as early as a hundred years ago this simplicity was noted by Pushkin who included in one of his articles long passages from the memoirs of John Tanner.

We highly appreciate the intentional indigence born out of abundance, the costly simplicity of Leo Tolstoi—the artist. In his *Cossacks and Hadji Mourat* he is as simple as his hunters and mountaineers whose dandified rags worn with the huntsman's peculiar smartness only serve to accentuate the necessary luxury of their expensive arms. We know that this sort of simplicity may be the result of either ancient culture or personal genius. The culture of the mountaineer, the genius of Yeroshka, the culture and genius of Tolstoi himself. We were highly pleased to read that Chekhov thought the best definition of the sea the one given by a schoolgirl— "The sea was big." We have seen

Gorki resolutely strip the later versions of his early stories of all the romantic adornments and work out the cleansed style of his memoirs, or of *The Artamonoffs*. We shared the joy of the journalist Koltsov when he was telling us, how after casting about for all possible attributes for "snow"—the snow was marble, the snow was violet, the snow was blue, the snow was like sugar—he delightfully caught at the "delicious white word" "the snow was white" and rejoiced in the joy of his future readers. We couldn't remain indifferent when reading bolshevist documents of such highly-convincing simplicity as the January 1905 proclamation or speeches by Lenin and Stalin. They, as well as our best masters of literature, are in favor of simplicity, that costly synthetic simplicity of socialist realism, which necessarily implies a high degree of professional craftsmanship. But there also exists another sort of simplicity. We know the affected simplicity of a Shklovski, a Hausner, a Gabrilovich, tortured, strained ever in search of new forms of conception and style. But Gabrilovich and Hausner have a purpose. They know what they are after, when stamping out the inertia of verbosity. They want to find a new language for the new themes and the new experiences of man in second birth. It is the simplicity of the period of transition.

Even in the elaborate, naïve simplicity of John Dos Passos, by means of which he occasionally tries to cover up his helplessness and his inability to find his way through the complexity of our time, even in this helpless simplicity we can detect a desire to see and understand those who are out to save the world and those who desperately interfere with their efforts.

In this respect Hemingway's simplicity is often affected, not unfrequently vicious, and always hopeless.

Hemingway's perception of the world is keen to the extreme, but his understanding of it as reflected in his works is intentionally primitive. It is a sort of muscular and tactual perception. He feels the world as the weight of a trout pulling at the line. "Ag was cool and fresh in the hot night." "The grass was wet on his hands as he came out"—this to mean that Nick has just got out of the tent on all fours, in a word—"The snow was white." And this is not bad at all.

His crudity is not bad in itself either, the more so as it is only seeming: "It is awfully easy to be hard-boiled about everything in the daytime, but at night it is another thing." (*The Sun Also Rises*). "Hardboiled but mild-hearted"—Hemingway certainly is, and if the latter quality shows particularly in his novels, he seems to be trying to make up for it in the short stories. In most of these he is above all afraid of sounding sentimental and strives to be utterly simple, dry and affectedly clumsy. Let's open one of his books at random, and we are sure to bump into something like this:

> "Let's get drunk," Bill said.
> "All right," Nick agreed.
> "My old man won't care," Bill said.
> "Are you sure?" said Nick.
> "I know it," Bill said.
> "I'm a little drunk now," Nick said.
> "You aren't drunk," Bill said.
> He got up from the floor and reached for the whisky bottle.

After reading Hemingway's parodies of himself like the one just quoted we see how easy it must have been for Curtis H. Reider to ridicule his affected clumsiness.

Indeed, such a dialogue by Reider as:

> Then I turned and saw Gerty.
> "Hello," she said.
> "Hello," Ernie said.
> "Hello," I said. . . .
> "Tweedleboom the rumdum," Joyce said.
> "Hello, I said," Ernie said. . . .
> "Sit down down," Gerty said.
> I sat down. Ernie sat down. We all sat down.

is but a cliché of many similar passages from Ernie Hemingway and his forerunners. Stopping to look more attentively you will see that Hemingway's clumsiness and audacity hide the wary reticence of a man whose nerves are taut, a man shellshocked by life and ready to scream on the slightest provocation. He can talk of the simplest things alone and that only in undertones, if not a whisper. Even when all is boiling within him, even when like Jake he has just given away his love to another man or has hopelessly twisted his own life as his heroes so often do. At times this reserve becomes merely infantile simplification, or, as in the case of Krebs—downright crudity.

Hemingway's heroes are infantile American fashion. Theirs is not the weak-minded lisping of the "ramolis" admirers of pseudo-childish nonsense, it is simply the fancy of a strong and healthy youngster for the playthings of men—the pipe, the gun, the bottle, the fishing nets, the brothel, to a certain point the badge of an arditti. Which alone would not matter so much. What matters is that these whims blind him to the greater, the truer problems of life, that they screen out life itself by the blinders of self restriction, the devil-may-care tone, the resort to gastronomy. "Say," said John, "how about eating?" "All right," I said—this being the solution Hemingway professes to offer for many a truly tragic situation. What matters is that as time goes on we perceive more and more of the snobism of the too-subtle primitive in Hemingway's treatment of the hopelessly tangled complexity and the cynically stripped image of death. More and more often we see him present horror and perversion in pseudo-simple tones. And in the long run this simplicity turns into its reverse—into a desperate complication; Hemingway no longer deals directly and simply with things either simple or complex, but deliberately simplifies things making them yet more complicated.

Hemingway's simplicity is nothing new to the American reader who has his own tradition of honest simplicity. When reading the manifestoes of the imagists, the interpretations of American culture by Waldo Frank, Mumford and others one is ready to believe that the spirit of Thoreau is alive in American literature and his influence will yet bear fruit. In our days the wanton growth of the machine age, disfigured by the clutches of capitalism and the sinister ghost of philistine comfort and contentment have driven the American intellectual to Rousseauism, to intellectual vagabondage, to the simple life.

A liberation from abstract rhetoric and convention was advocated by the American imagist poets as early as 1912. Even earlier than that Gertrude Stein made her first experiments with analytical prose. Immediately after the war Sherwood Anderson produced specimens of lyrical prose of the same pseudo-simple sort.

But imagist poetry was food for writers and poets only. Gertrude Stein was hopelessly unintelligible. To go through the boredom of reading her affected sing-song incantations was a hard job, they were a revelation of a new art fit only to be studied by professionals. Sherwood Anderson was obsessed by the mysticism of sex, was floundering in the swamp of static psycho-analysis, thus screening from sight his new, though not consciously realised intonation and manner. In Hemingway's writings one hears at times both the artless intonation of Sherwood Anderson, and the complicated primitive of Gertrude Stein, but the thing to be noted is that this technique, so deliberately and brilliantly assimilated, is part and parcel of Hemingway's intrinsic self. Nick Adams, still alive in Hemingway, wields this technique in an easy and natural way, thus bringing the experiments of Gertrude Stein and the psycho-analytical studies of Sherwood Anderson into the sphere of genuine art.

Maybe it is just the Nick Adams part of Hemingway that is so much in arms against the bloodless scholastic simplicity of the neo-humanists, wearing the garb of antiquity and reactionary ideology; also against the cold-blooded virtuosity of that specialist in nightmares Faulkner and of his kind. In *Death in the Afternoon* Hemingway draws a definite line beyond which he leaves both "the long preserved sterility" of the "children of decorous cohabitation" and the prolific thrill-monger William Faulkner. Coming as it did in the postwar years, the simplicity of Hemingway was very much to the taste of American readers who, their eyes now open to the reality and deceit of the Wilsonian era and starving for simple truth, were delighted to welcome the precise, laconic, lucid and refreshing stories of Hemingway's first book, stories that, like the icy water from a brook, made your teeth ache. Hemingway became the pet and the prophet of the Lost Generation but nothing could make him swerve one inch from his lonely path. He did not care for permanent seclusion in the "ivory tower" of the esthetes; settling in it for a time only he cut the windows wider, hung the walls with fishing-nets, rods, hunting bags, boxing-gloves and banderillas; but he used it only as his working-room, and didn't stay in it long, for he was busy hunting and fishing and boxing and wandering all over the world. Still he didn't make a single step to meet the tastes of the readers of the *Saturday Evening Post*. He didn't lower his art. He didn't condescend to provide explanatory notes for his transparently-clear cryptograms.

Year after year Hemingway steadily elaborated his main lyrical theme, creating the peculiar indirectly personal form of his narrative (Soldier's Home, Now I Lay Me), sober on the surface, yet so agitated; and as the years went by, the reader began to perceive the tragic side of his books.

It became more and more apparent that his health was a sham, that he and his heroes were wasting it away. Hemingway's pages were now reflecting all that is ugly and ghastly in human nature, it became increasingly clear that his activity was the purposeless activity of a man vainly attempting not to think, that his courage was the aimless courage of despair, that the obsession of death was taking hold of him, that again and again he was writing of the end—the end of love, the end of life, the end of hope, the end of all. The bourgeois patrons and the middle-class readers tamed by prosperity, were gradually losing interest in Hemingway. To follow him through the concentric circles of his individualistic hell was becoming a bit frightening and a bit tedious. He was taking things too seriously. In early days both critics and readers had highly admired the "romantic" strength, the "exotic" bull-fights, "the masculine athletic style;" but now Hemingway's moments of meditation, his too intent gazing at what is horrible, his self confessed weakness, the tenseness of his despair disturbed their balance, so essential to them "in the conditions of the crisis they were living through." They were not long in discovering new pets. They found the icily-academical Thornton Wilder and that cold virtuoso Faulkner more to their taste. Hemingway was perfectly aware of this coolness. In *Death in the Afternoon* we find a few significant dialogues with the patronising old lady. In the end of each chapter Hemingway entertains her with stories and talk. At first the old lady is interested and asks quite a number of questions; but by and by she gets bored with Hemingway's professionally honest attitude to the cruel Spanish sport and his too frank exposition of its seamy side. She makes faces and begs to be told something "amusing yet instructive." Hemingway makes her listen to a chapter of his "Natural History of the Dead." In answer to a similar request from the "jolly critic"—

> *Why do you frown? Now leave this freakish strain*
> *And with gay songs the people entertain—*

Pushkin said in his "A Joke"—*Look what a view is there* and proceeded to draw a nihilist picture of the bare and stripped country-side. Hemingway's cruel parody of "A familiar history of the birds"—his blood-curdling Natural History of Cannon-Fodder is in its way still more nihilistic.

On hearing it to the end the old lady acidly remarks: "This is not amusing at all. You know I like you less and less the more I know you," and soon she disappears for good from the pages of *Death in the Afternoon* accompanied by the author's "aside." "What about the Old Lady? She's gone. We threw her out of the book finally. A little late you say. Yes, perhaps a little late."

Hemingway's latest books in which he has given up entertaining old ladies and is developing his main lyrical theme with a frightening seriousness are no longer enjoyed by old ladies, or critics or the bourgeois readers in general. A vacuum is forming about Hemingway. He has squared his accounts with the philistine, has given a good dressing down to the Neo-humanist esthetes; he hasn't the courage to join the ranks of his former brothers in arms—now "proletarians of art"—for they have taken upon themselves the tremendous and for him unbearable task of saving the world. Solitude, a path through the vacuum—lion hunting, dwelling on morbid subjects, the motto: *Winner Take Nothing*. And we see the book thus entitled met with indifference by the critics and readers and with a sense of alarm by those who are fond of Hemingway and realise which way he is tending. And it is exactly "the proletarians of art" whom the crisis has taught many a lesson that realised it most painfully. The erstwhile esthetes are now members of writers' committees; they have visited the mining districts of Kentucky, they have received a piece of first hand knowledge of the theory and practice of class-struggle. It is the first time that the "proletarians of art" have clearly understood that class struggle is no "idle invention" of Karl Marx's, that it is bound to draw them in and to grind them between its mill-stones. And having understood that much, many of them have decided to cast their lot with the real proletariat, with the working class: their first step was to change from non-social esthetes to radicals. And for these who had once been in the same camp with Hemingway, his books acquire a new value, that of a document fixing and condemning the wrong course that brought the writer to an impasse. For this class of readers Hemingway's books are a warning of the peril that threatened their own artistic growth. They are a memento that in our time even a perfectly sound man is in danger of social and artistic decay if he follows the individualistic way and remains within the confines of bourgeois society; that new courses and a new way out of the impasse are now to be sought.

First the pet of the American youth that had seen the war at the front or in the rear,—then the prophet of the "lost generation" and the impertinent favorite of his bourgeois patrons—then a maniac alarming with his growing unrest and finally a vicious degenerate and a bogey for some, and for others—a man in supreme distress, sending out SOS signals. This is how from far away we picture the evolution of Hemingway in the eyes of his American readers.

Is there really no way out of the impasse to which Hemingway has come? His writings of the last years are few and strained, or else extremely special, such as his treatise on bull fighting. Another circle has come to completion. The question is which way Hemingway will turn now. Will it be another concentric circle of his individual hell or a step up leading from under the ground to the open spaces of realism to which he is obviously tending. In the story "Fathers and Sons" there is a promise of a novel about his father and his own boyhood. Even if in writing it he should embrace the course of naïve autobiographism as so many American writers have done, his craftsmanship, applied to simple and well-known material, is in itself a pledge of success: and one might "wish him luck, and hope that he will keep writing," a wish he vainly expects from his bourgeois critics; still writing not about Death, alone, but about work and craft and life as well.

The Nick Adams in Hemingway is an incorrigible realist. He can stand no lie or sham—either in life or in art.

> "If a man writes clearly enough any one can see if he fakes. If he mystifies to avoid a straight statement, which is very different from breaking so-called rules of syntax or grammar to make an effect which can be obtained in no other way, the writer takes a longer time to be known as a fake and other writers who are afflicted by the same necessity will praise him in their own defence." (*Death in the Afternoon*).

Hemingway himself, when he finds it necessary, has courage to break the traditional intonations and forms. He knows every device of his writer's trade to perfection but in this case he is an idealist like his Mexican gambler, who unfortunately for himself loves the risk of an honest game for its own sake and "suffers great losses thereby," at least in the opinion of the orthodox modernist innovators, who don't seem to relish Hemingway's taste for intelligible simplicity.

When necessary he knows no fear or compunction whatever. No theme however risqué or repulsive can become obscene when handled in his straightforward and precise manner. And this first of all because he doesn't wallow in it. Hemingway's indecency is either an experienced nightmare which he must put on paper in order to get rid of it or else a deliberate insult at all the old and young ladies and gentlemen that turn up their noses at the Chicago and Verdun stockyards alike. He points at what he feels must be pointed at and does it straightforwardly. "So far, about morals, I know only that what is moral is what you feel good after and what is immoral is what you feel bad after."

But the trouble is that his courage is limited and in some fields as for instance the social one, deliberately so; his values are as profoundly sceptical and cynical as bourgeois society itself.

A bull has gored a picador's horse and the entrails hang down between its legs in a blue bunch, while blood pumps from the gored belly. "I wish they didn't have the horse part"—Hemingway makes one of the spectators say. "They are not important" —his companion answers, "after a while you never notice anything disgusting." Hemingway's sight is confined to his walled in world. He is wearing blinders.

When in his first book he makes an attempt at sketching the portrait of a Hungarian revolutionist you hardly recognise Hemingway, so flat the result is. But within his chosen field he is invulnerable.

He knows how to name things, how to make us feel them, how to reveal new features in them. His books can teach you the technique of trout fishing, skiing or boxing, bullfighting and above all—the trade of a writer.

"The Old Newsman" Hemingway relates that in the days of the Greco-Turkish war "his correspondent's output—something on this order: 'Kemal inswards unburned Smyrna guilty Greeks,' was to appear as, copyrighted by Monumental News Service,

'Mustapha Kemal in an exclusive interview today with the correspondent of the Monumental News Service denied vehemently that the Turkish forces had any part in the burning of Smyrna. The city, Kemal stated, was fired by incendiaries in the troops of the Greek rear guard before the first Turkish patrols entered the city,'" you could almost believe that Hemingway is unconsciously comparing his crisp and weighty stammer to the trite academical verbosity of Booth Tarkington & Co. Like Hemingway the reporter of the olden days, Hemingway the writer is now sending us telegraphic versions of his stories. And back of the sober and dark grotesque of his puzzling text you often hear a cry of despair or at least a signal of coming disaster.

This newsman, unlike the free and easy know-nothings of the editorial offices, is very exigent to himself.

> "The trouble with our former favorite is that he started his education too late. There is no time for him now, to learn what a man should know before he will die . . . First you have to know the subject; then you have to know how to write. Both take a lifetime to learn." ("Old Newsman Writes")

Hemingway takes up an extremely honest stand with regard to his material, he spares no pains in order to approach it closely just as the brave and scrupulous matador is not afraid to work "close to the bull." This is adequately illustrated by his depressingly-conscientious treatise on bull fighting. At first it seems a pity that in order to master a subject like that so much labor should have been wasted. But then you remember the remarkable though peculiar literary qualities of *Death in the Afternoon.* You remember that it was while studying bull fighting that Hemingway found the material for many an unforgettable page in his other works, you remember the description of the fiesta in *The Sun Also Rises.*

And you see that to be able to produce these pages he was bound to go through the strenuous laboratory work which he describes on page 10 of his treatise: *Death in the Afternoon:* I was trying to write . . . mentally shut his eyes.

Hemingway is reserved and frugal—he keeps to the strict self-discipline of the exacting master. He is never tired of pruning off all that can be dispensed with: convention, embellishment, rhetoric, leaving only what is essential and indispensable. You won't find one ounce of "metaphorical fat" in the prose of this sportsman. You won't find more than one image or simile in a whole story, sometimes in a whole novel.

Hemingway knows how to be brief. In his story "The Killers" he might easily have told at great length what offense it was the obliging fellows had come to avenge or how they ran Ole Andreson from town to town, from state to state. But Hemingway has no wish to do so and produces a theory to explain why he usually drops a number of links that go to make his stories. See *Death in the Afternoon* page 183 ("If a writer of prose. . . . . . hollow places in his writing.")

He has no faith in the power of the word. Whatever you say and however you say it you will express nothing anyway. A good formula for this idea that Hemingway never put into words is Tyutchev's line. "Each thought when utter'd, is a lie." (Silentium).

The application of this theory is Hemingway's method of using the strictly worded hint, the combination of precision and laconicism, of *demi-mot* and *mot juste*; it is the canonization of expressive suggestions that he uses to avoid the necessity of either giving up the world for good or definitely accepting it. He doesn't adhere to the pure keys of the literary "well-tempered Clavichord." He is in search of new harmonies, unstable yet convincing, of novel means of expression by hints, by merely fixing external gestures and situations. Whole stories are nothing but a euphemism, the entire story "Hills Like White Elephants" for instance, pivoting on one unspoken word.

The awkward tone of everyday talk, halting and hesitating, is the best way to tell of an intimacy about to be broken, or of the increasingly painful feeling of life and love going, with the sensation that "we are cut of it all," and that all that is left is "look at things, and try new drinks." The talk is over. The low mild-looking wave has passed leaving nothing but a swell. but somewhere at the shore it will turn into a fierce surf. And it will catch up the boat and hurl it on the rocks.

Only a writer of Hemingway's rank can thus convey the most intimate, the most subtle moods by an accumulation of external details; not by the word which is powerless, but by an opposition of words; not by directly expressed thought which is inexpressible, but by an impulse, by pulling a bell that is to reverberate later in the reader's mind; by a scrupulous selection of external and trivial things, i.e. in fact by straining to restrict his power to see.

Even the reader used to the obviously unintelligible style of Joyce or Gertrude Stein wants a key to solve Hemingway's puzzles simple though they look on the surface. Even to him this puzzling question may occur: "What's it all about?" Hemingway supplies the key though it is not easy to find it. The accumulation of detail in his stories looks unnecessary—naturalistic until suddenly you perceive a phrase thrown in as if inadvertently to blend the "unnecessary" details into a single logical chain thus creating a complete and very essential background. The main theme shows through the trivial talk and it is in most cases an uncanny and significant theme.

On careful reading you are sure to find in most of Hemingway's works such a key disclosing the hints and the implications of this or that story. Take the unspoken word "abortion" in "White Elephants"; or the casual remark "You oughtn't to ever do anything too long" (An Alpine Idyll), or "He didn't want it. It wasn't worth it . . . While the boys are all settling down" (Soldier's Home), and so on. But in their own way the average readers who fail to find this key and reproach Hemingway with writing on nothing are still right. So are the shrewder readers who accuse him of deliberately veiling his meaning. Hemingway is indeed to be blamed, for he doesn't care for being easily understood, he wishes to meet his reader on equal terms, to lift him up to the heights of his own shrewd art.

The same theory of expressive suggestion leads Hemingway to

project the dénouement of his stories into the future as if expecting the reader himself to supply the end. And this is certainly not the right thing to offer to bored readers like the old lady we have already met; the natural question for them to ask is, "And what then?" On hearing out one of the stories the old lady drops the disappointed remark:

> "And is that all of the story? Is there not to be what we called in my youth a wow at the end?"–Ah, madame, it is years since I added the wow to the end of a story. Are you sure you are unhappy if the wow is omitted? (*Death in the Afternoon*).

The typical American story with a plot, like those of Aldrich, O. Henry and others may be compared to a box of surprises, to a thrilling chess game with an intriguing opening, a tense mid-play and a brilliant and unexpected end-play. We are sure to see their dénouement for the social function of this sort of story is to captivate, divert and lull to sleep, whether by admiration or pity, by genuine harmony or by harmony that is false. Now the surprises that Hemingway's stories contain are not in their plot but in their psychological development. They are rather like chess problems—the chessmen being practically brought up to the decisive point but the problem ending in what looks like a stalemate. Actually however they imply a mate and in most cases the mate to the hero is so well prepared dialectically that any trifle can supply the decisive impetus and once the impetus is given and things have been set in motion, the mate is inevitable at whatever move the author chooses to stop the game.

The social function of such stories is not to solve or even to set any questions but rather to evoke them in the reader's mind. They convey the unrest and confusion that obsess the author and there can be no harmonious solution. Most of the stories break off at half-time. In "The Killers" for instance, the chessmen are shown in the "end-play," without any digressions into their past and the game begins with the check to the hero. Any moment he may turn up in Henry's lunch room to meet the instantaneous mate. But the game is artificially prolonged; unlike the traditional "murder story" this tale has no apparent ending although the end is clearly foreseen. Whatever will happen—whether or not Ole Andreson is ultimately run down by the Killers—he is a finished man, the passive anticipation of death has already killed him.

Hemingway has really learned to construct his stories. His very short stories are not loose sketches but sometimes *very* short novels.

He has parted with metaphor only to pay the more attention to composition. "Prose is architecture, not interior decoration, and the Baroque is over."

There is a solid backbone to all of his stories. At about the time when Dos Passos wrote *Manhattan Transfer*, Hemingway, too, introduced into American literature—the type of book interspersed and held together by impressionist epigraphs.

At first sight there seems to be no connection whatever between the epigraphs of *In Our Time*, and the basic stories that go to make that book, but then you begin to perceive that a certain connection actually exists between them, sometimes based on analogy and sometimes on contrast.

For instance in Chapter I what might connect the story and the epigraph is the theme of expected and much dreaded death and the different ways men find to escape the fear. Darkness for the adjutant; death itself for the Indian.

In Chapter VII in the epigraph the shock of war and a fit of naïve religious feeling imbibed in early days; in the story—Krebs feeling an alien at home as a result of the shock and a conscious revolt against the false prayer that is being imposed on him.

In Chapter XII—the acme of craftsmanship and technique—a praise to bull fighting and skiing.

In Chapter XIV and XV—the greatest contrast imaginable between the grim epigraph and the idyllic story.

The book as a whole is held together by the introductory epigraph and the tail-piece. In the epigraph the author's American friends question him about Europe and the French girls. In the tail-piece Greeks want to go to America; an ironical transfusion and the emphasised vanity of meeting aspirations.

The same function of compositional clamp is borne by the identical setting recurring three times in Hemingway's triptych "Homage to Switzerland" and by the numerous parallelisms in stories such as "Soldier's Home" and "Cat in the Rain."

But besides serving as backbones these persistent repetitions of external details fulfill a psychological function as well. They are a means for the author to reflect in his style the utter boredom of the philistine Eden: "I want a cat" (Cat in the Rain), "He didn't want it. It wan't worth it" (Soldier's Home), "Would you like a drink of something" (Homage to Switzerland), and similar intense reiterations recur again and again taking the place of psychological analysis.

The leit-motif is the principle on which Hemingway builds all of his works, or rather all of his art. Hemingway's leit-motif is either his general basic theme—the theme of war, the theme of the end of human relationships, the theme of death and void, or else it is the special backbone of this or that work. Thus repeated fragments of the phrases "everybody was drunk," "going along the road in thc dark" hold together the first epigraph of the book *In Our Time*. Thus the story "Cross Country Snow" seemingly so simple is held together by the parallelism—the pregnant girl at the inn and Nick's pregnant wife—and by the basic theme of free snow-swept spaces, all of it being but a prologue to the impending complication—the skiing trip over, back to the States, the kid born—farewell to freedom. The mournful "there ain't anything to do now"—is the burden of "Killers"; so is the ominous sound of the rain in "Cat in the Rain" and especially in *A Farewell to Arms*. Hemingway uses this method with great skill, but even here the skill turns into weakness. His themes are few, they break into fragments.

Book after book brings him to his starting point, the concentric circles lead back to the underground. "An Alpine Idyll" repeats the motifs of "Cross Country Snow," "White Elephants" shows the explosion of what you felt brewing underneath the inaction of "Cat in the Rain." The theme of the loss of things most dear, the theme of death is to be found in nearly every story. True, each time the theme recurs, it gains in depth and intensity but to break free of the enchanted circle either the force or the wish is lacking.

There was a time when Hemingway knew how to laugh. Let us remember for instance the softly-humorous scene, when Nick Adams thoroughly drunk but thoroughly practical converses with Bill on a "high plane" in the story "The Three Day Blow," or the amusing tippler Peduzzi in "Out of Season." But as the years go by we see Hemingway more and more often, basing his restless stories on a pointed contrast, verging on a ghastly grotesque.

If they still have any humor left it is a direful and morbid humor. We may say of Hemingway what Victor Hugo once said of Baudelaire: *Il a creé un nouveau frisson,*—the shudder at the simple horror of everyday existence.

In line with his book *Men Without Women* where female characters indeed appear in only two of the stories, Hemingway writes a book about the poignant love affair between the mutilated Jake and a woman of Brett's temperament.

Even in his earliest stories he liked to oppose the keen sensation of life to the sudden intrusion of peril or death (Indian Camp); his later stories remind you more and more often of grim jokes, suffice it to recall "The Killers," "An Alpine Idyll," "Homage to Switzerland."

Most of all Hemingway is interested in people. "The hardest thing in the world to do is to write straight honest prose on human beings." He makes but a sparing use of settings giving only as much as is necessary for action to develop. As a rule his landscape has a psychological function to fulfill. In "An Alpine Idyll" Hemingway wants to show people incapable of sustained purposeful effort, people who seek to avoid questions that cannot be solved, who want to be lulled to sleep. And we see all the setting, every detail of it taking part in the lulling.

You are tired of skiing, blinded by the snow and the sun,

hypnotised by the sawmill you see from the window with the saw constantly moving back and forth, by the drowsy crows, and by the sun reflected in empty glasses; you are stunned by the appalling anecdote about the lantern in the teeth of the dead woman and dulled by the dinner with its inevitable dose of wine; and from a certain point of view all this is not so bad for it leaves no time to think.

The landscape in *A Farewell to Arms* is in itself an acting character—it is the ominous rain. In other cases it is the Maritza "running yellow almost up to the bridge," and the rain again, as a background for the stream of refugees flowing along the muddy roads. Or a car-window view of France in the story "A Canary for One," the arrivals and departures of which remind you by the laconic and impetuous manner in which they are presented of similar arrivals and departures in the books of John Dos Passos. But in the rare cases when Hemingway develops his method of description to its full length it is apt to tire the unhardened reader. After following Nick four or five times down the hill or passing a dozen bends of the river in search of trout you begin to feel as tired as Nick himself, much as you admire the author's perfect precise manner of fixing the stream of perceptions.

Hemingway's art is as contradictory as his nature. He stubbornly adheres to his creative principles with no guiding idea to relieve them, no high purpose to justify them, no faith in victory to quicken them. So he often slips into a parody of himself, he comes to an impasse. Art for art's sake only serves to reveal and emphasise the void and desolation that have formed within him.

3

Summing up we see in Hemingway: his affirmation of life and a torpor at the vision of death, his fullblooded pessimism and his restrained despair, the cynical sincerity of many of his pages and his sceptical Catholicism, his skillful clumsiness and complicated simplicity, the tautological brevity of his dialogues and the precision of his hints, finally his mirthless spasmodic smile—all this tangle of conflicts has its roots in the tragic disharmony *mens morbida in corpore sano*, the mental discord that threatens to bring about the disintegration of the body and its decay.

A latent supply of reticence and of optimism not yet fully spent distinguishes Hemingway from the "writers of hatred," "engineers of death." There is not much in him to be compared to the blaspheming Celine sadist frenzy and his affected longing for nonentity. Hemingway merely looks unblinking at what awaits us all—at death. He has seen the front. He knows the taste of death too well to relish it. And perhaps it is Aldington, that other, even more harassed and sophisticated man from the front who of all the writers of this group may be placed nearest to him.

And then again he may have moments of envy at the quiet ironical hopelessness of T. S. Eliot who has taught him more than merely quoting Andrew Marvell.

The orthodox innovators have for Hemingway a feeling of wary distrust. They particularly dislike the taste this rebellious disciple shows for intelligible simplicity. "He looks modern, but smells of museum," says Gertrude Stein who on the whole is very fond of him. Hemingway has known a passing infatuation for decadent art, but he realises perfectly well that it is impossible to approach the problems set and solved by the classics if one's method and possibilities are those of decadent art. Is it not this that he means when speaking of the modern style in bull-fighting:

> "In the old days the bulls were usually bigger than they are now; they were fiercer, more uncertain, heavier, and older. They had not been bred down to a smaller size to please the bull-fighters, and they were fought at the age of four and a half to five years instead of three and a half to four and a half years. Matadors often had from six to twelve years of apprenticeship as banderilleros and as novilleros before becoming formal matadors. They were mature men, knew bulls thoroughly, and faced bulls which were brought to the highest point of physical force, strength, knowledge of how to use their horns and general difficulty and danger. The whole end of the bullfight was the final sword thrust, the actual encounter between the man and the animal, what the Spanish call the moment of

> truth, and every move in the fight was to prepare the bull for that killing. . . . It is the decadence of the modern bull that has made modern bullfighting possible. It is a decadent art in every way and like most decadent things it reaches its fullest flower at its rottenest point, which is the present. It is impossible, day in and day out, to fight bulls that are really bulls, huge, strong, fierce and fast, knowing how to use their horns and old enough so that they have their full growth, with the technique that had been developed, starting with Juan Belmonte, in modern bullfighting. It is too dangerous." (*Death in the Afternoon*).

While fully appreciating the high skill of the modern matador and the modern decadent poet he himself keeps aloof of the tasks the decadents are out to solve. In his best works he has shown that he can be genuine, simple and integral almost to the point of classicism. But the people he depicts are broken and crippled by life however simple and realistic the method of their presentation. They are in constant search of some support, even if it is only unsuccessful technical Catholicism and what they find is the mental discord, the scepticism and nihilism of a Mr. Frazer. Hemingway wants to see the world as a whole, in that particular tiny part of it on which he is working. But he cannot achieve this aim by fusing the scattered things he knows into a single unbroken world philosophy. The necessary illusion is created by a gradual chopping off of all the roots holding him to the ground and by a seclusion in the stone cell of the "Ivory Tower."

The balance of the half-healthy man is permanently disturbed, the man has torn himself away from life, he is uprooted and drying up. All that was good in him turns into evil. Art is there, it has been achieved but there seems to be nothing for him to speak about except himself and the void within him. Hemingway's fate is a tragical illustration of what awaits the stragglers, those individuals who have lost their way through the period of transition. In his books Hemingway seems to be more and more hopelessly admitting that if he should follow this course he will really take nothing even though he win. Hemingway is now facing Flaubert's old problem—the never ending torture of dissatisfaction on the way to achieving art for art's sake. Although he has never formulated his doubts as to his art, or the course he is following, these doubts have for a long time been persistently materialising in his works, in the recurring images of impotence of body and soul and of nihilistic scepticism.

In some of Hemingway's latest works we detect signs showing that for him "the time of stern maturity is nearing" (Bagritski). A mental crisis is at hand, a crisis in his outlook. Thoughts are beginning to obsess Hemingway. True, so far these are but the ravings of sick Mr. Frazer suffering from insomnia, but nevertheless it is a step forward as compared to the nights when that same Mr. Frazer having silenced his radio to a whisper was learning to listen to its murmur without thinking. Now he thinks. Naturally, enough, his thoughts turn on all sorts of dope. We have no delusions whatever.

It would be hard to expect a precise and consistent way of thinking of a man who has just said, "Many times I don't follow myself with pleasure." But time will not wait. Let Mr. Frazer not imagine that the nihilistic nightmares that haunt his sleepless nights are "only insomnia that many must have." The way from the trenches to the confessional, from the bullfighting arena to the ring where even the winner takes nothing, from Big Two Hearted River to a Clean Well-lighted Place—this is indeed a terrible way. The way of Stavrogin that we know so well from Dostoyevski. Let Mr. Frazer not put too much faith in his failing powers.

And to conclude with:—reading Hemingway is a bitter and instructive business. His problem is to us an illustration of how the bourgeois machine uses first-class human raw material to turn out perfectly manufactured and skilfully disguised human waste —a consummate literary craftsman, a perfect sportsman and globe trotter, a man reduced to stupor by having gazed too long at the repelling and yet fascinating mask of Nada.

ELLIOT PAUL

Hemingway and the Critics

1937

When a book by Ernest Hemingway is published it should be received gladly. He is a talented artist, one of the best we have. Nothing he has written has been without interest. Some readers like one short story better than another. Personally I prefer "Hills Like White Elephants." And of the novels I think the new one *To Have and Have Not* is by far the best—style, subject matter, dialogue, and all. That is not the point. What I mean to say is that he is entitled to respectful consideration. Instead, a considerable portion of the reviewers become surly, flippant, in some cases insulting. Harry Hansen says Hemingway "has turned himself into a hack," Herschel Brickell "sees no reason why intelligent readers of fiction should bother with the book," Louis Kronenberger calls into question Hemingway's intelligence and states that the writer does not "understand" a woman he himself created.

One of the stuffiest and most tedious writers of a generation of bores in England finds Hemingway's "raucous and swaggering masculinity" "rather tiresome." Obscure young journeymen come up with remarks like these: "Almost everything that can be wrong with a novel is wrong with this one." "*To Have and Have Not* is essentially an empty book." "As real as a sewer."

Sinclair Lewis, who (all Swedes to the contrary) has never done anything mildly approaching Hemingway's least work, to whom Hemingway's intensity and artistry could never be possible, sounds off in a way that must disgust even his closest friends and his family. One columnist who has been around enough to know better comments on Hemingway's "excessive use of alley talk." Such phrases as "just a great big boy at heart . . . and mind," "as a thinking being he has a very great deal to learn," "evidence of no mental growth whatever," "mental innocence," come from men who have by no means distinguished themselves as thinkers. Of course, the public pays no attention to these disgruntled professionals but buys the book merrily, enjoys it, and understands it. Nevertheless, the manifestation of bad taste and unfairness meted out to Hemingway by those who are paid to keep the public informed is disgusting. No other American writer would be subjected to such an impertinent barrage, no matter what he published. The same men who carp about the degree of greatness of a sincere and sensitive writer whose talents are no longer in question, each week are extraordinarily gentle with the most abject tripe. No one is deceived.

Of course, a few modest men saw the worth of *To Have and Have Not* and disdained to amplify the absurd legends that have been published in news columns about Hemingway's personality and his activities. Charles Poore, Malcolm Cowley, Lewis Gannett, Granville Hicks, even *Time Magazine*, were appreciative. It is to their credit.

It may be too late, in view of the misinformation that has been circulated about Hemingway for years, to say that he is a shy and diffident man, eager for appreciation and constructive criticism, not at all sure of himself, a gay companion, and a loyal friend. It is true that he is a good boxer, an expert fisherman, and an accomplished tennis player, but like most men who know how to handle themselves, he is not at all belligerent, never ostentatious, in fact, conspicuously gentle and considerate. Hemingway does not seek personal publicity. He abhors it, but having been a reporter off and on for years, he feels obliged to be accommodating to other newspapermen, and many times they have taken unfair advantage of his kindness.

To Have and Have Not must mean a great deal to Hemingway. I cannot go along with those who believe that he hates most of his characters. Quite to the contrary. He is almost dangerously fond of them. There is not a writer in America who treats his people with such extraordinary, almost feminine, delicacy or who is capable of so many shades of meaning, in the lines and between them.

Harry Morgan, the hero of *To Have and Have Not*, has the qualities which characterized the builders of this nation in happier days. He is strong and courageous, ambitious and proud. Men respect and fear him. He lets nothing stand in his way. He would not harm a fly unless it seemed imperative to do so. To his wife he is loyal and affectionate, and she loves him and follows him unquestioningly. Other women are frightened and attracted by his force and virility. He is poor but resourceful, and instead of choosing a moderate and conservative path (such as running a filling station) he wants to take greater risks for greater gain.

This giant of Key West does not expect to own a railroad or a steel foundry, thus controlling the destinies of thousands of his fellow men and adding to the might and renown of the U.S.A. He does not dream of cornering wheat and driving his rivals to suicide. He lives in our own time, in our own country. The epoch of great industrial conquest is passed. He hopes, instead, to keep his wife and his two daughters from going hungry. There is open to him at a crucial moment in his career, a relief job paying six dollars and a half a week. That would keep starvation from his home but not hunger, so he does not take it.

With odd jobs, such as serving on the police force and fishing in another man's boat he gets a motor boat of his own, and when tourists flock to Havana to try to catch the big fighting fish Morgan takes them out and tries to show them how. He earns thirty-five dollars a day, the standards of living in his family improve. What brings him to his awful death is a daring attempt, after many dignified failures, to recoup his fortunes. There is no need of the mumbo jumbo of Marxian phraseology to point out the differences in opportunity between the pioneer days and the present or the dangers and terrors lurking in our wasteful decaying civilization. Hemingway has been reproached for violence which is inherent in the life he so honestly and shrewdly observes. His accurate ear makes it seem ridiculous to delete and falsify the words ordinary Americans use daily for emphasis and to mark the climaxes of their speech. Surely the bar-room scene with the war veterans ranks with the Cyclops episode in Ulysses and the orgy in Farrell's "Studs Lonigan." Reviewers who are shocked by expressive words and disgusted by violent scenes were born too early or too late and should, for the sake of their health and the public's convenience, take up some other line of work more sheltered.

Concerning the touching episode revealed by a conversation between Harry Morgan and his wife in bed, the divergence of opinion becomes slightly ludicrous. Herschel Brickell writes that it is "so far on the indecent side that it is not even possible to suggest what it is about," while Clifton Fadiman describes the same passage as "a conversation as beautiful as it is unashamed. . . . Just three pages . . . unforgettable." George Stevens says, "There is an excellent two-page scene between Harry and his wife, written in human terms."

Reviewers are unanimous, however, in believing that Hemingway dislikes Richard Gordon and the typical array of well-to-do or wealthy men and women who have money and, even with that, are unable to live enjoyably. I must enter a lonely protest. I have read and reread the parts about Gordon, and it seems to me Hemingway is sorrier for him than for anyone else in the book. Gordon wants peace of mind as desperately as Morgan wants money for his family. He is unsuccessful in his philandering, his wife wounds his self-esteem by reciting all his shortcomings and her discontents. He writes badly and knows it and suffers accordingly. He cannot even find relief in drink. Strangers sock him on the jaw. His rival takes him home and pities him.

It would seem at first glance that Mrs. Laughton, who loiters in Freddy's bar, is vulgar and futile, but her quick discernment concerning Morgan and her breathless "Gee, he is beautiful" raises her for a brief moment, as Harry is going to his death, to the level of a Saint Veronica.

To comment adequately on the poignant moments and scenes, to dwell upon the frightful implications that comfortable folk can ignore little longer, to pay tribute to the beauty and human understanding in Hemingway's derided masterpiece would take more words than are contained in the book itself. I am confident this will be done in due time. Meanwhile, I sincerely hope that Hemingway will not be discouraged or depressed, that he will know there are many who are grateful to him and are looking forward eagerly to his next book.

Cowley finds Hemingway not as "great" as Tolstoy or Thomas Mann but "perhaps as good" as Mark Twain. Stevens thinks Jules Romains did a better job in *The Proud and the Meek.* Some commentators are sure *To Have and Have Not* is not as good as *The Sun Also Rises* and *A Farewell to Arms*, others place it between them. Such comparisons are permissible but quite pointless. How would it seem if I said that I do not consider Clifton Fadiman, Louis Kronenberger, or Herschel Brickell to be in the class with Coleridge, Sainte-Beuve, or Ralph Waldo Emerson but that they were perhaps as good as Mencken, and surely much better than Dr. Joseph Collins?

DELMORE SCHWARTZ

Ernest Hemingway's Literary Situation

1938

1

"Mr. Hemingway is preëminently the wise guy." Such was Ezra Pound's succinct and idiomatic remark, which is mentioned for the sake of naming this popular and superficial aspect of his writing and immediately moving past it. It is worth saying, so that one can be aware of how much more his writing contains than cleverness, and of how very often the cleverness is a way of getting important feelings and attitudes upon the page. And now that this new novel presents an attempt to deal with the class structure of society, a review of this new book will be aided greatly by trying to get a whole and round view of what his writing has actually been concerned with besides cleverness and bright sayings.

Other aspects must be eliminated also. One must forget about the public figure, the legend, the athlete and sportsman, the American Byron, the one for whom Gertrude Stein has a weak-

---

From the *Southern Review*, Vol. III, Spring, 1938. Reprinted by permission of the author.

ness, with whom Morley Callaghan boxes and Max Eastman wrestles, and the professional funny man for a magazine whose chief purpose is the advertisement of men's clothing. These are very interesting aspects, no doubt, and Charles Scribner's Sons and the circulating libraries will not fail to appraise them at their true value. But one must forget about them if one is interested in serious criticism of a serious writer. It is precisely these aspects which obscure the serious writer: one would not be astonished if they obscured the writer from himself at times. The serious writer is the one who tells us that he was working for a certain feeling of life and death, and that it is important to be critical of mysticism because mysteries actually exist.

Once a good writer has written five or six books, there is always a pattern present. The pattern can be observed in its simplest terms merely by watching for recurrent themes, or in a more detailed fashion. The important thing obviously is the writing itself, as a specific thing. The pattern is to be discarded as soon as it has been used or is useless. It is there, but the only reason for abstracting it is to aid one's gaze and get near as possible to the actual thing to be read. With this apology, and knowing well that one will not fail to forget some important element, I would like to name the pattern in Hemingway's writing as briefly as this: there is an extraordinary interest in sensation; there is an extraordinary interest in conduct and the attitudes toward conduct; and there is always the background of war, either one which has recently been concluded or one which is going on. Sometimes the background takes the form of the imminence of death, but it is the same thing, actually, because it is there for the same reason, to draw forth certain kinds of conduct. It would be neat and very helpful, if there were a clear link between the interest in sensation and the interest in conduct, but I am afraid that I can find none. It is true that during a time of war and when one is writing about war there will be a great heightening of sense-awareness because of danger, but Hemingway's interest in sensation is directed to daily gratification of the sense-organs as well as the feelings of peril.

One need not dwell very long on the attention paid to sensations. It is responsible in Hemingway for much good writing, and especially for the clean and hard character of the descriptive passages, which are also affected, I think, by certain kinds of modern painting. One interesting point may, however, be made. Any psychologist will tell us that the term *sensation* is very abstract because the whole history of the organism responds to any stimulus and actively determines its nature, so that we are experiencing our own past as much as the stimulus. But if a naked sensation is possible, then Hemingway is often engaged in describing it, and this seems to be significant of the fact that his characters are separate and alone at the present moment, having little or no history. They usually have a nationality, but mostly for the sake of their conversational idiom, which, as I intend to try to show in a moment, is the most characteristic aspect of Hemingway's style. Good eating, good drinking, good sport, good sexual intercourse, good landscapes—all these subjects have to do with sensation rather than with a more complex human experience, and these subjects constitute the texture of the writing.

By contrast, the interest in conduct and the attitudes toward conduct is central. The conduct with which Hemingway is chiefly concerned must be distinguished sharply from behavior, and the meaning of the word in which it is equivalent to human action. For it seems, of course, that every storyteller is concerned with conduct. With very different kinds of conduct, however, with the ultimate ends of human existence, with the *mores* of a given time or race. In no exact sense is the fiction of Hemingway about the one, nor the other, nor is it about the habits of daily living (as in *Ulysses*), nor ideas (as in *The Magic Mountain*), nor the way of life of a whole class (as in *Buddenbrooks*), nor human passion amid an environment (as in *Wuthering Heights* or *The Return of the Native*), nor existence in every aspect (as in Tolstoy), nor the existence of a given society (as in Balzac), nor sensibility and time (as in Proust and Virginia Woolf), nor in moral obsessions of a special kind (as in Dostoyevsky and Gide), nor with the bureaucratic structure in which all human effort is involved (as in Kafka), nor with the growth and trials of character (as in George Eliot). This is a prolix list of negative examples, but they will serve to indicate the limitations of Hemingway's art as well as the kind of conduct in which he is not interested. Hemingway does not resemble any of the writers just mentioned; he does not resemble Gertrude Stein or Sherwood Anderson, although he has of course learned a method of style from them; he certainly does not resemble his imitators, but if a comparison is necessary, one could say, without meaning to be pretentious or astounding, that among novelists he most resembles Jane Austen, who was also very much interested in a special kind of conduct. Although she was not likewise concerned with sensations, she also used conversation for the sake of a kind of rhetoric.

There is a definite code by which characters are judged and by which they judge each other and which often provides the basis of the conversation. It is important to recognize that the code is relevant, and only relevant, to a definite period of time and to a special region of society. Courage, honesty, and skill are important rules of the code, but it is these human attributes as determined by a specific historical context. To be admirable, from the standpoint of this morality, is to admit defeat, to be a good sportsman, to accept pain without an outcry, to adhere strictly to the rules of the game and to play the game with great skill. To be repugnant and contemptible is to violate any of these requirements. It is a sportsman-like morality, or equally, the morality of sportsmanship. It extends its requirements into the region of manners and carriage, and one must speak in clipped tones, avoid pretentious phrases, condense emotion into a few expletives or deliberately suppress it—noble, to borrow a pun from William Carlos Williams, equals no bull.

Examples are, in fact, too plentiful. Cohen, in *The Sun Also Rises*, is a prime example of one character who violates the code again and again. He does not play the game, he discusses his emotions at great length, he does not admit defeat with the lady whom he loves, and when he is hurt, he lets everyone know about it. Thus he must be one of the damned. He comes up against the blessed, the secular saint of Hemingway's morality, when he meets the matador who has won the lady whom he loves, and, being a good boxer, knocks him down again and again, only to have the matador take unending punishment and get up from the floor each time with no word and without being knocked out, until Cohen is finally defeated by the fortitude, the moral ascendancy, of the matador, and can only begin to cry and to wish to shake hands. In turn, the lady in question obeys the code and gives up the matador because she too recognizes his sanctity of character, and because "it isn't the sort of thing one does," and because she does not want to be "one of those bitches that ruins children." As this instance suggests, the whole code can be found explicitly in the book about bullfighting as well as in the stories.

Whether a person is capable of living up to the code can be found out fairly well in sport. As C. K. Ogden has observed, the notion that modern sports are amusements is absurd—genuine recreations are one thing and involve no contest, but most games are actually among the most searching forms of existence. The best way, however, in which one's character is tested is by one's conduct in the face of death. It is, I think, this concern with conduct which directs Hemingway's plots to violent situations so often. And here again, one can recognize Hemingway's just intuitions, for one can scarcely doubt that the peril of dying is the most essential trial of any human being. But one would like, in passing, to protest against the frequent statement that Hemingway is interested in death, a notion which he himself seems to like. An interest in death is very unusual in the writers of our time, and it is with regret that one feels compelled to deny it of Hemingway. But he explains, in *Death in the Afternoon*, that he went to the bullfights because he wanted to see violent death "now that the wars were over"—a significant phrase—

and the bullring was the only place to see it. He wanted to see violent death, not "the complications of death by disease, or the death of a friend, or someone you have loved or have hated": which means, clearly, that he was not at all concerned either with dying, nor with the dead—which would be a truly impressive concern for a modern writer.

The morality in question has its own Arcady. The priest who is held up for admiration in *A Farewell to Arms* speaks of his own country, Abruzzi, where "the roads were frozen and hard as iron, where it was clear, cold and dry and the snow was dry and powdery and hare-tracks in the snow and the peasants took off their hats and called you Lord and there was good hunting." And we are given another version of it in the short stories about Switzerland—where the point in each story is the clear-cut integrity of the Swiss—and also in the story called "A Clean, Well-Lighted Place," a café "which is clean and pleasant and well-lighted and the light is good and there are shadows of the leaves."

But there is always the background of the war and the despair consequent upon it. It is this which distinguishes the code sharply from the ones which it might seem to resemble very much, the codes of the gentleman, of chivalry, and of sport, of the past. For there is no reason for obeying the code, no sense that somehow it sustains a society and a way of life. Obedience to the code is an act of desire with no other basis, and the matador is admired and Cohen is condemned with the implication that everything is relative, if one cares to think about it. The values by which we live have been ruthlessly laid bare by the bloodshed, at one extreme, and by the political speeches and propaganda, at the other extreme. There is a remarkable passage in *A Farewell to Arms* (much quoted, unless memory deceives me, when the book first was published) in which the destruction of values is explicitly recognized [A soldier says to the hero: "What has been done this summer cannot have been done in vain."]:

> I did not say anything. I was always embarrassed by the words sacred, glorious, and sacrifice and the expression in vain. We had heard them, sometimes standing in the rain almost out of earshot, so that only the shouted words came through, and had read them, on proclamations that were slapped up on billposters over other proclamations, now for a long time, and I had seen nothing sacred, and the things that were glorious had no glory and the sacrifices were like the stockyards at Chicago, if nothing was done with the meat except to bury it. There were many words that you could not stand to hear and finally only the names of places had dignity . . . Abstract words like glory, honor, courage, or hallow were obscene beside the concrete names of villages.

And yet, although the hero of this book deserts from the army, and although it is true that the abstract words have become obscene, it is nevertheless precisely glory, honor, and courage which constitute the ideals of conduct in all of Hemingway's writing. Given the historical situation, given the war and the post-war world, the characters grasp these values by a fiat of will, as if they existed in a vacuum without support or basis. It is impossible to resume the desires and ambitions and the whole way of life which made existence supportable before the war occurred. One must send dispatches to a newspaper or get one's living in some other fashion not related to one's essential life, and then one will be free, for a time of holiday, to seek the intensity of feeling which was the one positive gift of the war. There are too many homosexuals in the drinking-places (much homosexuality has developed as a result of the war) and the *nouveaux riches* (who have become rich during the war) are also too prominent; and perhaps one has been wounded in the war and rendered impotent, or perhaps one's girl has died during the war. The reader will recognize the circumstances of *The Sun Also Rises*; but whatever the specific context, the situation is identical. In a story called *A Way You'll Never Be*, a shell-shocked soldier says: "Let's not talk about how I am, it's a subject I know too much about to want to think about it anymore."

And there is, to complete the pattern, an outline at a distance of a morality and way of life which transcends the whole situation. There are figures in the background who are not in that state of privation in which values lack a firm ground. When these figures come forward, there is always the implication that they are naïve and do not know what has happened and that the world has moved on: but in their naïveté and ignorance, they are nevertheless whole and integrated, a way which we'll never be. Twice or three times, Catholicism provides the basis for these figures, and in recognition of the superiority involved, the hero sometimes prays, or is very courteous and friendly to a priest, and the priest himself, though he is baited, is set forth as a lovable figure. Yet when the priest in *A Farewell to Arms* asks the hero to go to his own happy country, in the passage already referred to, the hero does not go, although he had wanted to go, but he went instead "to no such place but to the smoke of cafés and nights when the room whirled and you needed to look at the wall to make it stop, nights in bed drunk, when you knew that that was all that there was," and then, in the morning, "a sharp dispute about the cost."

There is one intricate method of style which bears the weight of the whole complex of attitudes, conduct, morality, and the disintegration of values. The method of style is constructed in the medium of conversation (and it is in his modification and extension of the rhetorical possibilities of speech that Hemingway has, I think, made his most valuable contribution to writing), and the speech is, by no means, as Wyndham Lewis maintains (having, as usual, nine or ten axes to grind) "the rhythms of proletarian speech. . . . the voice of the 'folk,' of the masses, who are the cannon-fodder." The conversation is, on the contrary, a great heightening of the kinds of speech of our time, an exaggeration in which the whole pattern is embodied. *The foreigner* is necessary for this rhetoric. The foreigner carries over into English the idiom of his native tongue, and in that modified English he makes clear the fact that he is living by the values which constitute the code. If, at times, it happens that the honorable one is an American and the foreigner is without honor, this makes no difficulties or falsity, for the honorable Americans are given a style of speech all their own, and the foreigner is made to speak like an American. The method is a fine example of how a writer's style and his values are fused. In the story called "The Gambler, the Nun, and the Radio," a significant story in other respects also, we get the whole conversational system in action. A Mexican gambler has been shot and is being questioned by an American detective who wishes him to reveal his assailant and who tells him that he is going to die:

> "Listen," the detective said, "this isn't Chicago. You're not a gangster. You don't have to act like a moving picture. It's all right to tell who shot you. That's all right to do."

Here we have, of course, the concern with conduct set forth in usual American speech. The Mexican gambler understands English very well, but nevertheless this statement must be translated into his own terms, into a stylized foreign version. The translation is performed by a writer who is sick in the hospital at the same time:

> "Listen, amigo," said Mr. Frazer (the writer). "The policeman says that we are not in Chicago but in Hailey, Montana. You are not a bandit and this has nothing to do with the cinema."
>
> "I believe him," said Cayetano softly (because he is badly wounded this is not the cinema). "Ya lo creo."
>
> "One can with honor denounce one's assailant. Everyone does it here, he says."

For emphasis, one ought to note that *the moving picture* becomes *the cinema* and *that's all right* becomes *one can with honor*, and the background is taken care of very well by the statement that everyone does it here, everyone denounces one's assailant to the police here.

Many other examples could be given, and will come readily to the mind of every reader of Hemingway.

Before going on to consider the new novel, it ought to be

noted that the morality which seems so much the substance of Hemingway's writing is a fairly limited one. It is, as has been said already, peculiarly qualified by and linked to a specific historical background and a few definite situations. The morality cannot be directed to other kinds of situation and other ways of life without a thoroughgoing translation. It is a morality, to repeat, for wartime, for sport, for drinking, and for expatriates; and there are, after all, a good many other levels of existence, and on those levels the activities in question fall into place and become rather minor. Consider, for example, how irrelevant the morality would be when the subject matter was family life. The style, as has just been shown, is likewise focused upon certain key situations and contexts, and relative to them, and inseparable from them. This defines Hemingway's limitations as a writer, and it indicates that a genuine transformation would be needed if the same writer were to attempt to deal with the class structure of society directly. But this is precisely what Hemingway has tried to do in this new novel.

2

To Have and Have Not is a stupid and foolish book, a disgrace to a good writer, a book which should never have been printed. It contains passages of good writing, and the parts of three good short stories—when one of these parts appeared in *Esquire* as a short story, it was much better there, and not broken up by the interposition of a chapter. But elsewhere and for the most part, it is appalling as a literary product: the conversation is repeatedly false, or rather falsetto, and the descriptive passages sometimes read like improvisations.

The central character of the book is Harry Morgan, a fisherman who has been earning his living by chartering his boat for fishing trips. When a wealthy man who owes him almost a thousand dollars for two weeks of fishing departs without paying him, Harry Morgan is driven to crime. Driven is scarcely the exact word, since he is naturally a violent man and he has recently rejected an offer to smuggle Chinese into the United States for no scruple other than prudence: he says that he is afraid human cargo will talk. Once launched upon his criminal career, the responsibility for which rests upon the welshing rich man, Harry Morgan makes rapid progress. He is forced to kill one Chinaman in order not to kill twelve others, and soon, while smuggling rum, he is badly wounded by the Coast Guard, loses an arm, and has his boat taken from him by the police. Finally, still trying merely to earn a living for his family, he engages to take four Cuban revolutionists back to Cuba after they have robbed a bank, and they, launched upon a career of adventitious violence, kill his assistant for no good reason, and are killed by him, but not before one of them manages to get a bullet into him, leaving him slowly bleeding to death of a stomach wound. The action of this whole passage is written very well. Harry Morgan does not die, however, before he has announced his conversion to the belief that all those who are, like him, merely trying to make a living, can get nowhere without solidarity. Hemingway tries very hard to make actual Morgan's realization of this fact, in his speech about it, in the half-delirium before he dies, but the whole dialogue is completely false. Quoted apart from its context, the falsity may not be as obvious as in the book itself, but the effort to syncopate the sentences, to resort to expletives, and tough-guy diction must be transparent:

> "A man," Harry Morgan said, looking at them both. "One man alone ain't got. No man alone now." He stopped. "No matter how a man alone ain't got no bloody . . . chance."
>
> He closed his eyes. It had taken him a long time to get it out and it had taken him all of his life to learn it. . . . Harry Morgan looked at them but he did not answer [they, captain and mate, have asked the dying Morgan if he wants anything]. He had told them but they had not heard.

Throughout the narrative the rôle of the rich is underscored very heavily and they are presented in an unrelieved nastiness which amounts to little else than the worst caricature. There is, for example, the yachtsman, a member of the Administration, we are told, who sails by Harry Morgan's boat when he lies in it wounded, and wishes to get him and turn him over to the police because he thinks catching a bootlegger is better than catching fish. There are also passages in which Harry Morgan discusses the social problem with another of the "have nots," and these conversations are ridiculous despite Hemingway's perfect ear for conversation, and they are made more ridiculous by the effort to make them convincing by using a hard-boiled diction. There is the effort to make Harry Morgan an admirable character by observing him from the standpoint of his wife who celebrates him at some length because of his sexual powers.

And the progress of the story is as poorly constructed as it possibly could be by a writer who said once that writing is architecture and not interior decoration. The book begins in the first person singular of Harry Morgan, shifts to straight narrative, shifts to the first person singular of another person, resumes the straight narrative, which later becomes indistinguishable from a form of essay or biography, changes again to the first person singular of Morgan's wife for two pages, and concludes with straight narrative.

Such shifts in the standpoint would be less intolerable if there were any effort to make them systematic, and were it not for the fact that when the book is more than half completed and Harry Morgan is bleeding to death on his boat, we begin what is virtually a new book devoted to the break-up of the marriage of a writer who, crudely enough, is also writing about the social problem, but not—of course—like Hemingway. He is brought forward partly as another example of the contemptible lives of the "haves," partly to be a type of the insincere writer who, following literary fashions, is writing a novel about a textile strike. The most crude instances of the vicious literary attitude of the writer are given, and he is also condemned because he does not make love properly. Soon, however, the marital relationship becomes very interesting for its own sake, the writer becomes pathetic and moving, and the social theme has been lost sight of again. It is regained by bringing the writer to a saloon where there are abused, exploited, and punch-drunk veterans engaged in beating each other up. Here again the writing is very good in parts. The writer manages to get into a conversation with several of the veterans, one of whom, conveniently enough, turns out to be not only a communist, but also a reader of the writer's novels and their severest critic. The only relationship which the story of the writer bears to the story of Harry Morgan is that of geographical propinquity, and also there is one moment, the worst in the book, when the writer passes Morgan's wife in the street and mistakenly supposes her to be unsatisfied sexually, rather than one who is very well pleased.

But this is by no means all. Still feeling, one would suppose, that the theme has not received adequate exemplification, there is a new break in the narrative, again on the basis of geographical location, and we are treated to a series of brief character studies of the rich who are about to go to bed in their yachts in the harbor of Key West on the night that Harry Morgan is dying. Some of these studies are in themselves very well written—one of them suggests, almost, a Jamesian augmentation in Hemingway's style. One of them concerns the relationship of a homosexual millionaire and one of his friends who will, six months after the end of the book, we are told, commit suicide because he has too small an income. It is at this point that we get a neat little editorial to the effect that the income which will be too small is one hundred and seventy dollars a month more than those on relief are getting. Another character study is that of a grain broker who has no past to look back upon but one consisting of successive betrayals for the sake of wealth. And lastly, we get a fine little close-up of a movie star whose lover has just become too drunk to make love to her and fallen asleep. These people are not related to each other, and their only relation to Harry Morgan is the fact that he is poor and they are rich, and they are near each other, spatially speaking.

The weakness of the structure and the commonplace character of the conception is in itself enough to show how poor the book is. This judgment can also be reinforced by examining the specific conversations, which are often farcical in their effort at satire, or simply false. But I do not think it is necessary to engage in further quotation of particular passages.

What is more important is the way in which Hemingway has shifted his literary situation[1] without changing or modifying his style and method at all. First of all, he is writing about a theme which he does not know anything about and as a result the conception of character is constantly false. The immediate cause of Morgan's resort to crime, the fact that he has not been paid for his boat by the rich man, is not convincing as an explanation for the simple reason that he has been displayed as a violent individual to begin with, and thus one to whom crime would in no way be a degeneracy of character. Another curious attribute of the situation is that Harry Morgan has been getting thirty-five dollars a day during the fishing season and thus would presumably be one with a petty bourgeois mentality with regard to the economic situation and ripe for fascism. Another difficulty is his ability to generalize the evil from which he suffers, his ability to see it as a matter of the class structure and requiring solidarity. It would seem that, given Harry Morgan's mentality as presented in the book, he would tend to think always in terms of individuals, to fix evil-doing on individuals, on the man who did not pay, for example; and at most, if he did generalize about the matter, to make it a question of race-prejudice, or prejudice against the nationality of the individual who has wronged him. It is not exact to say that Harry Morgan is a criminal, but he is

[1] I borrow the notion of literary situation from Mr. Allen Tate's illuminating essay on Emily Dickinson in *Reactionary Essays on Poetry and Ideas.*

criminal enough in his whole manner of approaching things, and the criminal is the one, among all, who presupposes and requires property relationships, so that the conversion of Harry Morgan at the end of the book comes bluntly against the fact that criminals when dying do not seem and cannot seem to understand their defeat as an exposure of the futility of individualism, the need of solidarity, and the evil of property relationships.

To repeat: in order to shift from the literary situation which I have tried to elucidate as the basis of Hemingway's writing and in order to grasp the social theme directly what is required is a reorientation of style and method. If it is felt, that is to say, that the social theme must be handled directly, then the satirized writer in *To Have and Have Not* has at least chosen a subject matter proportionate to his theme in deciding to write about a textile strike, and thus taking up the evils of finance-capitalism in precisely the situations which show the conflict between the workers' need of wages and the employers' need of surplus value. In order to write about this, one needs what has been called "a Marxist imagination," the best example of which is to be found in Trotzky's *History of the Russian Revolution.* It is the kind of imagination which Hemingway does not have, and exactly because he has an imagination of another sort. Perhaps he might, by a miracle of development, manage to acquire one, but it is at least certain that the social theme as involving the class structure of society cannot be grasped merely by deciding to write about it; especially after one has created a complicated instrument for describing the lives of individuals who are engaged in leisure-class pursuits, and are trying to maintain a code of values in a warring or post-war world.

Is it necessary, however, to handle the social theme directly? It would seem evident, on the contrary, that the character of the society in which we live, the hell of finance-capitalism, is revealed most adequately in certain important aspects by *The Sun Also Rises* and *A Farewell to Arms.* We see clearly how the simplest and most unoffending values are mercilessly perverted, abused, and befouled by modern war. Or, to put it even more crudely, the contemptible lives of the rich as they have previously been depicted by Hemingway are sufficient examples and sufficient judgments of our time, given Hemingway's own values. No other examples are possible for him, given his style, his interests, and his perceptions (all three are actually one), and he deceives himself and betrays us when he abandons them for an abstract paradigm, which falls apart at every moment in his book.

And now, as it happens, it seems to be possible to round out the picture patly, for, without for a moment doubting the good will involved, we read that Hemingway is once more in the midst of a war, sending dispatches about the battles to a newspaper syndicate, knocking out another correspondent who has doubted his motives and insinuated his bravado, and writing a play about the war in a Madrid hotel amid the intermittent bombardments. I think it is not too much to say that we can hope for the best, both for the literary cause and the other one, so far as Hemingway is involved in it, because it is by no means a metaphor nor fanciful to say that he has now gone home.

EDGAR JOHNSON

Farewell the Separate Peace

The Rejections of Ernest Hemingway

1940

1

Few modern writers reveal a more consistent intellectual development than Ernest Hemingway. In both his themes and the meaning he has found in them he has moved steadily and even logically from the earliest work of *In Our Time* to the significant orientation of *The Fifth Column*. The logic of this development has for the most part remained unnoticed by critics who have failed to realize that Hemingway, far from being a child of nature, is in fact an intellectual. They have presented him, consequently, as a sort of savage endowed with style, gifted but brainless, and the angry darts of *The Sun Also Rises* as those of an *enfant terrible* planting them with deadly but unconscious naïveté, a child lisping in banderillos for the banderillos came.

During the last few years, especially, there has been an entire chorus depreciating Hemingway's understanding. Raised first

---

From the *Sewanee Review*, Vol. XLVIII, No. 3, July-September, 1940. Reprinted by permission of the author.

among the more serious reviews, the cry was swelled by emulative pipings from even the daily book-gossipers; it reached a climax of comic fatuity in the solemn judgment of one of these that "as a thinking being he has a very great deal to learn." Sometimes by dogma, sometimes by derision, Hemingway's claims to everything except a kind of instinctive flair for writing have been denied and the logical integrity of his work misunderstood. It would be persuasive but it would be an error to seek the roots of these misjudgments in political feeling. They already existed in germ long before Hemingway ever fought for loyalist Spain, long before he had any politics except the rejection of politics; and even now they may be uncovered in journals of every shade of opinion. The reasons lie rather, I believe, in the fact that Hemingway is an intellectual who has renounced intellectualism.

Writers in our time may safely attack almost all things, save only the intellectual and his values. They may sneer at Main Street and howl against Wall Street, they may mutter darkly against the perfection of the Constitution, they may even snipe at the outworks of learning and science. But let a writer defame the holy of holies, intellectualism itself, and he is torn to shreds by all the feline tongues of the intelligentsia, male and female together. Aldous Huxley, to be sure, impaled them upon the sharpened stakes of satire and escaped untorn—at least, until his current phase pacifist mysticism—but largely because his very attack implied an altitude of brow so much loftier than even high-browism as to reaffirm its essential values. Hemingway, however, like D. H. Lawrence, has quarreled, although not so fundamentally and all-inclusively, with the root-assumptions of bohemian-aesthetic intellectualism. And like Lawrence he has been derided as a sort of modern Heidelberg Man, incapable of understanding the things he despised.

Hemingway is himself partly responsible for these misapprehensions. He has sympathetically portrayed simple and ignorant people: prizefighters, matadors, boys, jockeys, whores, bartenders, waiters. He has savagely mauled the futile crew of post-

War expatriates and perverts and pseudo-literary sophisticates, the wealthy and the idle and the vicious, drifting from bar to brothel in Paris, Madrid, New York, and Florida. A skilled amateur boxer, he has almost paraded a rather fractious muscular virility and laid himself open to a good deal of kidding about hair on the chest, to which he has responded with an angry and humorless bellicosity. He has breathed a lot of fiery sentiments about bulls, blood, and death, and a good deal of truculence about his fellow-craftsmen.

None of these facts, however, really makes Hemingway the chest-pounding atavism of the caricatures. Neither brawn nor the scorn of bad writers implies absence of brain. It is rather simple-minded to assume that only the simple-minded can sympathize with or understand the simple. It is rather worse than that to read Hemingway's satire on sophistication as the howl of a savage against what he cannot comprehend.

If Hemingway rejected obvious subtlety and repudiated highbrowism he rejected them not through incapacity but comprehension, rejected them in a way because rejection has been the principle of his intellectual growth. Indeed, Hemingway's development as a writer has been almost dialectical: thesis followed by rejecting antithesis, the resolving synthesis fusing the values of its predecessors, and then being rejected in turn as Hemingway worked through its flaws. Its stages should be sufficient to refute those critics who find in his career "evidence of no mental growth whatever."

2

In Our Time is marked by the obvious influence of Sherwood Anderson. It contains stories about tramps and ex-prizefighters, Indians and lumberjacks, Nick Adams making fumbling and adolescent discoveries in sex and drinking, the son of an aging jockey (in "My Old Man") wounded and bewildered by the revelation that his father was crooked. And the idiom also holds an echo of the medium in which Anderson reflected his own naïve and nebulous wanderings through a mysteriously complicated world.

But even here Hemingway was never merely the disciple of Anderson. The stories with Anderson-figures are alternated with chapters portraying the suffering and brutality of war, the shooting of stickup men by the police, matadors bungling a difficult kill and being mobbed by a jeering crowd, a killer being hanged. And both groups are tied together, not by the vague and puzzled mysticism of Anderson, but by a sensitive awareness of cruelty: the blind cruelty of nature or sexual instinct or physical breakdown reinforced by the active cruelty of man: a foreshadowing of Lieutenant Henry's outcry against the universe in *A Farewell to Arms*. The simplicity of Hemingway's style, moreover, is not the simplicity of Anderson, so little removed from childishness, but a simplicity that has passed through the sophisticated criticism of Gertrude Stein, the simplicity of an analytical mind that has deliberately rejected complexity as a method. It seems simple because it is stripped and transparent, but it is packed with cumulative suggestion revealing depth within depth that may be overlooked on a first reading.

Nevertheless Hemingway had been influenced by Anderson; and he was sharply aware of the absurdities he had been skirting. In *The Torrents of Spring* he rejects Anderson, parodying his sex-mysticism and infantile symbolism with a burlesque as good-humored as it is hilarious. There are both wit and laughter in the way characters are always going "out into the night" until finally the Negro cook in the lunchwagon opines of yet another missing couple that "they must have gone out into the night"; and a ludicrous Andersonian veracity in that perky little bird whom the hero modestly keeps inside his shirt but exhibits to especially favored ladies.

Meanwhile, with *The Sun Also Rises*, he had rejected Anderson's yearning and frustrated characters for Jake's disillusioned post-War friends. The *naifs* of *In Our Time* had dumbly suffered the cruelty and the pain; Jake and his friends have exhausted words, and after words the progressive violences of drink, sex, bullfights, drugs, and perversion. In the very same step, then, Hemingway rejects these wasters and idlers and lost intellectuals. If the adolescents and the pugs and the simple-minded and the illiterates didn't have the answers, neither did the aesthetes and the sophisticates in their dreary world of urban futility. Indeed the superiority lies with the simple and the brave, with Pedro Romero loving the risk of sharp death in the arena, and Manuel Garcia (in "The Undefeated," from *Men Without Women*), old, sick, fighting in a style no longer understood by a public debauched with theatricality. These and the jockeys and pugs are better than the empty and decadent good-timers to whom they give a galvanic thrill. When Brett sends away Pedro Romero the point is clear: the only decent gesture of which the sophisticated is capable is to go away and leave the simple uncorrupted.

It is a mistake, of course, to think of Jake as a child of nature, the same mistake as thinking of Lieutenant Henry, in *A Farewell to Arms*, in that way. Jake's idiom is bare and unpretentious, but the reason is that Jake is tired of all the big words, tired of society, tired of civilization. And Jake is afraid—like Henry again—of being betrayed by the tenderness he still has in him. He is full of the wisecracks of a man trying to masquerade as a hard guy: "I mistrust all frank and simple people," he says of Robert Cohn, "especially when their stories hang together"; and, again, "he realized . . . that the fact of a woman caring for him and wanting to live with him was not simply a divine miracle." Jake is in many ways a transparent mask for Hemingway himself, hating and disgusted with the characters of his story, and yet feeling an unhappy pity for them too.

But if Jake has seen through the world of the aristocrats and the intellectuals, he has been no more impressed by the newspaper overlords for whose columns he turns out cablegrams or the bankers and brokers who with them rule the modern world. His rejection is sharpened to universality by Hemingway's next novel. In *A Farewell to Arms* it is society as a whole that is rejected, social responsibility, social concern. Lieutenant Henry is in the War, but his attitude toward it is purely that of a spectator, refusing to be involved. He is leading a private life as an isolated individual. Even personal relations, of any depth or intimacy, he avoids; he drinks with the officers and talks with the priest and visits the officers' brothel, but all contacts he keeps, deliberately, on a superficial level. He has rejected the world.

Such an attitude is possible only to a sensitive and reflective person. Henry is no naïve barbarian. He was studying architecture in Italy when the War began; he makes ironical remarks about sculptures and bronzes; his reflections and conversation contain allusions to Samuel Johnson, Saint Paul, Andrew Marvell, and Sir Thomas Wyatt. His flight from responsibility is the ultimate of the flight that Jake and Brett and Mike were trying to effect with drink and bullfights and sex. He is evading responsibility and emotion, taking refuge in simple primary sensations. Successfully, so far as the War is concerned: "I was always embarrassed by the words sacred, glorious and sacrifice and the expression in vain . . . Abstract words, such as glory, honor, courage, or hallow were obscene beside the concrete names of villages, the number of roads, the names of rivers, the numbers of regiments and the dates."

It is hardly possible to miss the intensity here trying to masquerade as a hardboiled indifference, endeavoring to shore itself against the immeasurable cruelty of things and the callous glibness of words. Even more than Jake, Henry is immuring himself in an ivory tower of trying not to feel. But an indifference preserved in the face of such underlying emotion is precariously held. It breaks down upon his meeting with Catherine Barkley.

"God knows I had not wanted to fall in love with her. I had not wanted to fall in love with any one." Emotion has found an entering wedge, although Henry tries even now to draw a circle enclosing themselves alone. The world without is the enemy. "Because there's only us two and in the world there's all the rest of them," Catherine says. "If anything comes between us we're gone and they have us." Henry deserts, he escapes to Switzerland with Catherine. He no longer even reads about the fighting. "I was going to forget the war. I had made a separate peace." (So the dying boy in one of the interchapters of *In Our Time* whispers to his fatally wounded comrade, "You and me, we've made a separate peace.") But momentarily Hemingway tries to ignore the implication that the only separate peace is in death. He will solve the problem of dealing with the world by taking refuge in individualism and isolated personal relationships and sensations. He too will make a separate peace.

But the separate peace soon turns out to be impossible. Hemingway's honesty and understanding will not allow him to pretend it is successful. Catherine undergoes a prolonged and painful childbirth, and ultimately she dies. "You did not know what it was all about. You never had time to learn. They threw you in and told you the rules and the first time they caught you off base they killed you." In the end, then, one could not be a candle-holder and look on. Life caught you up, willy-nilly, by your instincts, by your sensations, by your emotions, caught you in a trap; and the better you were the harder it dealt with you. "If people bring so much courage to the world the world has to kill them to break them, so of course it kills them. . . . It kills the very good and the very gentle and the very brave impartially. If you are none of these you can be sure it will kill you too but there will be no special hurry."

Such is the result of trying to reject society and reject responsibility. It seemed to lead back with intensified bitterness to the vision of cosmic cruelty underlying *In Our Time*. Life was only an endless abrasion and destruction, even more harsh to the intelligent and the good than to all the others. To them it brings "only the remorseless devaluation of nature . . . which bears away of our great hopes, emotions, and ambitions only a few and soon disintegrating trifles." The end of the road was blank disheartenment, despair for life and civilization and mankind.

3

A Farewell to Arms was published in 1929, and its conclusions prolonged themselves from that time into 1933. It was the mood behind both the fantastic spleen of *Death in the Afternoon* and its heroic apotheosis of the matador. If death was all—searing and sudden or prolonged with humiliation—then courage was the only virtue. The courage of the bullfighter, no more useless than all other courage, was a self-sufficient value, daring and inflicting with grave and serene style the annihilation of death. The same mood dominated *Winner Take Nothing*, whose stories are conceived in a cynicism that extends even to their handling, for though there are brilliant flashes of writing they are mainly so trivial and shoddy that they appear almost to have been flung out with a sneer of indifference. Dialectically, although with bitter emotional overtones, Hemingway had reached a stage equivalent to the skepticism of Descartes when he had brought himself to doubt everything except his own existence, a stage preparatory to a new departure.

It lasted, however, through the composition of the first draft of *To Have and Have Not.* That version, Malcolm Cowley tells us in a review of the published volume, had been finished nearly a year before, and ended in "a mood of utter discouragement." Hemingway destroyed large parts of the manuscript after returning from Spain, and rewrote the end. In revising, Hemingway rejected all his previous rejections and thereby struggled through to affirmation.

The plan of *To Have and Have Not* synthesizes both the themes and the characters of all his previous fictions. There are the sham artistic and literary cripples and luxurious idlers of *The Sun Also Rises*, hollow joy-riders substituting appetite and impulse for conviction and ideals. There are the simple and the unsophisticated of so many of the short stories, the reliefers, the ex-Service men roaring in the bars, the bouncers. There are the gentle and the brave, the fisherman Albert Tracy supporting a family of kids, Harry Morgan the tough guy on his own, devoted to and adored by his heavy and aging Marie. Harry Morgan presents as hard a surface to those outside as any of Hemingway's gangster killers, but honesty, straightness, and courage lie underneath. He is the man-against-the-world, the heroic individual, like the Garcias and Romeros in the daily risking of his life, the pitting of his wits against circumstance; like Lieutenant Henry in that he stands alone, fighting only for himself and his own, but unlike Henry in that his mood is not passive isolation but struggle.

All three kinds of rejection that Hemingway has previously dealt with are thus posed in *To Have and Have Not:* the intelligent rejection of the merely biological plane of living, the sophisticated rejection of all responsibility except that of self-indulgence and having a good time, and the philosophic or heroic rejection of letting the world go its ways and standing for personal ties alone. The simple and the ignorant, the instinctive and unreflective, are always defeated in the end because they do not understand. Hemingway can respect and like them, as he always has; he sees that their strength is not enough. And yet their virtues are precisely what the sophisticated have lost: "The simplicity which is so large an element in a noble nature," as Thucydides observed, "was laughed to death and vanished out of the world." To the third way of rejection we shall presently return.

Hemingway's satire on the sophisticates and writers is bitterer than ever before. The fat bohemian tourists at Freddie's bar, Richard Gordon shoddily following the latest literary fashions by writing a novel about a strike in a garment factory, and leaving his Helen while he goes off to tea and fornication with a wealthy nymphomaniac whose husband looks on shadowily from the doorway, the homosexual musicians and yachtsmen, the wife of a drug-consuming movie director taking refuge in self-abuse while her lover is lost in drunken slumber: the illustrations mount to pure horror.

The revulsion reaches its peak in Helen's denunciation of Richard and of love: "Love is all the dirty little tricks you taught me that you probably got out of some book. I'm through with you and I'm through with love. Your kind of picknose love. You writer." And all the end of the book is full of desperation and doom, of suicide in the background, people taking "the long drop," shooting themselves with automatics, "those admirable instruments . . . so well-designed to end the American dream when it becomes a nightmare." But if there is horror, there is pity too: Professor McWalsey pitying Richard Gordon, Hemingway pitying his own characters, as McWalsey goes back to his bar saying, "I will now return to the anaesthetic I have used for seventeen years and will not need much longer."

Against these spiritual failures we have the strength, tenderness, courage, ingenuity, and manhood of Harry Morgan. In him are fused the qualities of all those figures with whom Hemingway has formerly stood, and added to them, a heroic stature. But even heroic stature Hemingway finds insufficient; and in this last rejection—and it *is* rejection, for all his admiration for Harry Morgan—Hemingway reaches a logical affirmation transcending negation.

The simple brave had fought, but they had never understood. Jake had been made a passive onlooker by a physical mutilation. Henry had seen and reflected and tried to stand aside, but had been caught, by his very humanity, within the trap. Morgan is almost as simple and nonreflective as Manuel Garcia, and, like him, he is undefeated because he is not broken. Like Jake and Henry, however, he has taken the measure of the world—not pessimistically or philosophically, but almost without thinking about it, and gone through life standing alone, for himself, his wife, and their girls. But unlike Henry, he fights the world; it is by trying to win a separate victory that he seeks a separate peace.

And it is this very isolation, as Hemingway now perceives, that has ensured disaster. Harry Morgan does not know it, but the materially well-fed and voracious, riding prosperous, very victorious, and fighting for themselves alone as much as he, are in reality even more defeated. Hemingway has drawn together all his threads, and realized that it was the very core of his earlier positions, the separate peace, that needed to be rejected. Morgan sees the light before the end, while the light is fading from his eyes, and he does not blame the universe. He sees now that he has been beaten because he has tried to stand alone and fight alone. "'One man alone ain't got. No man alone now.' He stopped. 'No matter how a man alone ain't got no bloody . . . chance.'" "It had taken him a long while to get it out," Hemingway concludes, "and it had taken him all his life to learn it." But it is the logical climax of Hemingway's development. It is true, as various critics have pointed out, that his counterpoint in *To Have and Have Not* is not entirely successful. He fails to bring his two worlds together. Harry Morgan and the sophisticates touch, but they do not intermingle. And Harry's realization of the reason for his having had a hopeless struggle all his life is too sudden and too unprepared for. Nevertheless *To Have and Have Not* is a better book than almost any of the critics have allowed. The earlier chapters, both those where Morgan speaks for himself and those where Hemingway reveals him in action and dialogue, the fishing scenes, the chink smuggling, the warm, strong, and tender relation with Marie, are among the best writing Hemingway has ever done; they build up the picture of the man with an assurance and solidity that Hemingway has never excelled. And his bohemian wastrels and weaklings, mere sketches as all of them are save Richard and Helen Gordon, are more truly lost than any he has portrayed before. Seen with a bitter and mournful pity, they are indeed the hollow men, wandering in despair or jerking galvanically through the mists of Hades, a gray world of doom.

It is not they, however, who convey the tone of the book, but Harry Morgan, given the clue to victory even in the hour of defeat. That tone is clarified and strengthened in what Hemingway has written since. His recent play, *The Fifth Column*, has not only a new vitality but a high-spirited sense of fun in the midst of seriousness that Hemingway had all but lost since *The Torrents of Spring*. The comic and still authentic hotel manager, with his fantastic English dialect, is only one example of this gaiety. "Is bright," he defends the failings of the hotel electrician. "But the drink. Always the drink. Then rapidly the failing to concentrate on electricity." And, explaining how furious is the weak-kneed Preston, whom Philip has kicked out of Dorothy's room, at being supplanted, he adds, "Fills him with, how you call, jellishness."

The change bathes in a new light Hemingway's former themes of death and love against the world. He still sees the courage to face death well, to be sure, as supremely heroic, but it is not death for death's sake now, not death as a gesture, it is death for a cause. Philip says of the Lincoln Battalion, "It's such a good battalion and it's done such things that it would break your damn heart if I tried to tell you about it."

And romantic love, the nineteenth century dream, *égoisme à deux*, the love of Catherine and Henry that was an ivory tower against the world, is crumbling away; Hemingway refuses now to harmonize it into the tragic Liebestod of *A Farewell to Arms*. There is a girl in the play "named Dorothy," he says, "but her name might also have been nostalgia." She has for Philip "the longest, smoothest, straightest legs in the world," and he loves her in the night, but "the things of the night" which were all-embracing for Henry are not enough for Philip. They are a distraction from his real business in the world, gilded pitfalls for the warrior and nets of hair for the hunter. "Never believe what I say in the night," he bursts out bitterly. "I lie like hell in the night."

Philip's real business is voiced by his fellow-worker Max while bombs explode in the streets of Madrid to the scream of children and the yelping of mutilated dogs. "You do it for all men. You do it for the children. And sometimes you do it even for the dogs." The same words speak for Ernest Hemingway. "In going where you have to go, and doing what you have to do, and seeing what you have to see," he says, "you dull and blunt the instrument you write with. But I would rather have it bent and dulled and know I had to put it to the grindstone again and hammer it into shape and put a whetstone to it, and know that I had something to write about, than to have it bright and shining and nothing to say, or smooth and well-oiled in the closet, but unused."

Hemingway is no longer merely an inverted aesthete and intellectual. He has rejected his previous rejections, rejected a philosophy of atomic individualism and irresponsibility foregoing the world. He has rejected the ivory tower of a literary athleticism living for its own taut musculature alone. He has analyzed each of his own positions in turn, rejecting its weaknesses, embodying what in it was strong in a new synthesis of honorable emotion fortified by intellectual clarity. "Where I now go I go alone, or with others who go there for the same reasons I go." He has fought his way out of defeatism.

Those who might believe that this was no very great achievement would be wrong. For the important thing about Hemingway is that he has earned his philosophy, that he has struggled to reach it, overcome the obstacles to attaining it. That is why Hemingway's affirmation means more than the affirmation of a whole bandwagon of sociological novelists like Richard Gordon, whom Hemingway poses significantly in the middle of *To Have and Have Not.* Such novelists have already tumbled off the bandwagon of Proustian subtlety or brightly glittering sophistication to scramble on the bandwagon of fiction about strikes in garment factories, and such novelists may, as likely as not, scramble into Jew-baiting tomorrow. Incapable of their facile leap, Hemingway has had to fight his way through to affirmation, fight in his blood and fight in his brain. He has earned the right to reject rejection.

For the good, the gentle and the brave, he now tells us, if they do not try to stand alone and make a separate peace, defeat is not inevitable. His life-blood dripping into the bottom of the boat, Harry Morgan realized it at the end of his career. Philip Rawlings realized it in the blood and terror and tragedy and splendor even of a dying Madrid. Hemingway has realized it there too, and the realization may well be for him the very beginning of a new and more vital career.

MAXWELL GEISMAR

Ernest Hemingway: You Could Always Come Back

1942

1. THERE AND BACK

'You could always come back,' said the Hemingway who stood in exile among the green hills of Africa, about the American culture he had renounced. And it is with a writer who left us and came back that we must deal. With Ring Lardner we saw the history of an artist so much a part of his society that he could imagine no other; and who ends by condemning that society so completely that he must also question his own work and life. In Hemingway we have the artist who starts with Lardner's conclusion. Here we take up our history at the point which formed the tragic termination of '29's favorite child. For the basis of Hemingway's early writing is a total renunciation of all social frameworks; the separation of the writer from the common activity of his time; the acceptance of a profound isolation as the basis for the writer's achievement.

This voyage of Hemingway to the extremes of solitude and back has its drama. In many ways it is a spiritual act as courageous and bold as any of his famous, violent episodes. It has its enigmas. Beneath the 'discipline' of Hemingway's style, the strictly modulated feelings, the flat tones which were to impress themselves upon a section of American prose, there lies a temperament that is fresh and new in literature. Hemingway's character is deep and complex, ruled over by a sort of rigidity, an iron restraint which, however, allows the spirit's true visions to slip through from moment to moment, to tear themselves out from under his discipline, to emerge and create the wonderful tension of his best work. His temperament has its weakness also, its temptations, forebodings, and fears. Does it seem strange to talk of Hemingway in these terms? This writer who is to travel alone into the shadows of death, the author who has given us so many immortal studies of strength, the story-teller specializing in toughness, the advocate of the boxer, the matador, the revolutionary, and the killer? The artist who has above all proclaimed courage as his supreme value in life, the daring hunter of big game who, with his writer-protagonist of 'The Snows of Kilimanjaro,' may equally declare he has 'sold vitality, in one form or another, all his life'? To these dilemmas do our hidden forces bring us.

Like Lardner, Hemingway is another western American boy, a doctor's son, born in Illinois in 1898. His youth was spent in the Michigan woods whose quality he catches so nicely in his early tales of our last stretch of frontier. In Hemingway's first book, 'In Our Time,' we meet the young Nick, his family, the hunting and fishing trips in these Michigan forests, the encounters with Indians, Nick's introduction to reading, drinking, first friendships and early love—a wonderfully idyllic youth that Hemingway does not forget. He went to a Michigan high school, no further formal education; like Lardner, too, he became the journalist of a small-town newspaper. During the First World War Hemingway enlisted with the Italians; saw, recorded, and was wounded. The impact of this experience coming directly upon his adolescence was to condition a part of his writing; there are other factors, however, operating beneath this. There was a sharp break now with his environment. Europe in 1921, and we see the middle-western boy surrounded by Parisian bohemians, among them those who believed the salvation of literature lay in the lack of punctuation, Gertrude Stein, Ezra Pound, Ford Madox Ford, and William Bird who published the work of the young Hemingway, sometimes rejected by others as merely 'sketches.' These were exciting times in Paris, Ford tells us. 'Young America from the limitless prairies leapt, released, on Paris. They stampeded with the madness of colts when you let down the slip-rails between dried pasture and green.' We are to suppose that the dried pasture was the United States of the twenties; there was certainly enough stampeding. Among the new aesthetes Hemingway would advance, with 'rather the aspect of an Eton-Oxford, husky-ish young captain of a midland regiment of His Britannic Majesty . . . balancing on the point of his toes, feinting at my head with hands as large as hams, and relating sinister stories of Paris landlords.' Fiestas and Spanish bullfights, the trailing of the kudu in Africa, and there came the long decade of Hemingway's rebellion, isolation, and search for the meanings of death. In his writing now there was the abrupt transition from the 'Nada,' echoing his despair, to the Florida of Lardnerian yachtsmen still grimly bent on pleasure. Hemingway was home again. Home; and then he was in the midst of the Spanish Civil War; the isolated chronicler of man's fatal impulses transformed into the Cassandra of social crisis.

Living this life with its twisting turns and sudden reverses, and apparently so remote from our own manners and shores, Hemingway must be seen as a typical figure. The underlying causes of his art are, I believe, particularly American. In his evolution Hemingway is to anticipate the new literature of the nineteen-thirties, the transition from Lardner's dead end to new faiths—however extreme, erratic, or, as with Hemingway himself, imperfectly realized, faiths which were nevertheless to form the dominant literary tradition of America in social change. But Hemingway is more than typical. Our written patterns do not altogether define him. There is a sort of magic touch with him, an inherited depth and reaching awareness in the midst of his obvious and sometimes exasperating limitations. Magic is a delicate adjective nowadays, an embarrassing admission for the literary analyst to propound. And yet at the end of Hemingway as at the start, we can do little better than admit it: a confession, an evasion perhaps, and with these we have a sense of gratitude that in the age of formulas we are still allowed to feel some mysteries of creation.

2. WOODS OF MICHIGAN TO CAPORETTO. It has been the common view to attribute the solitary position which is at the bottom of Hemingway's work to the post-war reaction, and to class him with other social rebels as the English D. H. Lawrence, the French Jean Giono, or the German Rainer Maria Rilke, those who during or after the World War moved away from a society whose international murder they could no longer tolerate. We cannot deny the importance of the war in Hemingway. With his first collection of stories, 'In Our Time,' published in 1925, Hemingway himself established such a pattern. In the series of alternating episodes which comprise the volume we see first the adventures of a sensitive American adolescent; one without, however, the typical traits of most literary adolescents. It is almost impossible to convey the admirable quality of these early Hemingway stories, seeming so light in their fiber and yet so rich in feeling, the tone which marks 'The End of Something' or 'The Doctor and the Doctor's Wife.' And in a lighter vein we have such sections as the incomparable, if inebriated, 'Three Day Blow':

> 'What are you reading?'
> '"Richard Feverel."'
> 'It's all right . . . It ain't a bad book, Wemedge.'
> 'What else have you got I haven't read?' Nick asked.
> 'Did you read the "Forest Lovers"?'
> "Yup. That's the one where they go to bed every night with the naked sword between them.'
> 'That's a good book, Wemedge.'
> 'It's a swell book. What I couldn't ever understand was what good the sword would do. It would have to stay edge up all the time because if it went over flat you could roll over it and it wouldn't make any trouble.'
> 'It's a symbol,' Bill said.
> 'Sure,' said Nick, 'but it isn't practical.'

In these plain tones, of course, is heralded the new style, the new manner, the new philosophy which, along with Lardner, would influence a generation. This is literary revolution as well as literary criticism.

The contrast with the alternate half of 'In Our Time' is startling, and intended so. The juxtaposition with these early, lyrical sketches already represents the full reaction of Hemingway as the war novelist. Quite abruptly as the volume indicates, the war scenes placed directly against the Michigan woods, Nick is plunged into horror. Here in this new world of battle, suffering, and death, every accent is tortured. Pain no longer emphasizes the peace of living; now indeed there is no peace to balance or even to intrude upon the province of pain, as if it were immutable, immemorial. The entire structure of this new world, the anatomy of war, all its tissues are saturated with suffering:

> They shot the six cabinet ministers at half-past six in the morning against the wall of a hospital. There were pools of water in the courtyard. . . . One of the ministers was sick with typhoid. Two soldiers carried him downstairs and out into the rain. They tried to hold him up against the wall but he sat down in a puddle of water. The other five stood very quietly against the wall. Finally the officer told the soldiers it was no good trying to make him stand up. When they fired the first volley he was sitting down in the water with his head on his knees.

No protest could be much more effective, no rhetoric more eloquent, I suppose, than this impartial, expressionless recording of 'facts' in wartime. It is only, indeed, by noticing that these facts recur endlessly, that the monotone of terror never changes, that we may fully realize the intention of Hemingway's objective, almost statistical diagram of things as they are.

The quality of Hemingway's war reaction becomes, however, somewhat curious. Its emphasis comes to rest not on intelligence, or action to avert such scenes or to eliminate their future possibility; nor on any moral intention to renounce such horror as incompatible with all human effort. There is rather a sort of inevitable acceptance of it. The recording of war scenes, so intense, is also, as it were, motionless. The maimed, bleeding, sick human beings; the army mules, their forelegs broken, who must drown slowly in water hardly deep enough for drowning; the water too with its 'nice things' floating around in it; these humans and animals and the scene of warfare itself are shown as if frozen, as though the writer were doing a 'still' of them which has no continuation, and does not even culminate in death but remains fixed in its endless dying. The scenes of horror are indelible. If there is a protest in their recording, it is a protest which itself must continue endlessly. Both the sickness in the world outside the writer, and the sickness within him as he observes the world, will continue in their rigid, static relationship, in this equation of pain which has no equivalent.

Thus, while the early Nick was in the midst of his life, however casual it may have been, the later Nick, in the midst of extreme tension, has withdrawn. While the young Nick was functioning, if only to read and drink and hunt, the older Nick is watching. (It is a terrible sort of watching, to be sure, insistent, an observation which is almost compulsive in its fixed stare.) We may see this more clearly if we recall the larger body of war literature in which Hemingway belongs, the work of Arnold Zweig or Erich Remarque, for example, H. G. Wells, or Henri Barbusse, or Jules Romains. If these writers do not often compare with Hemingway in their statement of the war's shock, their accent lies more fruitfully on human effort rather than Hemingway's rigid embracing of disaster; on the human will if it is only to question the inevitability of Hemingway's scene. And in the weaker sections of Hemingway's new craft we may see more clearly what in its perfection we suspect. In his over-emphasis, sometimes flippant or ostentatiously virile, or with a sort of disdainful bravado, Hemingway shows us his defenses. 'It was a pleasant business. My word yes a most pleasant business.' This is just a little too jolly, and in these phrases we may often see Hemingway's post-war attitude in the process of construction. Such an attitude, of course—at its best, this intense but immobile observation, and often descending into a callous acceptance of a mannered boredom—is understandable both in its moral and psychological aspects. The latter runs into the 'weariness' of the post-war generation; a weariness resulting from the extremes of the war experience itself; in the face of which the psyche must retreat to protect itself, and after which the routine existence of civilized society—a life operating under the usual conventions and restrictions—could make little impression. The activities of peace, all the complex relationships and tensions of normal life were no longer vital. And in moral terms, the artist, having assumed Hemingway's rôle of the spectator, disclaims his responsibility for the war world of horror and agony which he, certainly, had never made.

A variety of later stories—'The Revolutionist,' 'In Another Country,' 'A Simple Enquiry,' 'Now I Lay Me,' 'A Way You'll Never Be'—affirm the various phases of Hemingway's thesis: the suffering of the war, the resistances and defenses of his people, their ways of ignoring the scene around them which apparently they cannot control. Perhaps no other contemporary writer, in fact, has brought us so many vivid studies of the war's impact on the defenseless human temperament; the almost unbearable episode which closes 'A Natural History of the Dead' is typical of these. In 'Soldier's Home,' one of the earliest of his stories and still perhaps the best of them, we have the story of Krebs, who went to the war from a Methodist College in Kansas, and returns after the war to his home town. The town, the family and friends of Krebs, even his father's car are still the same. 'Nothing was changed in the town except that the young girls had grown up.' But Krebs was changed. He no longer had the desire to become part of the town's life. Even the attractive young girls who appealed to him now lived 'in such a complicated world of already defined alliances . . . that Krebs did not feel the energy or the courage to break into it.' From a distance, from his front porch as they walked on the other side of the street, Krebs liked to watch the young girls in their round Dutch collars and silk stockings, but when he was next to them 'their appeal to him was not very strong':

> He did not like them when he saw them in the Greek's ice cream parlor. He did not want them themselves really. They were too complicated. . . . He did not want to get into the intrigue and the politics. He did not want to have to do any more courting. He did not want to tell any more lies. It wan't worth it. . . . He did not want any consequences. He did not want any consequences ever again. He wanted to live along without consequences.

Nowhere more clearly than in the story of Krebs has Hemingway given us his underlying attitude—this living along without consequences, the emotional withdrawal from experience and moral renunciation of life's responsibilities; this looking at things henceforth from a variety of porches rather than participating in all the streets of life. And 'A Farewell to Arms,' four years after Krebs, gives the unified history of the events which led up to such a conclusion.

Returning to read the famous novel after all the prefaces by Parisian bohemians like Ford Madox Ford, and the excitement of the American popular reception, is, I believe, still a fine experience. For the book is without doubt as fresh today as in 1929, as gay and moving. Against the gaiety, the warmth of 'A Farewell to Arms,' Hemingway portrays, of course, the cumulative degeneration of the human temperament under the conditions of war. The novel is a series of human defeats within one continuous and terrible sequence: the rains, the cholera, the soldiers who mutilate themselves rather than go on fighting, the growing weariness of the Italian army which led up to Caporetto, the degeneration of Rinaldi himself who is symptomatic of the novel's pattern, and at its start is so quick and alive. Contrasted against this in turn, in the love of Lieutenant Henry and Catherine Barkley we have another antithesis of increasing joy. The love and the despair are constantly related, intensely intertwined, and in the end almost gain the feeling of life and death themselves: the death preying upon the living organism of the lovers' hope, eating into the flesh and destroying the form from page to page. Yet each change of form, each advance of destruction makes the life of the novel more vital, the life we know must yield, but in the manner of its yielding asserting itself beyond its destruction.

'A Farewell to Arms' in this sense lies quite outside of the pattern of Hemingway's development which we have been showing. For the feeling of tragedy in the novel comes precisely from the struggle to participate in life despite all the odds, from the efforts of the lovers to fulfill themselves in a sterile world, from the exact impact of the human will which Hemingway has negated. Yet even here we must notice that Lieutenant Henry turns his back upon our society after Caporetto. Following his personal objectives he abandons his friends, his responsibilities as an officer, the entire complex of organized social life represented by the army and the war. This farewell to arms is accomplished without request or permission. Lieutenant Henry, in fact, deserts, and his action is prophetic of his author's own future movement. 'You and me,' says Nick to the Rinaldi of 'In Our Time,' 'we've made a separate peace.' And Hemingway's separate peace was to embrace the woods of Michigan as well as Caporetto, the activities of normal times as well as war, and even at last the ordinary purposes of the individual's life within his society, as well as the collective purposes of society as a whole.

Hemingway's withdrawal from experience and denial of human

responsibility, in short, are to run their course in his work from Nick and Krebs of 'In Our Time' for some ten years until 'The Green Hills of Africa' in 1935. The implications of this appear throughout his stories for the decade. His work has little significance, indeed, without the framework of revolt and isolation which gives it unity. That it has sometimes been misinterpreted in this respect, his novels seen from an immediate or fragmentary view, is due primarily, I believe, to the fact that Hemingway gives so little articulation to his dominant attitude. It is rather by piecing together his fragments of editorial expression that we may approach anything like a logical statement of his position. It was only in 'The Green Hills of Africa' that he himself gave a fuller view of the matter:

> If you serve time for society, democracy, and the other things quite young, and declining any further enlistment make yourself responsible only to yourself, you exchange the pleasant, comforting stench of comrades for something you can never feel in any other way than by yourself. That something I cannot yet define completely but the feeling comes . . . when, on the sea, you are alone with it and know that this Gulf Stream you are living with, knowing, learning about, and loving, has moved, as it moves, since before man, and that it has gone by the shoreline of that long, beautiful, unhappy island since before Columbus sighted it and that the things you find out about it, and those that have always lived in it are permanent and of value because that stream will flow, as it has flowed, after the Indians, after the Spaniards, after the British, after the Americans and after all the Cubans and all the systems of governments, the richness, the poverty, the martyrdom, the sacrifice and the venality and the cruelty are all gone as the high-piled scow of garbage, bright-colored, white-flecked, ill-smelling, now tilted on its side, spills off its load into the blue water, turning it a pale green to a depth of four or five fathoms as the load spreads across the surface, the sinkable part going down and the flotsam of palm fronds, corks, bottles, and used electric light globes, seasoned with an occasional condom or a deep floating corset, the torn leaves of a student's exercise book, a well-inflated dog, the occasional rat, the

> no-longer-distinguished cat; all this well shepherded by the boats of the garbage pickers who pluck their prizes with long poles, as interested, as intelligent, and as accurate as historians; they have the viewpoint; the stream, with no visible flow, takes five loads of this a day when things are going well in La Habana and in ten miles along the coast it is as clear and blue and unimpressed as it was ever before the tug hauled out the scow; and the palm fronds of our victories, the worn light bulbs of our discoveries and the empty condoms of our great loves float with no significance against one single, lasting thing—the stream.

We notice, moreover, that if this view of Hemingway's position is more complete than any other statement of his, it is still in effect one sentence. Such a sentence to be sure! So complex and modulated, and representing so much of the bewilderment and despair of the post-war decade: consigning us, and all our works, our victories, discoveries, and great loves, to oblivion in these haunting and elegiac cadences; and holding in its rhythms again so much of the passive, the drifting, and solitary individual on the unfathomable waters of existence. And as Hemingway with such a statement left behind him the European framework of society, this the final fruit of Lieutenant Henry's desertion at Caporetto, he also abandons his own American culture. Again we generally perceive this as a fact rather than a manifesto, marked not by Hemingway's references to America but rather his lack of references. We shall notice a little later the factors leading to this decision; here we see only the statement which Hemingway gives us on his decision:

> It is easier to keep well in a good country by taking simple precautions than to pretend that a country which is finished is still good. . . . Our people went to America because that was the place to go then. It had been a good country and we had made a bloody mess of it and I would go, now, somewhere else as we had always had the right to go somewhere else and as we had always gone. You could always come back. Let the others come to America who did not know that they had come too late. Our people had seen it at its best and fought for it when it

> was well worth fighting for. Now I would go somewhere else. We always went in the old days and there were still good places to go.

As Hemingway had previously condemned all our work to the depths of the Gulf Stream, blue and unimpressed, now he has added our continent itself. What a tremendous renunciation of human effort this is, which can sweep away a continent, as rich, as young, as powerful as ever! What a supreme and final contempt for the common existence of humanity, our customs, songs, and land! And so renouncing the smells of peace as well as the 'comforting stench' of comrades in war, the land of his birth as well as that of his adoption, our native earth in addition to our social patterns, Hemingway is to follow alone the narrow and tortuous path of the rebel.

Such, then, is the reaction of our American writer, in the interpretation of Hemingway's art which sees him primarily as the product of the post-war disillusionment. It is our belief, however, that to remain content with the interpretation of Hemingway as the war novelist is somewhat limited. We intend to show that in terms of his own personality Hemingway's rebellion against society is more complex than this, deeper, and antecedent to the war itself; and that the sociological factors conditioning this rebellion are also more profound. To accomplish this we must follow him along the path of his exile for the middle period of his writing. We must consider him, as Hemingway himself might insist that every human being be considered, without benefit of society, a single individual on a spiritual expedition, indeed, to avoid all societies. It is, to be sure, a long and perhaps dangerous search for the critic, as for the author whom we follow; a solitary excursion of the psyche into the last enigmas and shadows of life. Yet to avoid it is to lessen the meaning of Hemingway. What are the truer causes, what are the consequences of Hemingway's safari into the haunted and isolated regions of the spirit's darkness?

3. THE MATADOR AND THE KUDU. 'The day of death,' we are told in the wisdom of the Preacher, 'is better than the day of one's birth'; and perhaps no American writer has come to explore the ultimate truth of Ecclesiastes more deeply than Hemingway. It is indeed this 'day of death' which was to preoccupy him steadily from now on, and was to fill the bulk of his mature work; a day of doubt and torment which was to last a decade.

In the transition from the Hemingway who is defined by the boundaries of the European war to the new Hemingway who has renounced the boundaries of society, we may notice, first of all, what our more strictly Marxian critics have rather conveniently ignored: how often the 'sociological' patterns of Hemingway seem to reflect a particular temperamental stress. The actual passages we use so convincingly to establish the disillusionment of Hemingway themselves indicate a sense of futility which is earlier and stronger than the war. In the midst of Hemingway's war action, we may feel the elements of an internal struggle more crucial perhaps than that which Hemingway is describing:

> It was a frightfully hot day. We'd jammed an absolutely perfect barricade across the bridge. It was simply priceless. A big old wrought-iron grating from the front of a house. Too heavy to lift and you could shoot through it and they would have to climb over it. It was absolutely topping. They tried to get over it, and we potted them from forty yards. They rushed it, and officers came out alone and worked on it. It was an absolutely perfect obstacle.

But this 'absolutely perfect obstacle' is to appear and reappear so often in Hemingway's work, sometimes changing its shape but never its meaning until we are tempted to speculate whether life itself is for the writer Hemingway simply a larger sort of absolutely perfect obstacle. We cannot dismiss it as a symbol of merely external action. The battles of the war, themselves the expression of the larger strain of the era of modern industrialism, were also for Hemingway the convenient framework for the manifestation of a spirit itself in the throes of conflict.

Again the post-war reaction of resignation and of renunciation that Hemingway expressed in the story of Krebs, and which, as we saw, became his own dominant attitude, corresponds to an inner reality. We may hazard the speculation that the secret of 'The Sun Also Rises' lies here—in the exact and rare meeting of the writer's individual temperament with the ostensible demands of his subject. For if 'A Farewell to Arms' is Hemingway's master work of the war itself, 'The Sun Also Rises' is that of the epoch which followed. What portrait of the 'lost generation' is more convincing, eloquent, accurate, full of sympathy which does not soften its perceptions? In 'Antic Hay' or 'Point Counter Point' Aldous Huxley has the intelligence of Hemingway but hardly the feeling. The 'Rainbow' volumes of D. H. Lawrence, whose post-war studies approximate Hemingway's, lack the incisiveness of 'The Sun Also Rises,' the clear purpose and the craft which fulfills it. Has it been questioned, as Thomas Wolfe was to question and turn the phrase in a new direction, whether there ever was in fact a lost generation? After 'The Sun Also Rises' there had to be one. All of us have known our own Lady Bretts and Jakes, these gifted and despairing souls, revealing their disillusion in a variety of nuances in the vain hope that perhaps they also were out of Hemingway. Vainly we say, for it was only in a novel that a lost generation could feel its plight with such intensity and live it out with magnificence. Yet paradoxically the novel was so real that it took us another generation to discover that being lost was a delicate art in itself; and our own Lady Brett Ashleys, so beguiling in literature, were apt to be boring in life.

For in this union of Hemingway's temperament with the post-war attitude, it is the writer's beliefs which very subtly control his people's; which dominate his setting and, using it as the perfect projection of his feeling, carry it beyond his private convictions into the realm of universal connotations. Why must these modern lovers continually nourish the passion that is denied them? Rather like reversing the ancient fable of Pygmalion, Brett is the perfect woman who has turned to marble, for Jake at least; but why must Jake continue moulding this marble; as all the personages of the novel constantly emphasize the methods of their own destruction? The lightest conversation in 'The Sun Also Rises' seems quite inevitably to turn the screw upon the wounded spirits of this group of pleasure-seekers. And we see finally how the entire action of the novel—this torturing and self-torture—takes place in Parisian cafés, along the fishing streams of the Basque country, and, as its climax, in the orgiastic rejoicing of a southern fiesta—in a setting, that is to say, of almost absolute pleasure. Yet, if this is the life of joy, it seems we might do better through deliberately seeking pain.

We see, in fact, that the lost generation is, in the end, much more than lost. Just as none of us could live up to the disillusionment of Hemingway's people, none of us, or few, could be so overwhelmingly ineffectual. Hemingway's post-war generation is frustrate with an intensity and cunning of purpose, with a natural and unconscious knowledge of the best methods to defeat itself, with an almost diabolical sense of frustration. If these people are meant to be representative, they must derive not merely from a disorganized society but from, so to speak, an entire genealogy of frustrated ancestors, from a race of the disillusioned. What we have in 'The Sun Also Rises,' as a matter of fact, rather than an 'objective' history of the lost generation, is the functioning of an immensely delicate imagination guiding these people so skillfully that they seem to be genuine, independent personalities—an imagination tormented as well as intricate which in the actions of its characters is revealing the depths and the shades of its own anguish. 'The Sun Also Rises' is a complete and beautiful treatise on this sort of anguish, physical and spiritual, profound and light, intentional and accidental, delivered upon others and self-determined. Toward this every episode, almost every line in the novel contributes its exact weight, the most careless gesture or phrase of Hemingway's characters seeming to provide the one stroke in the pattern hitherto missing.

That is what the novel is, really, and as we know, reality is neither quite so accurate nor artistic. There is, indeed, only one thing the matter with 'The Sun Also Rises.' It is not like life.

That it was like Hemingway, however, the years following it were to show. After this novel, Hemingway's theme becomes more sharply defined. The sequels to 'The Sun Also Rises' and to all of Hemingway's war novels reveal even more clearly that, in the precarious interaction of the temperamental and the environmental which we are tracing, the balance seems to lie with the factors of Hemingway's personality. For now it is the nineteen-thirties. Now the war and the post-war have both slipped away to give us that moment of peace in our time, the illusion of permanence in which so many tragic historical errors were committed simply because the wish of men was for permanence, thus refusing to see, what was clearly shown, that under these conditions there could be no peace. And what is our writer saying? 'Death in the Afternoon' (1932), 'The Green Hills of Africa' (1935), and the bulk of Hemingway's mature stories are to tell us, and their answer is, I think, unmistakable. The war affected Hemingway, surely, yet many other temperaments were affected and recovered. With him the impression was so deep, so natural and final as to make it seem that the war experience released his energies rather than inhibited them. We may almost say, to paraphrase Voltaire, that if there had been no war, it would have been necessary for Hemingway to invent one.

Of these works, 'Death in the Afternoon' is often described as the most absurd, perhaps, of Hemingway's works. What is this major writer doing, with his consuming passion for bullfighting to which he seems to subordinate everything else in his life? We must agree with many of the objections raised by the critics. Here certainly are the imperfect attributes of Hemingway, the braggadocio, the rather sophomoric, sophisticated smartness which marked his earlier work. There are the mannerisms into which Hemingway sometimes falls. Yet these are the reflection of something more central, the marks of an uneasv spirit. Hemingway protests rather too constantly (as he was to do again in 'The Green Hills of Africa') the significance of his achievement, and his own pleasure, and the ignorance of those who would doubt his importance and pleasure. And there is a misplaced irritation which runs through the book, of which we never seem to find the true object; all the unhappy evidences of a morality which is disputing, by all sorts of indirection, its own moral values. The tone of 'Death in the Afternoon' is hence often wrong, denying and accusing, wrangling and quibbling; yet again often rich and amusing, and including some of Hemingway's sharpest studies of the human constitution.

But what sort of constitution? In these transparently bad moments, and in his superbly good ones, what after all is the enemy Hemingway is attacking, the friend he embraces? It is the conception of the matador, we may say, that has caught Hemingway's admiration: the dignity, courage, discipline, and honor, all these traits which are embraced in the Spanish 'pundonor.' 'Bullfighting is the only art in which the artist is in danger of death and in which the degree of brilliance in the performance is left to the fighter's honor.' This dignity and courage, however, the sense of man's virtue, comes out infrequently and against large odds: the fickle crowd, the sacrifice of the horses with their horrid disembowelings, the diseases, too, and sorts of death which overtake the matadors, the commercialism of the sport as a whole, the easy tricks and the commercialism of the matadors themselves. And the sense of man's virtue, rare, composed of such dubious components, lasts for only a moment: the moment when the matador and the bull are both ready for the kill; not when victory is easy; but when it is one strength against another, one skill, one will meeting its counterpart in the brief seconds of the last act of the bullfight.

In the final moment of decisiveness, then, which evidences the grand style of man, the bull is equally important; in a sense, more so. As the matador gains his dignity by facing death, and in the end, in one form or another, sooner or later, almost inevitably succumbing to it, the bull, even more surely, has less chance to escape it, and so gains a greater sense of crisis and tragedy. He is the victim, the sacrifice, the sufferer. He dies the death, not remotely or by chance, but through purpose here and now. Thus the actors of 'Death in the Afternoon' are double. The matador and the bull are united in the moment of fusion; they become one; the one who suffers and the one who makes suffer, to use Edmund Wilson's discerning phrase; the active and the passive elements in Hemingway's fundamental thesis; the matador who gains his power by killing and the bull through being killed. And beneath the formalized murder which joins these curious lovers lies the true protagonist of the book, death itself—'death uniting the two figures in the emotional, aesthetic, and artistic climax of the fight.' As 'The Sun Also Rises,' despite the narrative, was in fact a single treatise on the destructive instincts of the human temperament, 'Death in the Afternoon,' while it is ostensibly a text on bullfighting, is another such treatise on these destructive instincts carried to their ultimate conclusion. For the 'death' which Hemingway is here describing with such skill and brilliance is not merely the good death, but very often the evil death; not the physical, but the spiritual death; and not, of course, the final and big death alone, but all the little deaths we die from moment to moment—those of cowardice and frustration, of hatred, of guilt and expiation; of all our obscure longings for defeat and destruction which, like an immense and submerged antiphony answering and often guiding all our life instincts, run through the human temperament. In the pretty play of the matador and the bull which forms the core of 'Death in the Afternoon,' Hemingway, in short, has gathered together an elaborate and meticulous compendium, perhaps uniquely in the Anglo-Saxon literary tradition, of dissolution.

But while in his earlier work Hemingway's meaning came out clearly, here there are evasions. Hemingway is uncertain both about his audience's reaction and his own. What he could admit about our destructive impulses in their lesser form, he cannot altogether admit about their extension. It is the uneasiness as to his own purpose which brings forth the justifications, the complaints, evasions, denials which give 'Death in the Afternoon' its broken form:

> Killing cleanly [Hemingway says] and in a way which gives you aesthetic pleasure and pride has always been one of the greatest enjoyments of a part of the human race.

But Hemingway never quite reaches into the profound causes which make this killing the 'greatest enjoyment' for a very large part of the human race. And we must notice how many of the descriptions in the book are in reality not those of 'clean' killing with the attendant emotions of 'pleasure' and 'pride' and 'enjoyment.' Perhaps rather the opposite, and perhaps the majority of Hemingway's descriptions. 'Death in the Afternoon' is indeed, if you like, a text of unclean killings, of the horrors and diseases and various uglinesses of death, such as that of Gitanillo and other matadors and animals. The entire structure of the bullfight, with its 'classical form,' its strict requirements which Hemingway constantly stresses, in this sense is a sort of moral justification for Hemingway's concern with death, a concern which often breaks through his defensive structures and shows the very meaning to which he denies validity. The fact that Hemingway must so often stress the 'rules' of bullfighting—his contempt for the man or beast who breaks them, sometimes in what seem to the uninitiated very sensible ways—indicates his fear of the opposing forces within him. He must again defend his study of death in terms of Spanish ethics as opposed to Anglo-Saxon:

> Because they [the Spaniards] have pride they do not mind killing; feeling that they are worthy to give this gift. As they have common sense they are interested in death and do not spend their lives avoiding the thought of it and hoping that it does not exist only to discover it when they come to die.

What a curious statement, like so many others found here, formed of confusion and perception! What is the 'pride' which grants death, the death which is a 'gift' (as indeed it will come to be in the deep feeling of Hemingway)? It is certainly not wise to avoid the thought of death in our life. Neither is it wise to avoid the thought of living in the midst of death. And that 'Death in the Afternoon' does this in effect, that Hemingway's concern with death is a little more than the Spaniard's 'interest' in it, is obvious by now. The Spaniards, Hemingway adds, are not preoccupied by death. 'It has no fascination for them.' Can the writer say as much for himself? It was only a little later that Hemingway's protagonist in 'The Snows of Kilimanjaro' was to admit that with him death had been an obsession.

Then why must Hemingway deny his fundamental concern with the darker elements of the human temperament—with this pain and torment and suffering, with these destructive impulses common to us all, and commonly vented from moment to moment upon ourselves and our environment, unpleasant perhaps but powerful? If it is only in our modern era we have come to a more systematized knowledge of these forces, we have not come to this knowledge by falsifying our intention, or again by minimizing the forces. Yet, despite the uncertain self-realization of his theme, Hemingway's conflicts conditioning the volume, 'Death in the Afternoon,' is nevertheless a central book in Hemingway's development. For here at last he has accepted his true métier. During the period of his war writings there was around Hemingway the pressure of his immediate environment, forcing suffering and destruction upon him, and, so to speak, legitimizing it. 'The only place where you could see life and death, i.e., violent death,' Hemingway says, 'now that the wars were over, was in the bull ring.' We have seen that in effect Hemingway's 'life' is merely the brief prelude to his death. And now that the wars were over, seeking this death of his own wish, affirming it from his own convictions, he makes it truly his own. If death no longer generally exists, he must seek it out; battles being over, the bull ring must do, or the jungles of Africa, the matador or the kudu.

That he does seek it, and finds it, all of Hemingway's mature work bears witness. 'The Green Hills of Africa' in 1935 contains again the same central trinity of the hunter, the hunted, and death as the only resolution of the hunt. And despite the flat, invariable thesis of his own, Hemingway's, happiness which accompanies the record of his hunting of the kudu, we have such passages as this:

> Highly humorous was the hyena obscenely loping, full belly dragging at daylight on the plain, who, shot from the stern, skittered on into speed to tumble end over end. Mirth provoking was the hyena that stopped out of range by an alkali lake to look back and, hit in the chest, went over on his back, his four feet and his full belly in the air. Nothing could be more jolly than the hyena coming suddenly wedge-headed and stinking out of high grass by a *donga*, hit at ten yards, who raced his tail in three narrowing, scampering circles until he died.
>
> It was funny to M'Cola to see a hyena shot at close range. There was that comic slap of the bullet and the hyena's agitated surprise to find death inside of him. It was funnier to see a hyena shot at a great distance, in the heat shimmer of the plain, to see him go over backwards, to see him start that frantic circle, to see that electric speed that meant that he was racing the little nickelled death inside him. But the great joke of all, the thing M'Cola waved his hands across his face about, and turned away and shook his head and laughed, ashamed even of the hyena; the pinnacle of hyenic humor, was the hyena, the classic hyena, that hit too far back while running, would circle madly, snapping and tearing at himself until he pulled his own intestines out, and then stood there, jerking them out and eating them with relish.
>
> '*Fisi*,' M'Cola would say and shake his head in delighted sorrow at there being such an awful beast. Fisi, the hyena, hermaphroditic, self-eating devourer of the dead, trailer of calving cows, ham-stringer, potential biter-off of your face at night while you slept, sad yowler, camp-follower, stinking, foul, with jaws that crack the bones the lion leaves, belly dragging, loping away on the brown plain, looking back, mongrel dog-smart in the face; whack from the little Mannlicher and then the horrid circle starting. '*Fisi*,' M'Cola laughed, ashamed of him, shaking his bald black head. '*Fisi*. Eats himself. *Fisi*.'

A magnificent passage again, of which we may say, as with all the best of Hemingway, that any amount of rationalization, both self-deception and the projection of this outward, while hardly deceiving himself to assuage his readers, is worth its price. And we notice how this 'comic' hyena seems to compress into one the trinity of death which Hemingway has been describing, this view of man's hidden motivation which in the Spanish arena had elements of dignity, at least, and here seems more dubious. The hyena is the killer and the one killed. He is the hunter, now become a scavenger, who is being hunted. And caught, traveling in his 'frantic circles' (rather like our own), he snaps unaware at his own vitality. Impelled by the 'little nickelled death' within him (which, I suppose, we also carry in one form or another), he performs his ironic rôle, eating himself out in the fond illusion he is nourishing himself. We often hardly do better.

The hyena is typical of many other such dark and brilliant passages which form the center of Hemingway's work over this period. The choice is neither limited nor the passages accidental. Of Hemingway's stories, almost all the later ones confirm this; certainly the last four contained in 'The Fifth Column and the First Forty-Nine Stories.' If it is profitable to isolate the best of these, we may mention 'The Short Happy Life of Francis Macomber' or 'The Capital of the World.' And if it is possible to surpass them, we may mention 'The Snows of Kilimanjaro.' Perhaps indeed no story written by an American has a more profound and pervasive sense of dissolution than this. And here, more directly than before, Hemingway gives us—in an incomparable burst of disturbed emotion—the human guilt, the frustrations, the acts of destruction, the series of little deaths we cause or are stricken by, the losses we suffer by chance and by design before the final one, which are the truer elements of the pattern of destructive behavior he has been recording. For thus, always seeking the patterns of death in life, Hemingway has very seldom given us their full nature. His basic theme reaches us only in fragments. His truths do emerge in his work. But they break through it. They are hardly ever directly faced and dealt with. The human emotions which in Hemingway center around his search for death have their logic as well as their phenomena. Though we do not yet know all about them, or even perhaps very much about them, we know more—and almost every major writer dealing with them has known more—than Hemingway tells us. A play like Eugene O'Neill's 'Days Without End' is artistically uneven, yet it does make a full effort to understand the destructive impulses of its protagonist who is not unlike one of Hemingway's figures. Except in 'The Snows of Kilimanjaro,' there is hardly with Hemingway such a sustained and whole attempt to reach into the annihilation which he has embraced as his own.

Our long and uneasy development from inanimate to organic matter, the evolution of the race, the history of man under civilizational restraints, the study of human maladjustment, all teach us differently. The death instincts at the center of Hemingway's creation are not at all so broken and causeless as he would seem to have them. Though we seek to destroy perhaps more often than we should like to believe, we do not seek to destroy without reason: some very good reasons. If Hemingway's element of destruction, very much like his 'little nickelled death,' resides in all of us also, making us, like the animal, both hunters and hunted, unlike the animal we have, at any rate, a fuller consciousness of the forces which urge us into our devouring and self-devouring actions. If modern man is still unfortunately governed by these deep, fatal, irrational feelings, his little triumph is that now at least he recognizes himself. Yet Hemingway's people, so concerned with suffering as in 'In Our Time,' so engaged in torment as in 'The Sun Also Rises,' and finally so obsessed with death in 'The Green Hills of Africa' and 'Death in the Afternoon'—these people and Hemingway himself give us no adequate motivation for their dominant concern. So real, so full of life, however destructive, so convincing in all their outward movement, they are yet like puppets in their true internal action: drawn upon the strings of forces which neither they nor their author seem to understand. With Hemingway, the destructive impulses are unchanging and causeless. Pretending to such power, such omnipotence, they are also impotent to understand themselves.

In his descriptions of these dark and submerged factors of the human temperament, Hemingway is easily comparable with the major writers before him who have also dealt with them—the Shakespeare of 'King Lear' or 'Timon of Athens,' or the Ibsen of the later plays, a Kafka, Proust, James Joyce, and in particular perhaps the Russian Dostoevsky. But we see that Hemingway describes these depths of our motivation in a reportorial sense. He is without the comprehension of the Europeans, without their fuller freedom of search and speculation. And if among these other writers he seems closest to the Russian, playing upon the same themes of guilt, expiation, and death, Hemingway is also a peculiarly Nordic Dostoevsky. For his writing is almost compulsive as well as reportorial. The absence of freedom and knowledge of his theme is less significant, I believe, than his wish to remain in ignorance; his writing, as it often seems, as if against his own will. Much of Hemingway's work seems emblematic of a conflict between his desires and rejections. A portion of the writer is unable or unwilling to deal with the other parts of his temperament. So we have the series of rationalizations, the protestations, the apologies and evasions which we have already noticed. Much of Hemingway's best achievement also, the dramatic tension marking his work, springs from his personal conflicts: this temperament so deep and so complex, tortured and inhibited, ruled over by a sort of iron discipline. And yet its true visions slip through from moment to moment, breaking through its restraints to emerge ambiguously, equivocally, themselves in torment. With other writers the word is a catharsis. With Hemingway it seems rather a weapon of coercion. In his work the reason, or the conscious and moral standards, fight against these visions of catastrophe rather than work with them; or retreat from them; or again in a sort of burst of frenzied effort attempt to destroy them. The boy in 'God Rest You Merry Gentlemen,' who mutilates himself rather than continue to endure his sexual desires, is symptomatic of the many other Hemingway protagonists who eliminate their problems rather than solve them.

And once we have reached the disturbed source of Hemingway's creation, we see the significance of his two dominant artistic effects. There is first the emphasis on action, virile and violent, which runs through his work. Yet the quality of this vitality is enigmatic also. It is an action so utterly self-engrossed, so heedless of consequences, as to suggest that it is a confession rather than an affirmation. In our lives such bold action is necessary at particular junctures. In Hemingway's work these junctures occur from moment to moment. The Robert Cohn of 'The Sun Also Rises' who answers all criticism with an uppercut is another typical Hemingway protagonist, and in Cohn this virility is not a rational value but rather the expression of an emotional weakness. Hemingway's courage is often that of desperation rather than reflection. It is really as if he were attempting something like the ancient ordeal by fire which sought to establish innocence through its immunity to flame. And thus, in the pattern of Hemingway's creative process, his constant emphasis on virile action accomplishes its double function. It at once reassures the writer as to his apparent fear of thinking through the basic problems of his work, and at the same time obviously removes the opportunity to think. It was Henri Bergson who advised his pupils to think like men of action and act like men of thought. With Hemingway the axiom has been somewhat simplified. His people act as if thought were unthinkable.

And we notice how the other dominant mood of Hemingway fits into the pattern, the scenes of blank despair running parallel to those of concentrated action. Throughout Hemingway's work how many protagonists there are like the punch-drunk 'Battler,' the condemned victim of 'The Killers,' the veterans of 'To Have and Have Not'—those whom 'circumstances' place beyond the possibilities of thinking! Reflection and now even action are impossible for them. They await their fate with a magnificent but impotent resignation. We remember the Billy Campbell of 'A Pursuit Race' who, at last abandoning the effort to keep up with life, has shot himself full of dope and retired to his bed. 'They got a cure for that,' says his manager. 'No,' William Campbell says. 'They haven't got a cure for anything.' The Hemingway figure, his moment of blind and frenzied struggle against the forces of life having dropped away, places himself in the true and final position of drugging himself against the knowledge of these forces. Hemingway's emphasis on action is itself, of course, a sort of drug; here the pattern emerges without evasion. How full, indeed, of opiates is Hemingway's work; this emphasis which is summarized so eloquently in Frazer's monologue in 'The Gambler, the Nun, and the Radio.' Usually Frazer avoided thinking, Hemingway tells us, 'except when he was writing.' But now he meditates on the remark of the Mexican Marxist: 'Religion is the opium of the people . . .'

> Yes, and music is the opium of the people. Old mount-to-the-head hadn't thought of that. And now economics is the opium of the people; along with patriotism the opium of the people in Italy and Germany. What about sexual intercourse; was that an opium of the people? Of some of the people. Of some of the best of the people. But drink was a soverign opium of the people, oh, an excellent opium. Although some prefer the radio, another opium of the people, a cheap one he had just been using. Along with these went gambling, an opium of the people if there ever was one, one of the oldest. Ambition was another . . . along with a belief in any new form of government. . . . But what was the real one? What was the real, the actual opium of the people? He knew it very well. It was gone just a little way around the corner in that well-lighted part of his mind that was there after two or more drinks in the evening; that he knew was there (it was not really there of course). What was it? He knew very well. What was it? Of course; bread was the opium of the people. Would he remember that and would it make sense in the daylight? Bread is the opium of the people.

The true meaning of Hemingway's dominant artistic mood becomes clear. The emphasis on frenzied action which characterizes his work is merely the masculine counterpart of the passive emphasis on opiates, until all forms of life are seen as themselves drugs to soothe us rather than any sort of stimulant toward knowledge, or intelligent behavior. Whatever we may try to do, or be, is in the end an action to avoid the fact. And this passage anticipates too the final 'solution' of Hemingway's conflicts, caught as he is between the major working of his temperament toward the destructive instincts of man and the restraints of his spirit which apparently prevent him from following through this effort to any full conclusion. In 'A Clean, Well-Lighted Place' Hemingway reaches this solution in another of these magnificent, despairing passages. It is late in the café where the story takes place. The old man who is drunk wants to stay on. The young waiter is impatient, but the other waiter agrees with the old man. 'I too,' the other waiter says, 'am of those who like to stay late at the café. . . . With all those who do not want to go to bed. With all those who need a light for the night.' And each night, the older waiter continues, he is reluctant to close the café because there may be someone who needs it—

> 'Hombre, there are bodegas open all night long.'
>
> 'You do not understand. This is a clean and pleasant café. It is well lighted. The light is very good, and also, now, there are shadows of the leaves.'
>
> 'Good night,' said the younger waiter.

'Good night,' the older waiter says, and he, like the Frazer of the previous story, continues the discussion in his own mind:

> 'It is the light of course but it is necessary that the place be clean and pleasant. You do not want music. Certainly you do not want music. Nor can you stand before a bar with dignity although that is all that is provided for these hours. What did he fear? It was not fear or dread. It was nothing that he knew too well. It was all or nothing and a man was nothing too. It was only that and light

> was all it needed and a certain cleanness and order. Some lived in it and never felt it but he knew it all was nada y pues nada y pues nada. Our nada who art in nada, nada be thy name thy kingdom nada thy will be nada in nada as it is in nada. Give us this nada our daily nada and nada us our nada we nada our nadas and nada us not into nada but deliver us from nada; pues nada. Hail nothing full of nothing, nothing is with thee. He smiled and stood before a bar with a shining steam pressure coffee machine.'
>
> 'What's yours?' asked the barman.
>
> 'Nada.'

But the 'nada' is not in itself a clear or positive solution. It has been the considered verdict of many other writers, starting with Ecclesiastes, whom in so many respects our Hemingway resembles, that life is vain. Yet it has never been with the others so causelessly, so completely vain, a nothingness so blind and so blank: a despair without past or future, both so artistically incomparable and intellectually incomprehensible. We have noticed the apparent increase of Hemingway's conflict as in his work he came steadily closer to the central meaning of it. We must conclude that he was unable to follow through his direction. For the true illumination of the destructive impulses in life, he has substituted the emphasis on meaningless action, the reliance on the drugged consciousness to avoid thought, and now the final nada—the emptiness which covers the frustration of the writer who is unable to cope with his true material. This is the opiate of the spirit which, unable to reach solutions for its own turmoil, projects itself outward to declare that the world itself offers nothing to be solved. This is the nada which denies meaning because it has been unable to discover it: the nada which is a final spiritual death of the writer who for so long has been searching for the secrets of death.

For with Hemingway's nada we come to the conclusion of his safari into the wilderness of our life alone. Beyond war and peace, the collective organisms of security, beyond continents and customs, our discoveries, songs, laws, and loves, here is the solution offered us by our author in his pursuit of meaning, and like Ring Lardner so richly endowed with life's favors. 'Hail nothing, full of nothing, nothing is with thee.' And in his next novel, 'To Have and Have Not,' in 1937, Hemingway carries the lesson of 'A Clean, Well-Lighted Place' to its own end. Here in turn is a nothingness gone brutal, callous. 'To Have and Have Not' offers a portrait of suffering in which the writer has given up his attempt to understand suffering. The book is a sort of apotheosis of stale horror, a Walpurgis-night of delirious and sadistic orgies within a strictly ignoble framework. It might be difficult to reconcile this destruction, both so extravagant and trivial, with the careful and deep work of Hemingway at his best, if we did not realize that 'To Have and Have Not' is in this respect the last point of Hemingway's long isolation and rebellion. It is a release of the blocked and despairing temperament; but a release that is a surrender. The literary mind no longer wishes to understand or control itself. The all-consuming sense of nothingness has at last struck at the temperament which has been so beautifully projecting it. And in this way the lessening of Hemingway's craft which marks 'To Have and Have Not' seems to add to the total disillusionment of the novel. It is almost as if the final remaining stability of the writer, his art, so brilliant, so magnificent, always so much the product of an iron will, as if his art itself had now crumbled before the advancing corrosion of his thesis. And why should it not? Surely the nada which applied to all life must also apply to the art which records life?

Yet we notice that after these many years of solitary struggle, 'To Have and Have Not' is placed within the setting of the modern United States. 'You could always come back,' the African Hemingway said of the America he was deserting, and now he has. The biographer of the matador, the artist of Parisian cafés, the hunter of kudus, has returned from foreign boulevards and savage hills. With his return to the boundaries of states and societies, to all the social complexity he had renounced, we realize that 'To Have and Have Not' represents a crisis novel for Hemingway. Like the 'Mice and Men' of John Steinbeck, as we shall see a little later, this novel of negation is both a death and a resurrection.

4. NO MAN ALONE. Hemingway's temperament is thus curiously contradictory; yet when we look for its causes we find they are more than temperamental. The interpretation of him as the war novelist seems inadequate to explain the deep tensions of his art. And in the midst of our preoccupation with him as a unique personality, we may not ignore the sociological pressures antecedent to the war which helped to form this personality. We must remember that Hemingway is one of the few writers of the depths—of the buried forces of guilt, destruction, and death, our primitive impulses, the inversions and psychic aberrations, which we have been treating—to emerge from the American tradition: from our modern industrial ethics which, as we saw with Ring Lardner and will see again with Thomas Wolfe, reinforced the harsh mould of our puritan, pioneer, and provincial patterns.

In our past and present literature, indeed, we can think of few Americans to compare with Hemingway in his intention and achievement. Through our eagerness to compensate for the lack of these deeper values in our heritage we have, I believe, rather overinterpreted Herman Melville. Edgar Allen Poe, concerned with many of Hemingway's themes, and so becoming the model of the French Symbolists while relatively ignored in America, was often condemned to a false release of his talent. Hawthorne is in many ways perhaps the closest of these to Hemingway—with his 'cloudy veil' which stretched 'over the abyss of my nature.' And Hawthorne, arousing our intense interest with his studies of guilt and expiation, does not strike at our feelings, as Hemingway surely does. It is interesting to notice that these three who most closely perhaps approach Hemingway's métier are working somewhat apart from the strict American pioneer culture and before the deep impression of contemporary industrial society.

That both of these cultural pressures left their mark on the early Hemingway, 'The Torrents of Spring,' his second work, provides us with sufficient proof. Usually ignored, certainly the weakest of his books, 'The Torrents of Spring' is nevertheless one of the most illuminating in respect to Hemingway's creative motivation, for it provides us with an unequivocal judgment on the America of Hemingway's youth. Often uncertain in its satiric touch, the novel is a sort of mélange of Hemingway's early aversions, pertinent and irrelevant, deep or trivial. The somewhat infantile, the smart, the snobbish elements which disturb Hemingway's work are shown here. What concerns us primarily, however, is the novel's portrait of the American ethics. Scripps O'Neil, the hero, travels amongst the paraphernalia of the industrial age. He meditates profoundly, though with no appreciable effect, upon the locomotive, the barbershop, the telegraph office, the dynamo. In his youth he remembers being entranced by a fascinating electric sign in three colors: 'Let Hartman Feather Your Nest.' Feathering his nest to Scripps is making money. 'Ah yes, there was big money to be made in the furniture business if you knew how to go about it. He, Scripps, knew all the wrinkles of that game.' As with Ring Lardner, the Success Myth of the Twenties has transformed our national spirit into this sterile refrain. 'Ah, these drummers,' Scripps thinks, meeting a salesman who to him is the essence of our culture—

> Going up and down over the face of this great America of ours. These drummers kept their eyes open. They were no fools. 'Listen,' the drummer said. He pushed his derby hat off his brow and leaning forward, spat into the tall brass cuspidor that stood beside his stool. 'I want to tell you about a pretty beautiful thing that happened to me once in Bay City.'

Ironic echo of the American fate which Thomas Wolfe was to redeem from this context and return to us! And again Scripps, or Hemingway, meditates on the great sweep of America:

> Near there Gary, Indiana, where were the great steel mills. Near there Hammond, Indiana. Near there Michigan City, Indiana. Further beyond, there would be Indianapolis, Indiana, where Booth Tarkington lived. He had the wrong dope, that fellow. Further down would be Cincinnati, Ohio. . . . Ah! there was grand sweep to this America of ours.

But this 'grand sweep' of our land, we know very well, is in the end limited to steel mills, flashing electric signs, the furniture business, drummers, Indiana metropolises, and Booth Tarkington. Scripps works in the 'Peerless Pounder Pump' factory. He dines at Brown's Beanery, 'Best by Test.' After 'an endless succession of days of dull piston-collaring,' he meets a strange waitress; together they pursue the life of the mind, and fall in love. But there are no decent human relationships possible in this social context, according to the young Hemingway. Though Scripps finds his best friends among the Indians, even these primitives, we realize, have been affected by the blight of the machine age. If Hemingway has often returned to his Michigan scene with tenderness, that of 'The Torrents of Spring' has been corrupted by the factory. The American earth itself—the primal forest, the virgin land whose quality Hemingway catches so beautifully in his Michigan stories, the fishing streams and woodland haunts, the scenes of his young hunting and reading and drinking and early loves—has yielded its nourishment to feed the new mechanical colossus whose body tends the conveyor belt and whose spirit is absorbed in the fabrication of such dazzling electric advertisements. Perhaps it was not 'the passing of a great race' which Hemingway tells us is mourned by 'The Torrents of Spring.' But it was certainly for Hemingway the passing of the American land he had so early loved and which, now under the imprint of industrial society, he was here renouncing.

This background, so closely affecting his youth as Hemingway shows it, was obviously no support for the work he was intent upon. The American physical effort, so Hemingway felt here, was too much like Scripps O'Neil's 'endless succession of days of dull piston-collaring.' The America of spiritual effort was too much like Brown's Beanery, the 'best by test' perhaps, but hardly sufficient for the artist of the depths. The American background denied Hemingway by and large the values which he needed for his exploration of the deeper instincts of man. When we notice in Hemingway's work the persistent impulses toward Catholicism, these impulses denied, tormented and recurrent, the issue becomes clearer. For the ethics of Catholicism include the elements of human nature which are omitted by Hemingway's own American environment. Thus Hemingway is in a state of creative ambivalence. He is the writer concerned with the shadows and enigmas of man's life, arising from the American tradition outlined in 'The Torrents of Spring'—tougher, harder, practical, more elementary in its values, less observant of the areas of human motivation with which Hemingway is concerned, perhaps more 'sensible' and certainly less truthful. He is the writer close to the final mysteries of life who comes out of the society which has exploited the Indian and exalted the Engine.

That Hemingway was himself aware of this in his later work as well as in 'The Torrents of Spring' we recall from his statement that the Spaniards 'are interested in death and do not spend their lives avoiding the thought of it and hoping it does not exist.' Unlike the Americans. Yet we remember also the uneasy and evasive tone of his realization: Hemingway's inability to state the full nature of his own concerns. His American background, not only unequal to his demands as a writer, was often indeed in direct opposition to it. It not only withheld from him the freedom of thought, the knowledge, the spiritual values which he needed for his central purpose. It increased, I believe, the actual conflict we have noticed in his work. The repressions which seem to block Hemingway from the full comprehension of his material have, of course, a particularly 'American' ring to them. They too echo a society which, with its emphasis on work and material achievement, had little time for these disturbing factors of our behavior. American society has uneasily pushed Hemingway's problems away from its own consciousness in the hope, perhaps, often like that of Hemingway himself, that by ignoring them we may solve them. (Even now, I dare say, we may consider the dominant concerns of Hemingway's work as rather more 'Russian' than American.) That Hemingway must break away from his native tradition was inevitable. But then it had already conditioned him more perhaps than he realized; and that working in exile as he did, he could only reach his ultimate purpose in fragmentary, if sometimes quite superb forms, seems almost as inevitable.

The conviction of 'Torrents of Spring,' moreover—that the meanings of life with which Hemingway was dealing lie outside of the American framework—persists through his work. In 'A Very Short Story,' which was the early outline for 'A Farewell to Arms,' the original hero comes to an ignominious end in the United States:

> A short time after he contracted gonorrhea from a salesgirl in a loop department store while riding in a taxicab through Lincoln Park.

This, we see, is the American equivalent for the love of Lieutenant Henry and Catherine Barkley, so warm and rich and touching on a foreign shore! Or if Hemingway will grant us the echoes of genuine tragedy in 'One Reader Writes,' it is a tragedy that is incoherent and unaware. 'Maybe he can tell me what's right to do,' the heroine thinks, after writing to a newspaper columnist about her husband's syphilis:

> Maybe he can tell me. In the picture in the paper he looks like he'd know. He looks smart, all right. . . . He ought to know. I want to do whatever is right. It's such a long time though. It's a long time. And it's been a long time. My Christ, it's been a long time.

It was a long time, too, between 'The Torrents of Spring' and 'To Have and Have Not' where Hemingway returns to the

American scene—the decade of rebellion and exile which we have been tracing. Yet in his second novel on the United States, the quality of Hemingway's American reaction remains essentially the same. Here indeed he renders his harshest judgment on the past patterns of our society, summarized perhaps in his statement on American love as the focus for our human relationships. 'Love is the greatest thing, isn't it?' says Richard Gordon's wife in the novel:

> Slop. Love is just another dirty lie. Love is ergoapiol pills to make me come around because you were afraid to have a baby. Love is quinine and quinine and quinine until I'm deaf with it. Love is that dirty aborting horror that you took me to. Love is my insides all messed up. It's half catheters and half whirling douches. I know about love. Love always hangs up behind the bathroom door. It smells like lysol. To hell with love.

The happiest of Hemingway's human relationships has no happy end, we know, the most intense as well as the most transient of them resulting alike in the inevitable nada. Yet it is doubtful whether anywhere else in his work Hemingway's conception of a human passion is quite as frightful as this, so mechanical and sterile, detached from all human feeling. The 'rummies' and 'vets' who fill the pages of 'To Have and Have Not' are another illustration of the American tragedy which is perhaps best described in the legalistic phrase as 'incompetent, irrelevant, and immaterial.' But the sharpest example of its essentially broken nature comes with the Mrs. Tracy of the novel. Her husband brought home to her dead, she screams, 'Albert! Albert! Oh, my God, where's Albert?' In her despair and agitation she falls off the dock into the water, loses her dental plate, emerges to wail: 'Basards! Bishes! . . . Alber. Whersh Alber?'

It seems evident that in Hemingway's search for the dark and tragic abysses of the human spirit, there was no place for his work in America. And the only positive Hemingway could find to place against the power of the destructive instincts, the sense of man's dignity which was realized in the Spanish matador, also did not reside in America's commercial order. With Hemingway as with Lardner, the American meaning is blurred, bathos too often supplanting sorrow. 'I lost my plate,' says Mrs. Tracy in the midst of her tragedy. What single image could better convey Hemingway's judgment than this, itself so Lardnerian in tone? And for Hemingway it is our national dental plate, as it were, which has been swept away by the flowing and unperturbed waters of the Gulf Stream. In this respect the American nada is emptier than any other. Whatever has been in it of man's struggle, his courage, dignity, and grand style, transient at best and inevitably doomed, is here rendered indistinct by the prevailing pattern of our society. Here in America the rare and few accents of humanity's divine articulation have been reduced to a sort of grotesque mumbling.

The similarity of Hemingway's verdict with Lardner's, extending even into the quality of their imagery, is of course marked. Is it curious that these two of the distinguished talents of '29, and in some ways two such distinct talents, should come to an identical agreement on their time? It is illuminating. And with other corroborations, both in these writers and their successors, it is almost conclusive. For it is essentially the ethics of the twenties which Hemingway is dealing with in 'To Have and Have Not.' This is still the Florida of Lardnerian millionaires, playboys, and yachtsmen, so grimly intent on entertainment. In this framework Hemingway places his protagonist Harry Morgan. Morgan fights to make a living for himself and his family against the encroaching forces of the depression. Single-handed he plays against the odds, living out in his own struggle the individualistic code of the '29 era. But his career is an ever-sharpening disintegration. Morgan's jobs grow more dangerous; he himself grows more reckless; his final defeat is implicit, although the manner of it may still shock us. The individualistic motivation fails him. And in a scene which is saturated with the orgiastic destruction marking the novel, Morgan pronounces his final words on his own struggle. Shot in a fight with Cuban revolutionaries, he has been rescued by a Coast Guard cutter. The men standing around him are trying to learn the facts of the shooting. 'A man,' Morgan says—

> 'Sure,' said the captain. 'Go on.'
> 'A man,' said Harry Morgan, very slowly. 'Ain't got no hasn't got any can't really isn't any way out.' . . .
> 'Go on, Harry,' said the captain. 'Tell us who did it. How did it happen, boy?' . . .
> 'Who did it, Harry?' the mate asked.
> Harry looked at him.
> 'Don't fool yourself,' he said. The captain and the mate both bent over him. Now it was coming. 'Like trying to pass cars on the top of hills. On that road in Cuba. On any road. Anywhere. Just like that. I mean how things are. The way that they been going. For a while yes sure all right. Maybe with luck. A man.' He stopped. The captain shook his head at the mate again. Harry Morgan looked at him flatly. The captain wet Harry's lips again. They made a bloody mark on the towel.
> 'A man,' Harry Morgan said, looking at them both. 'One man alone ain't got. No man alone now.' He stopped. 'No matter how a man alone ain't got no bloody . . . chance.'
> He shut his eyes. It had taken him a long time to get it out and it had taken him all of his life to learn it.

With these words, of course, Hemingway might have been passing judgment on the egotistic morality of '29 which Harry Morgan embodied; on all the Lardnerian unique individuals. The last quarter of the novel, indeed, dealing with the Lardnerian aristocrats of the prosperity decade, is a superb satirical elegy on the passing of the age: Wallace Johnston, a yachtsman who had originally defrauded Harry Morgan, '38 years old, M.A. Harvard, composer, money from silk mills, unmarried, *interdit de séjour* in Paris, well known from Algiers to Biskra.' His guest, Henry Carpenter, '36, M.A. Harvard, money now two hundred a month in trust fund from his mother, formerly four hundred and fifty a month,' who 'with his rather special pleasures' is now postponing 'his inevitable suicide by a matter of weeks if not of months.' The sixty-year-old grain merchant who lies awake, on his handsome, black, barkentine-rigged threemaster, worrying about the report from the Internal Revenue Bureau which is pronouncing the end of his sensational success as a speculator.—These and others of the American industrial élite are showing the ravages worked on their lives by the new age of crisis. And their decline is marked in a memorable epitaph for '29:

> Some made the long drop from the apartment or the office window; some took it quietly in two-car garages with the motor running; some used the native tradition of the Colt or Smith and Wesson; those well-constructed implements that end insomnia, terminate remorse, cure cancer, avoid bankruptcy, and blast an exit from intolerable positions by the pressure of a finger; those admirable American instruments so easily carried, so sure of effect, so well designed to end the American dream when it becomes a nightmare, their only drawback the mess they leave for relatives to clean up.

Thus the final word on the unique and miraculous age of material power which Lardner and his fellows had thought so absolute and eternal. Lardner's nightmare had preceded that of his time by only a few short years.

'To Have and Have Not,' then, records the disintegration of Lardner's age of individualism. But for Hemingway the novel is critical in a double sense. Simultaneously, as the first of his new works dealing with modern social problems, it records Hemingway's farewell to the solitary course he himself has been pursuing. 'No matter how a man alone ain't got no bloody chance.' With these words also Hemingway might have been judging his own decade of isolation. In this respect 'To Have and Have Not' is the projection into artistic form of Hemingway's personal struggle, and the decision of the writer to move henceforth in new directions. Equally with his protagonist Harry Morgan, Hemingway might say it has taken him a long time to deliver such a verdict upon his own life, upon his own single-handed revolt against country and culture and the continents of man's work. Like Morgan, Hemingway has also been 'the man alone.' And now, seeing the error of his isolation, he may almost say in turn that, if his judgment was long in coming, 'it had taken him all his life to learn it.'

With the return of the expatriate artist and the rebellious individualist to the land of his birth and the patterns of society, we may ask ourselves how much of the frustration which marked the end of Hemingway's isolation was emphasized by the solitary nature of his search. In themselves, as we know, all such explorations as Hemingway's of the destructive impulses of human nature are very delicate. Our normal ignorance of these forces and our normal desire to remain in ignorance are perhaps dictated in part by Nature's long-tried wisdom. For most of us it is safer here as elsewhere to know too little rather than too much. And when such explorations are conducted, as by Hemingway, with no balancing forces of culture and country, it is little wonder the stress upon the artist becomes acute, the despair more pronounced, the sense of human weakness in the face of such enigmas greater. We may wonder how much of the futility, the lack of meaning in life which Hemingway summarized so eloquently in his nada, was not merely the product of his own inability to reach these meanings, but also of his sense that there was no purpose in reaching them? How much of the emptiness he saw before him in man's life was in fact the emptiness he felt behind him in his own life?

There are, moreover, other even more curious connections between the writer and the society he had repudiated. It is somewhat ironic to realize that in his total rejection of it Hemingway seems often to embody the fundamental motivation of post-war America. What is Hemingway's complete individualism as an artist but the extension of that which marked Lardner's commercial egotist? The 'I' which for so many years was the single star to guide Hemingway over foreign boulevards and African jungles is not, after all, very different from the self-absorption of the typical man of America's boom era. The artistic métier was simply replacing the economic. In the method of his renunciation Hemingway bears the sign of the society he is renouncing. Disowning his social and his human obligations in favor of 'art,' Hemingway was in the end very close to the business man of the twenties who spoke in similar terms of his own commercial achievement. There is a distinction, obviously, between Hemingway's genuine devotion to his craft and that of Lardner's commercial superman to himself. Yet this qualifies rather than alters the essential similarity of their patterns. The illimitable desert of pure individualism is the same wherever its boundaries may lie. Even the artist may not pursue the rich fruits of his unique temperament too far. In the midst of the 'I' there must still be the 'we.' He, like the rest of humanity, must lose his soul to save it.

And that in his method of opposition to his age often Hemingway proves himself typical of it is, I think, clear. The rejection of the American twenties need not imply, as it did with Hemingway, the rejection of America. The rebellion against one society does not necessarily imply a rebellion against all society. In Hemingway's apparent ignorance of this, his feeling so much like Lardner's that such a transient age as '29 was permanent, in the extremes of his reaction into almost total isolation, Hemingway is characteristic. And in the failure of his total individualism, however spiritual its objectives, we may see the final comment on the Lardnerian epoch. What could certainly never 'work' in the sphere of material achievement (we use the terms of American pragmatism by intention) could not work either in the realm of the spirit. This is the last and most profound death of '29: the true end of the age's egotism.

And so our rebellious, anti-social, and uniquely aesthetic individual, the artist Hemingway, must be viewed as something of a sociological phenomenon even at the moment of his total escape from society. It is usually so. The more desperately we shake off the chains of our humanity, the more they cling to us. No one is of no value to society however much he may try to be. Attempt as we may to cut through it, the circle of our human heritage moves around us. The omniscient Lord of the mediaevalists, scrutinizing every little blade of grass as well as monarchs of the realm, was merely the materialization of man's growing perception of the indivisibility of man. Yet if Hemingway reached the end of '29 in his own flight from it, he came back to record the age's death and his new birth. In 'To Have and Have Not' the rebel returned to all the human works he had condemned. And from now on Hemingway will deal with the crucial aspects of the contemporary world he has so often, and often so brilliantly, negated. His next novel and the play which formed its prologue show a major reorientation of his values. As the outlines of the prosperity decade gave place to those of exile, these in turn have brought us to a new social framework. So in his own career Hemingway will illustrate the transition of the American writer in the depression of the nineteen-thirties, the turning from Ring Lardner's dead-end toward new beliefs.

5. RETURN OF THE NATIVES. It is within the entire pattern of Hemingway's renunciation, exile, and return that his latest and most popular novel, 'For Whom the Bell Tolls,' must be appraised. Its limitations come directly out of the series of crises and transitions which have marked Hemingway to this point, his career embracing so much spiritual turbulence and seeming to include in it the decisions of an entire generation.

For when we compare 'For Whom the Bell Tolls' with comparable works of its own genre, the revolutionary novels of André Malraux, for example, or the anti-Fascist work of Ignazio Silone, the difference in quality becomes apparent. 'For Whom the Bell Tolls' hardly reaches into the depths and nuances of its theme. The protagonist of the novel, Robert Jordan, is fighting for 'the dignity of man,' for the Spanish Loyalists against the oppressive forces of native and foreign Fascism. But beyond the broad outlines of the Spanish Civil War, we are given relatively little of the impact of the struggle in either sociological or personal terms. Malraux's 'Man's Fate,' Silone's 'Bread and Wine,' or lately Arthur Koestler's 'Darkness at Noon'—these works are filled with penetrating insights on the patterns of social crisis, the gains and losses worked by such crisis upon the human temperament, the problems of human behavior today when individuals and societies are making inestimable decisions as to the future. Silone's 'School for Dictators,' again, reveals the background of specialized thinking which both the Frenchman and the Italian have poured into their human narrative. By contrast, the new concern of Hemingway with this material often seems romantic or immature for the writer of a major work of art. How could this not be true, after Hemingway's long isolation from precisely this sort of material? He has shown us his contempt for the 'politics' or the 'economics' or the great sociological movements which form the background for his new novel. Everything we might say on this issue, in fact, is admitted by the protagonist of 'For Whom the Bell Tolls.' The Spanish Civil War is his education, Robert Jordan continually emphasizes. 'It is part of one's education. It will be quite an education when it's finished. You learn in this war if you listen. You most certainly did.' In terms of Hemingway's own development we may surmise that the Spanish War was also a central part of his own education, or re-education, as a member of society. As the returning individualist, the knowledge which Hemingway gained often seems too new, too complex and foreign for him to integrate fully into the artistic structure of 'For Whom the Bell Tolls.' And the strain of his transition from the rebellious individualist seems to interfere with Hemingway's artistic achievement. Robert Jordan is not only an untutored apprentice, he is more or less undistinguished. Maria is on the whole more theatrical than substantial. She is a sort of compendium of the virtues of the modern proletarian mistress. She emerges to the heights of romance from the depths of the class-struggle. Yet despite the horrors heaped upon her and the fortitude with which she bears them, she is in the end hardly as appealing as some of Hemingway's more typical, vain, trivial, and quite useless leisure-class ladies.

The merit of 'For Whom the Bell Tolls' often resides, in fact, in the material which Hemingway has previously dealt with. The Spanish peasants and anarchists, the bullfighters and bandits —these lesser personages hold us where the major figures fail. So too in the novel there are the familiar forces of Hemingway's despair, of the destruction which for so many years has preoccupied him. If he is now fighting for the good life, Jordan is nevertheless surrounded by the omens of death which marked the doomed protagonist of 'The Snows of Kilimanjaro.' The pillaging of the Fascist town is more coldly brutal perhaps than any previous episode in Hemingway's work. The dynamiting of the bridge, which forms the plot of 'For Whom the Bell Tolls,' is hardly a creative act to begin with. And progressively more frustrating, it becomes an act of complex destruction worthy of the best Hemingway of the past. As Hemingway used the framework of the First World War to project his own emotional tensions, here again he often finds the destruction and death marking the Spanish War appropriate for his present concern with these negative forces of our temperament. And certainly in the ethics and practices of civil war he finds many suitable outlets.

Yet in the past, if Hemingway's expression of these elements was sometimes limited, its purpose was clear. Here it is ambiguous. At the center of 'For Whom the Bell Tolls' there is a basic confusion of Hemingway's intention. The novel attempts to be a constructive statement on human life. Yet Hemingway's underlying sense of destruction often contradicts this. As the story progresses, in fact, the older Hemingway accents of futility seem to increase. The 'Yes' of Robert Jordan is progressively minimized by the submerged nada of his creator. Hemingway is thus still apparently caught between his previous and future purposes. Intellectually, his affirmation of man and his life have become clear, but his emotions have not altogether accepted the mind's dictate. The patterns of negative belief which Hemingway has built up over his long period of isolation are not so easy to modify: the nada has left its imprint upon Hemingway's new positives. The conversion of our writer in crisis is, after all, not quite so simple. We can hardly remake the temperament of a lifetime by a single affirmation, however insistent, or loud. As we see in Hemingway's novel, the buried feelings may yet use, despite all our good intentions, our new intellectual transformation for their older purpose. This then is the last and most crucial dilemma for Hemingway's future, and that of some of his followers in the new period. Here is the last price that the prosperity era of American post-war society has demanded of its high talent—this luxury time, so splendid in materialistic vanity, so unique and changeless in its own eyes, priceless, and demanding such a high price of its artists; casting the blight of its gilded glory over its writers even in the midst of the new age of chaos which rang out its dazzling and empty splendor. 'You could always come back,' but you also paid for the trip.

Yet, stating this of Hemingway—and this is, I believe, the crux of his future work—and of 'For Whom the Bell Tolls,' we do not intend to minimize the book, its effect on its society, or, with these limitations, its importance in the growth of Hemingway himself. If the novel remains inchoate in its comprehension of the central social issues of our time, and sometimes inarticulate in its expression of them, it represents nevertheless a transitional step beyond that of 'To Have and Have Not' and the embryonic 'Fifth Column.' And this third step on the path of Hemingway's return to humanity expresses the possibilities inherent in Hemingway. If the study of the individualist Pablo remains perhaps the most effective single portrait in the novel, it is nevertheless a study of Pablo's conflict between self and society: a new theme for Hemingway, a rich theme for the artist who in his former period hardly considered such a thesis worthy of attention. With Pablo's statement after his desertion from his fellow Spaniards ('Having done such a thing there is a loneliness that cannot be borne') we perceive that Hemingway, the advocate of Lieutenant Henry's desertion at Caporetto with no such conflict, has come near to the source of much of his own previous feeling of corrosive solitude. In General Golz, again, Hemingway has achieved the outlines of a genuine tragic protagonist—Golz who ends the novel still 'believing in how things could be, even if they never were,' and who replies, on being told the Spanish offensive is futile: '*Bon. Nous ferons notre petit possible.*'

These are close to the potentialities of Hemingway's reorientation of values. We are not asking that he become a rotarian optimist or a party propagandist. Yet the true sense of man's depths and his tragedy, first denied to Hemingway by the social patterns of '29 and then in turn thwarted by his isolation, the tragedy of Ecclesiastes which at his best Hemingway so magnificently approaches, is possible only within the framework of man's effort. The supreme renunciation of The Preacher himself came, not from any withdrawal from experience, but from the middle of it. It was the verdict on man's struggle, not on its absence. And that this sense of high tragedy has been conspicuously missing from much modern art may lie precisely in the fact that Hemingway, like other moderns, could not find the materials for genuine tragedy in the '29 era, nor ultimately in isolation. With his return now to the common fate and the common lot Hemingway is thus enriching the potentialities of his work.

And if as yet much of this transformation of Hemingway manifests itself in merely intellectual affirmations, what surprising affirmations they are! It is Anselmo—the sweet man of peace in the midst of the war's horrors, the soldier who wishes to convert all and shoot none, Anselmo who is perhaps the purest example of the basic tenderness of Hemingway, so often twisted and warped into bitterness and here freed—who most sharply contrasts the old and the new Hemingway as he rebukes the guerrilla leader, Pablo:

> Now we come for something of consummate importance
> and thee, with thy dwelling place to be undisturbed,
> puts thy fox-hole before the interests of humanity.

A strange statement indeed for our own writer individualist, our hunter in the lonesome hills, the despairing spectator of man's fruitless struggle; the tormented follower of fiestas who eschewed the sweat of comrades on the battlefield for his African solitude; who consigned our works and loves and willing achievement to waters of oblivion for the residence in his own fox-hole of abstract art. The interests of humanity! A curious conclusion to be born from the passing of '29's industrial fiesta, its own savage jungles of commercial ethics and floridian paradises: the interests of humanity rising from the death of an age where interest meant only dividends, and humanity was the material for exploitation.

Whatever the imperfections of 'For Whom the Bell Tolls,' it must be seen as the decisive step in Hemingway's circuit of escape from the trap of the American twenties. Doing this, Hemingway has illustrated the direction of our writers in the thirties from Ring Lardner's impasse to new beliefs which are themselves based on the elements of social conflict whose culmination Hemingway has recorded in terms of the Spanish scene—beliefs, however erratic or extreme, or, as with Hemingway, imperfectly fulfilled, which are to be the dominant tradition of the new age of American expression in crisis. And it is no coincidence that with Hemingway the first step of his transformation took place in 'To Have and Have Not' which simultaneously recorded the end of the prosperity era. The death of '29 accomplished what apparently its life could not. To Hemingway and his successors whom we are now about to discuss, the American depression, changing the face of our culture within a decade, came as a sort of salvation. Making the writers of the thirties aware of the transience of our materialistic power which they had felt so inimical to creative values, the crisis gave them new directions. Like Hemingway they were willing to return to a society in chaos where, in one form or another, they had fled from its aspect of permanence. For chaos implied transition. And the transition held in it the hope, at least, of a new system of social values less rigid and less empty than those of the twenties. The cultural optimism of '29 produced the nothingness of Lardner and the early Hemingway. The crisis of the thirties brought in the new faith of the later Hemingway, Wolfe, Dos Passos, Steinbeck, a rising cycle of belief in our future, a restatement of the vision of Jefferson and Lincoln rather than that of Jay Gould and Henry Ford. The dissolution of our material splendor cut away, for the first time in a century quite so sharply, the spiritual blight which the advent of the industrial order laid, in 1860, upon these earlier meanings of American society. Filled as it was with social distress, the new era was to be one of spiritual affirmatives.

The depression of the nineteen-thirties was thus a sort of shock to our writers, rather like the insulin treatment in modern therapy, which brought them back from the shadows of apathy to American life at best, and active hostility at worst. This much of the expression of the thirties Hemingway anticipates in his own withdrawal and return to our common life, though the pattern will vary with our other literary figures, and with John Dos Passos and William Faulkner we have both an apparent exception to the rule and a real one. But we cannot deny that if the return to social sanity through shock is better than no return, it is in the end a method of desperation rather than a counsel of perfection. Our Americans are also to show its effect in their work of the decade, as Hemingway has already. The crisis of the new age has caught him well along in his career. Can he discover, who has discovered so much and left much unsaid, the genuine method of unifying his work and his times, the fusion of the 'I' and the 'we' which will further illuminate the tragic impulses he has made his own? We recall the phrase which summarized Hemingway's solitary position: 'a way you'll never be.' With such native capacities, the inheritance of wisdom and eloquence, the sense of bottomless intuitions we often have with Hemingway, the prophetic texture which marks his talent, will Hemingway now find a way to be? For what a marvelous teacher Hemingway is, with all the restrictions of temperament and environment which so far define his work! What could he not show us of living as well as dying, of the positives in our being as well as our destroying forces, of 'grace under pressure' and the grace we need with no pressures, of ordinary life-giving actions along with those superb last gestures of doomed exiles!

ALFRED KAZIN

Hemingway: Synopsis of a Career

1942

The lost generation's fatalism developed in Ernest Hemingway's hands into the freshest and most deliberate prose art of the twenties. What E. E. Cummings had suggested in his great war autobiography, *The Enormous Room*, was that the postwar individual, first as soldier and citizen, now as artist, was the special butt of the universe. As Wyndham Lewis wrote later of the typical Hemingway hero, he was the man "things are done to." To Hemingway life became supremely the task of preserving oneself by preserving and refining one's art. Art was the ultimate, as it was perhaps the only, defense. In a society that served only to prey upon the individual, endurance was possible only by retaining one's identity and thus proclaiming one's valor. Writing was not a recreation, it was a way of life; it was born of desperation and enmity and took its insights from a

---

From *On Native Grounds* by Alfred Kazin. Copyright 1942 by the author. Reprinted by permission of Harcourt, Brace & Company, Inc. This essay has been slightly revised.

militant suffering. Yet it could exist only as it purified itself; it had meaning only as it served to tell the truth. A writer succeeded by proving himself superior to circumstance; his significance as an artist lay in his honesty, his courage, and the will to endure. Hemingway's vision of life, as John Peale Bishop was to put it, was thus one of perpetual annihilation. "Since the will can do nothing against circumstance, choice is precluded; those things are good which the senses report good; and beyond their brief record there is only the remorseless devaluation of nature."

The remarkable thing about Hemingway from the first was that he did not grow up to this rigid code, or would not admit that he had. The background of his first stories, *In Our Time*, was the last frontier of his Michigan boyhood, a mountainous region of forests and lakes against which he appeared as the inquisitive but tight-lipped youth—hard, curt, and already a little sad. With its carefully cultivated brutality and austerity, the sullen boy in *In Our Time* revealed a mind fixed in its groove. These stories of his youth, set against the superb evocation of war monotony and horror, elaborately contrived to give the violence of the Michigan woods and the violence of war an equal value in the reader's mind, summarized Hemingway's education. Their significance lay in the number of things the young Hemingway had already taken for granted; they were a youth's stricken responses to a brutal environment, and the responses seemed to become all. Just as the war in *A Farewell to Arms* was to seem less important than the sensations it provoked, so the landscape of *In Our Time* had meaning only for what the youth had learned from it. To Hemingway in his early twenties, the criticism of society had gone so deep that life seemed an abstraction; it was something one discounted by instinct and distrusted by habit. It was a sequence of violent actions and mechanical impulses: the brutality of men in the Michigan woods, the Indian husband who cut his throat after watching his wife undergo a Caesarian with a jackknife, adolescent loneliness and exaltation, a punch-drunk boxer on the road. And always below that level of native memories, interspersed with passing sketches of gangsters and bullfights, lay the war.

> Nick sat against the wall of the church where they had dragged him to be clear of machine-gun fire in the street. Both legs stuck out awkwardly. He had been hit in the spine. His face was sweaty and dirty. The sun shone on his face. The day was very hot–Two Austrian dead lay in the rubble in the shade of the house. Up the street were other dead–Nick turned his head carefully and looked at Rinaldi. "Senta Rinaldi. Senta. You and me we've made a separate peace."

The glazed face of the Hemingway hero, which through its various phases was to become, like Al Capone's, the face of a decade and to appear on a succession of soldiers, bullfighters, explorers, gangsters, and unhappy revolutionaries, emerged slowly but definitively in *In Our Time*. The hero's first reaction was surprise, to be followed immediately by stupor; life, like the war, is in its first phase heavy, graceless, sullen; the theme is sounded in the rape of Lix Coates by the hired man. Then the war became comic, a series of incongruities. "Everybody was drunk. The whole battery was drunk going along the road in the dark— The lieutenant kept riding his horse out into the fields and saying to him: 'I'm drunk, I tell you, mon vieux. Oh, I am so soused.'— It was funny going along that road." Then the whole affair became merely sordid, a huddle of refugees in the mud, the perpetual rain, a woman bearing her child on the road. "It rained all through the evacuation." By the sheer accumulation of horrors, the final phase was reached, and the end was a deceptive callousness.

> We were in a garden at Mons. Young Buckley came in with his patrol from across the river. The first German I saw climbed up over the garden wall. We waited till he got one leg over and then potted him. He had so much equipment on and looked awfully surprised and fell down into the garden. Then three more came over further down the wall. We shot them. They all came just like that.

Hemingway's own values were stated explicitly in the story called "Soldier's Home," where he wrote that "Krebs acquired the nausea in regard to experience that is the result of untruth or exaggeration." The Hemingway archetype had begun by contrasting life and war, devaluating one in terms of the other. Now life became only another manifestation of war; the Hemingway world is in a state of perpetual war. The soldier gives way to the bullfighter, the slacker to the tired revolutionary, the greed of war is identified with the corruption and violence of sport. Nothing remains but the individual's fierce unassailable pride in his pride, the will to go on, the need to write without "untruth or exaggeration." As a soldier, he has preserved his sanity by rebelling quietly and alone; he had made the separate peace. Mutiny was the last refuge of the individual caught in the trap of war; chronic mutiny now remains the safeguard of the individual in that state of implicit belligerence between wars that the world calls peace. The epos of death has become life's fundamental narrative; the new hero is the matador in Chapter XII of *In Our Time*. "When he started to kill it was all in the same rush. The bull looking at him straight in front, hating. He drew out the sword from the folds of the muleta and sighted with the same movement and called to the bull, Toro! Toro! and the bull charged and Villalta charged and just for a moment they became one." The casual grace of the bullfighter, which at its best is an esthetic passion, is all. And even that grace may become pitiful, as in the saga of the aging matador in "The Undefeated." For the rest, defeat and corruption and exhaustion lie everywhere: marriage in "Cross Country Snow," sport in "My Old Man" ("Seems like when they get started they don't leave a guy nothing"), the gangrene of Fascism in "Chi Ti Dice la Patria?" The climax of that first exercise in disillusion is reached in the terse and bitter narrative called "The Revolutionist," the story of the young boy who had been tortured by the Whites in Budapest when the Soviet collapsed, and who found Italy in 1919 beautiful. "In spite of Hungary, he believed altogether in the world revolution."

> 'But how is the movement going in Italy?' he asked.
> 'Very badly,' I said.
> 'But it will go better,' he said. 'You have everything here. It is the one country that every one is sure of. It will be the starting point of everything.'

When Hemingway published those first stories in 1925, he was twenty-seven years old, and the rising star—"the surest future there," Lincoln Steffens recalled in his autobiography—in the American literary colony in Paris. Unlike most of the writers in the "lost generation," he had not gone to a university; after completing a round of private schools he had gone to work, still in his teens, for the Kansas City *Star*, a paper famous for its literary reporters. He had driven an ambulance on the Italian front before America entered the war, been wounded gloriously enough to receive the Croce di Guerra, and after 1921 had traveled extensively as a foreign correspondent. "In writing for a newspaper," he reported seventeen years later in the rambling prose of *Death in the Afternoon*, "you told what happened, and with one trick or another, you communicated the emotion aided by the element of timeliness which gives a certain emotion to any account of something that has happened on that day. But the real thing, the sequence of motion and fact which made the emotion and which would be as valid in a year or ten years or, with luck and if you stated it purely enough, always, was beyond me and I was working very hard to get it."

Hemingway's intense search for "the real thing" had already singled him out in Paris before he published *In Our Time*. In those early years, guided by his interest in poetry and his experiences as a reporter of the European debacle, he seemed to be feeling his way toward a new prose, a prose that would be not only absolutely true to the events reported and to the accent of common speech, but would demand of itself an original evocativeness and plasticity. What he wanted, as he said later in *Death in the Afternoon*, was a prose more intensely precise than conventional prose, and hence capable of effects not yet achieved. He wanted to see "how far prose can be carried if anyone is serious enough and has luck. There is a fourth and fifth dimension that can be gotten. . . . It is much more difficult than poetry. It is prose that has never been written. But it can be written without tricks and without cheating. With nothing that will go bad afterwards." Yet what he was aiming at in one sense, F. O. Matthiessen has pointed out, was the perfect yet poetic naturalness of a Thoreau. Hemingway's surface affiliations as a prose craftsman were with his first teachers, Gertrude Stein and Sherwood Anderson, who taught him the requisite simplicity and fidelity and—Gertrude Stein more than Anderson—an ear for the natural rhythms of speech. But his deeper associations went beyond them, beyond even the Flaubertian tradition of discipline and *le mot juste*. He did not want to write "artistic prose," and Gertrude Stein and Anderson, equally joined in their hatred of display and their search for an inner truth in prose, had certainly taught him not to. But he wanted not merely to tell "the truth about his own feelings at the moment when they exist"; he wanted to aim at that luminous and imaginative truth which a writer like Thoreau, on the strength of a muscular integrity and arousement to nature very like his own, had created out of a monumental fidelity to the details of life as he saw them. What he wanted was that sense of grace, that "sequence of motion and fact" held at unwavering pitch that could liberate the innate symbolism in every fact touched and recorded.

It was this that separated him essentially from Gertrude Stein and Anderson. Anderson was not fundamentally interested in *writing*; Gertrude Stein, who could help everyone in the world but herself, was interested in nothing else. The Hemingway legend, which Hemingway himself fostered in the Twenties, encouraged the belief that he was only a pure nihilist and coldly assimilative, even brutish in imagination. But nothing could have been more false. He brought a superb art to a minor vision of life, and it is as important to measure the vision as it is to appreciate the art. But his seeming naïveté was really an exemplary straightforwardness and a remarkable capacity for learning from every possible source. As a practicing artist he had the ability to assimilate the lessons of others so brilliantly that he seemed to impart a definitive modern emotion to everything he touched. He learned so brilliantly, indeed, that the extent of his borrowing has often been exaggerated. What is significant in Hemingway's literary education is not that he learned prose rhythm from the Gertrude Stein of *Three Lives*, the uses of simplicity from Ezra Pound and the cosmopolitan literary ateliers of postwar Paris, but that they gave him the authority to be himself. Despite his indebtedness to Mark Twain's *Huckleberry Finn*—for him the greatest book in all American writing—he had no basic relation to any prewar culture. Byron learned from Pope, but Hemingway learned to write in a literary environment that could not remember 1913. Even the literary revolution that found its appointed heir in him, an avant-garde forever posing under its Picasso, and talking modernism with a Midwestern accent, could not long claim him. Once Hemingway had learned the principles and tricks of his art, had made a literary personality out of the Midwestern athlete, soldier, and foreign correspondent; had created a new hero for the times in the romantically disillusioned postwar dandy, he went his own way in his search for "the real thing."

It was in his unceasing quest of a conscious perfection through style that Hemingway proclaimed his distinction. To tell what had happened, as he wrote later, one used "one trick or another," dialogue being the supreme trick. But "the real thing," the pulse of his art, was from the first to Hemingway that right blending of fact into symbol, that perfect conversion of natural rhythm into an evocation of the necessary emotion, that would fuse the various phases of contemporary existence—love, war, sport—and give them a collective grace. And it was here that style and experience came together for him. Man endured the cruelty and terror of life only by the sufferance of his senses and his occasional enjoyment of them; but in that sufferance and enjoyment, if only he could convey them perfectly, lay the artist's special triumph. He could now rise above the dull submissive sense of outrage which most men felt in the face of events. By giving a new dimension to the description of natural fact, he could gain a refuge from that confusion which was half the terror of living. What this meant was brilliantly illustrated in the association of the worlds of peace and war in *In Our Time*; the theme of universal loneliness in the midst of war that was sounded in the very first paragraph of *A Farewell to Arms* and attained its classic expression in the retreat at Caporetto, where the flowing river, the long grumbling line of soldiers, the officers who are being shot together by the carabinieri, seem to recede together in the darkness; the extraordinary scene in *The Sun Also Rises* where Robert Cohn, sitting with Jake and his friends at the bull-fight, is humiliated a moment before the steer is gored in the ring. In each case the animal in man has found its parallel and key in some event around it; the emotion has become the fact.

If "the real thing" could not always be won, or retained after it had been won, there were other forms of grace—the pleasures of drinking and making love, the stabbing matador dancing nervously before his bull, the piercing cry of the hunt, the passionate awareness of nature that would allow a man to write a sentence like "In shooting quail you must not get between them, or when they flush they will come pouring at you, some rising steep, some skimming by your ears, whirring into a size you have never seen then in the air as they pass." If art was an expression of fortitude, fortitude at its best had the quality of art. Beyond fortitude, which even in *For Whom the Bell Tolls* is the pride of a professional integrity and skill, there was the sense of nature paralyzed, nature frozen into loneliness of terror. No writer in all American literature after Thoreau has had Hemingway's sensitiveness to color, to climate, to the knowledge of physical energy under heat or cold, that knowledge of the body thinking and moving through a landscape that Edmund Wilson, in another connection, has called Hemingway's "barometric accuracy." That accuracy was the joy of the huntsman and the artist; beyond that and its corresponding gratifications, Hemingway seemed to attach no value to anything else. There were only absolute values or absolute degradations.

The very intensity of Hemingway's "nihilism" in his first stories and novels proved, however, that his need for an ideal expression in art was the mark of a passionate romanticist who had been profoundly disappointed. The anguish of his characters was too dramatic, too flawless; it was too transparent an inversion. The symbols Hemingway employed to convey his sense of the world's futility and horror were always more significant than the characters who personified emotions, and the characters were so often felt as personified emotions that the emotions became sentimental. The gallery of expatriates in *The Sun Also Rises* were always subsidiary to the theme that the period itself was lost; the lovers in *A Farewell to Arms* were, as Edmund Wilson has said, the abstractions of a lyric emotion. Hemingway had created a world of his own socially more brilliant than life, but he was not writing about people living in a *world*; he was dealing in stock values again, driving his characters between the two poles of a tremulous inner exaltation and an absolute frustration. What he liked best was to invoke the specter of damnation.

After that, *Death in the Afternoon* and the Hemingway legend. There had always been a Hemingway legend, and with good reason; like Bryon, he had always to live up to his own reputation. But the legend became ominous and even cheap only when Hemingway chose to treat it as a guide to personal conduct and belief; when, in fact, he became the most public of his own characters. After *Death in the Afternoon*, Hemingway's work became an expression of the legend, where the legend had been the first dazed response to his work. The sense of shock, the stricken malaise of his first stories were now transformed into a loud and cynical rhetoric. "Madame, all our words from loose using have lost their edge," Hemingway tells the Old Lady in *Death in the Afternoon*; and proves it by his own example. "Have you no remedy then?" she asks. "Madame, there is no remedy for anything in life." The pose, pretentious on one level, becomes merely tittery on another. The highjinks of the wastrels in *The Sun Also Rises* had suggested a tragic self-knowledge, a verdict on life as they saw it; Hemingway's own tone was now a little frantic. "So far, about morals, I know only that what is moral is what you feel good after and what is immoral is what you feel bad after." It was on a plane with the famous parody of Marx in "The Gambler, the Nun, and the Radio":

> Religion is the opium of the people—Yes, and music is the opium of the people— And now economics is the opium of the people; along with patriotism the opium of the people in Italy and Germany. What about sexual intercourse; was that an opium of the people? Of some of the people. Of some of the best of the people. But drink was a sovereign opium of the people, oh, an excellent opium. Although some prefer the radio, another opium of the people—Along with these went gambling, an opium of the people if there ever was one—Ambition was another, an opium of the people, along with a belief in any new form of government.

As the years went by, one grew accustomed to Hemingway standing like Tarzan against a backdrop labeled Nature; or, as the tedious sportsman of *The Green Hills of Africa*, grinning over the innumerable beasts he had slain, while the famous style became more mechanical, the sentences more invertebrate, the philosophy more self-consciously juvenile, the pleasures more desperate. Most of the lost generation had already departed to other spheres of interest; Hemingway seemed to have taken up a last refuge behind the clothing advertisements in Esquire, writing essays in which he mixed his fishing reports with querulous pronouncements on style and the good life. Then, eight years after the publication of *A Farewell to Arms*, when the Hemingway legend had already lost its luster with the disappearance of the world that had encouraged that legend with emulation and empty flattery, Hemingway wrote *To Have and Have Not.* It was a frantically written novel, revealing a new tension and uncertainty in Hemingway; but for all its melodrama, it was not cheap, and it was strange to note that it was the first novel he had written about America. The dry crackle of the boozed cosmopolitans eating their hearts out in unison, the perpetual shift of scene to Malaga or Paris or the African jungle—the best proof that Hemingway had become a true American success, at home and not at home in every part of the world—had been replaced by Key West, like the Paris of 1925 an outpost of the world in rot. It was by Key West that Hemingway had come home, and it was Key West, apparently, that for him became a working symbol of America in the depression: the noisy, shabby, deeply moving rancor between all those human wrecks, the fishermen and the Cuban revolutionaries, the veterans and the alcoholics, the gilt-edged snobs and the hungry natives, the great white stretch of beach promising everything and leading nowhere.

The Hemingway of *To Have and Have Not* was not a "new" Hemingway; he was an angry and confused writer who had been too profoundly disturbed by the social and economic crisis to be indifferent, but could find no clue in his education by which to understand it. Inevitably, he lapsed into melodrama and sick violence. To the Hemingway who had gained his conception of life from the First World War only to crash into the Second by way of international panic and the Spanish Civil War, mass suffering had always been a backdrop against which the Hemingway hero persisted by dint of his Byronic pride, his sense of grace. But this new crisis had to be endured with something more than artistic fortitude; every generation was caught up in it, every phase of contemporary culture and manners was transformed by it, as even his beloved Spain was being devastated by it. It was like Hemingway, of course, to pick for his new hero in the Thirties the pirate of *To Have and Have Not* and the international secret agent of *The Fifth Column*: the two men left in the era from Black Friday to Munich who could remain casual about annihilation! He was reaching for something in these two works that he could not identify satisfactorily or project with confidence, and it was inevitable that both Harry Morgan and Philip should represent the old tormented individualism passionately eager for human fellowship and contemptuous of it. The Hemingway hero was now a composite exaggeration of all the Hemingway heroes, yet nothing in himself. He was the *Esquire* fisherman and a GPU agent in Spain who found that he had to choose between the Spanish Republic and a Vassar girl; he was a murdering gangster who killed only because Hemingway wanted to kill something at the moment, and a sophisticated fellow-traveler who, when he heard the militia sing "Bandera Rossa" downstairs in the shell-battered Hotel Florida, cried: "The best people I ever knew died for that song." Yet Philip in *The Fifth Column* was not one of the best people; he was Jake Barnes making up for his impotence by murdering Fascists, and the Fascists were as unreal as the sick wisdom he and the perennial Lady Brett mumbled at each other in the midst of a civil war that was shaking Western society.

Whatever it was Hemingway tried emotionally to recover, however, he found in some measure in Spain; and he found it first in an extraordinary little story, "Old Man at the Bridge," that he cabled from Barcelona in April, 1938. "It will take many plays and novels to present the nobility and dignity of the cause of the Spanish people," he wrote in his preface to *The Fifth Column*, "and the best ones will be written after the war is over." "Old Man at the Bridge" was more than an introduction to *For Whom the Bell Tolls*; it was a record of the better things Hemingway had learned in Spain, an intimation of a Hemingway who had found the thwarted ideal clear and radiant again through the martyrdom or the Spanish masses. In the retreat of the Loyalist forces a Spanish officer encounters the last refugee from San Carlos, an old man who has been taking care of eight pigeons, two goats, and a cat, but has been separated from them and from his own people by the advancing Fascist armies. "And you have no family?" the Loyalist officer asks. "No," replies the old man, "only the animals I stated. The cat, of course, will be all right.

A cat can look out for itself, but I cannot think what will become of the others." "What politics have you?" the officer asks. "I am without politics," replies the old man. "I am seventy-six years old, I have come twelve kilometers now and I think now I can go no further."

It was in something of this spirit that Hemingway wrote *For Whom the Bell Tolls*, the work of a profound romanticist who had at last come to terms with the ideal, and who had torn down the old charnel house with such ardor that his portrait of the Spanish war was less a study of the Spanish people than a study in epic courage and compassion. The idealism that had always been so frozen in inversion, so gnawing and self-mocking, had now become an unabashed lyricism that enveloped the love of Robert Jordan and Maria, the strength of Pilar, the courage and devotion of the guerrillas, the richness and wit of Spanish speech, in a hymn of fellowship. "All mankinde is of one Author, and is one volume—No man is an Island, intire of it selfe." Nothing could have been more purely American than the love story of Robert and Maria, and no love story ever seemed so abstract an expression of an American writer's confidence in life and his reverence for Europe. Hemingway had apparently gained a new respect for humanity in Spain: and in the spirit of the Catholic devotion by John Donne which gave him his title, it seemed as if his long quest for an intense unity, the pure absolute fortitude and grace, had become a joyous unison of action and battle and love.

Yet *For Whom the Bell Tolls* is among the least of Hemingway's works. Its leading characters are totally unreal; as a record of the human and social drama that was the Spanish Civil War, it is florid and never very deep. And if one compares this work of his ambitious conversion, with its eloquence, its calculation, and its romantic inflation, with the extraordinarily brilliant story of this late period, "The Snows of Kilimanjaro," it is clear that the attempted affirmation of life in the novel, while passionate enough, is moving only in itself, while the concentrated study of waste and death in the story is superbly dramatic, in Hemingway's best vein. Hemingway's world is a world of death still, even in *For Whom the Bell Tolls*; and the great things in it, like the battle scenes or the pillage of the Facist town, flow with a carefully contrived violence and brutality in his old manner. But the Spanish war is essentially only Robert Jordan's education —"It's part of one's education. It will be quite an education when it's finished." The Hemingway "I" is still the center of existence, as only he could alternate between the war and Maria in the sleeping-bag so easily; as only he could seem less a man entering into the experience of others than the familiarly damned, familiarly self-absorbed, lost-generation Byron playing a part beside them. And the Hemingway hero is still "the man things are done to"—the war is something happening to Robert Jordan—still the brilliant young man counting the costs of his own life among the ruins. *For Whom the Bell Tolls* is thus an unsatisfactory novel, certainly unsatisfactory for Hemingway, because it is a strained and involuntary application of his essentially anarchical individualism, his brilliant half-vision of life, to a new world of war and struggle too big for Hemingway's sense of scale and one that can make that half-vision significantly sentimental.

The will is there, the reaching hope; nothing could be more false than the familiar belief that Hemingway wanted to go round and round the old nihilist circle. But as Robert Jordan lived and fought the war so curiously alone, so he dies alone, waiting for the enemy to come—the Hemingway guerrilla dying a separate death as once he made a separate peace, the last of the Hemingway heroes enjoying the final abnegation, and now the least impressive. That separate death and abnegation were all there before, and they were very good before. Good when the hunter was alone in the hills, the matador before his bull, the quail skimming through the air. Good when Gertrude Stein could teach a young man fresh from war to write "perfect" sentences, and the triumph of art was equal to the negation of life. Good when the world could seem like a Hemingway novel; and the "I" was the emblem of all the disillusionment and fierce pride in a world so brilliant in its sickness; and the sentences were so perfect, spanning the darkness. It did not matter then that the art could be so fresh and brilliant, the life below its superb texture so arid and dark. For Hemingway's is one of the great half-triumphs of literature; he proved himself the triumphal modern artist come to America, and within his range and means, one of the most interesting creators in the history of the American imagination. But if it did not matter then, it matters now—not because what is supremely good in Hemingway is in any way perishable, but because his work is stationary, because there is no real continuity in him, nothing of the essential maturity of spirit which his own poetic insight has always called for. It matters now that Hemingway's influence has in itself become a matter of history. It will always matter, particularly to those who appreciate what he brought to American writing, and who, with that distinction in mind, can realize that Hemingway's is a tactile contemporary American success; who can realize, with respect and sympathy, that it is a triumph in and of a narrow, local, and violent world—and never superior to it.

Technically and even morally Hemingway was to have a profound influence on the writing of the Thirties. As a stylist and craftsman his example was magnetic on younger men who came after him; as the progenitor of the new and distinctively American cult of violence, he stands out as the greatest single influence on the hard-boiled novel of the Thirties, and certainly affected the social and left-wing fiction of the period more than some of the writers could easily admit. No one except Dreiser in an earlier period had anything like Hemingway's dominance over modern American fiction, yet even Dreiser meant largely an example of courage and frankness during the struggle for realism, not a standard of style and a persuasive formula, like Hemingway's, that would color the manners of a whole generation and make its real effect, where it had begun, in the smaller truth and larger slickness of American journalism. Hemingway is the bronze god of the whole contemporary literary experience in America.

EDWARD FENIMORE

English and Spanish in "For Whom the Bell Tolls"

1943

In the following passage of his novel *For Whom the Bell Tolls* Hemingway expresses a sensitivity to the suggestive value of words in themselves which I conceive to underlie his whole handling of language in the book. His American protagonist, Robert Jordan, thinks (p. 166):

> And if . . . there is only now, why then now is the thing to praise and I am very happy with it. Now, *ahora*, *maintenant*, *heute*, Now, it has a funny sound to be a whole world and your life. *Esta noche*, tonight, *ce soir*, *heute abend*. Life and wife, *Vie* and *Mari*. No, it didn't work out . . . Take dead, *mort*, *muerto*, *todt*. *Todt* was the deadliest of them all. War, *guerre*, *guerra*, and *Krieg*. *Krieg* was the most like war, or was it? Or was it only that he knew German the least well?

It may be worth emphasising that this is not at all an exuberant heaping up of words, but a savoring, no matter how inconclu-

From *A Journal of English Literary History*, Vol. Ten, Number Two, June, 1943. Reprinted by permission of the author.

sive, of the suggestive power of particular words.[1] For our perception of the Spanish which is assumed to be spoken throughout the book, we have in Jordan a center of consciousness explicitly aware of that language as an objective thing. " 'For us will be the bridge and the battle, should there be one,' R. J. said, and saying it into the dark he felt a little theatrical but it sounded well in Spanish" (p. 43). And further along: " 'Back to the palace of Pablo,' R. J. said to Anselmo. It sounded wonderful in Spanish" (p. 199). The sense of language thus appears as a constant element of the "view from without," the non-Spanish looking in upon the Spanish world; and the value of phrase and idiom is in the effect produced on a consistently assumed English ear. The austere and amusing and grandiose—in so far as these, in Spanish, ring on the English ear—move with the same elements in scene and character, are justified by these latter and, to an even greater extent, contribute to them.

The most elementary of such cases is perhaps that of words which echo the odd yet recognizable in English and are effective because of this echo-value—for instance the "rare" and "much" (the blond one with the rare name . . . much horse . . . thou art much woman, etc.). These are of course direct translations from the Spanish, in which they also appear: ". . . the deaf man nodded. '*Sí algo raro, pero bueno.*' " But the reason for the choice for these among presumably innumerable Spanish idioms is to be sought in the English value—in one sense a slang value as in this (p. 212):

> "Very rare, yes," Pablo said. "Very rare and very drunk . . ."
>
> He's rare all right, R. J. thought, and smart and very complicated.

Jordan's thought in English, and the peculiar quality of his silent "rare" comes naturally to American lips and ears. The line, in

[1] It has been remarked to me that these lines also reflect, and in a sense point to, the international nature of the Loyalist organization and the body of men of whom R. J. is representative. But this point does not strictly fall within my limits here.

short, amounts to a partial explanation of Hemingway's fondness for the word. It reflects a variety of tones, including Shakespeare's "What is the news of the court?—None rare, my lord" (*Winter's Tale*, I, 2, 367), or the Abbey stone's "O rare Ben Jonson." To the modern ear there is just enough of the ironical in a context not necessarily so, to make such Elizabethan examples pleasant; and it is this piquant added tone which is borne by the constant carrying over of the Spanish *raro*.

To some extent the same thing may be said of *mucho* but the case is less simple. For example: " 'That,' said R. J., pointing to one of the bays . . . 'is much horse' " (p. 13); or: " '*Eras mucho caballo*,' he said, meaning 'Thou wert plenty of horse' " (p. 313). This second example is especially interesting in view of the translation accompanying it—a translation deliberately unidiomatic, in order that what the English ear feels to be rough and primitive in the Spanish should not be weakened.[2] In each case the English endeavors to approximate the Spanish by transferring, as the Spanish at least appears to do, a quantitative estimate to a qualitative plane, but doing so without losing the essentially crude vigor which it finds in the original. The English cannot of course really make this transfer. What it can do is to make literal meaning clear, leaving the peculiar nature of the original idiom to remain, objectively perceived and hence an important trait in the portrayal of this Spanish world.

The *mucho* of these phrases has, like *raro*, its echo value, but one of a different kind. There are at least two threads of familiarity: one, the resemblance between *mucho* and "much" which makes the English ear highly sensitive to the Spanish usage; a second, the pidgin-English function of "much" in the role of "very" and "many." The two threads are perhaps really one, for we are especially conscious of Spanish usage when it appears to be along pidgin-English lines. We are all no doubt familiar with the second of these threads if only from overhearing the "Ugh!

[2] As a general thing there is no hesitation in translating into colloquial English. Cf. p. 108: "*Qué pasa, cobardes?* What is the matter, cowards?"

Heap much pale-face in alley" of backyard Mohawks. When Spanish *mucho*, then, is used in a manner conflicting with the proper use of English "much" the echo in an ear still objectively conscious of Spanish will hold something of the primitive. "Much horse," "much woman" mean, literally, nothing in English. Yet they are highly suggestive of meaning. It is no literal translation, but what might be termed "phonetico-semantic" translation.

Nevertheless it is not easy to draw a sharp line here, for relatively close is a construction in which the word is again in a grammatical though not wholly familiar place, and Hemingway's "translation" of the Spanish perhaps holds something of this. Caesar says (*Ant. and Cl. 2.6.5*): "Let us know If 'twill tie up thy discontented sword And carry back to Sicily much tall youth That else must perish here." There is more than a mere collective here, for *youth* evokes both the young men and the quality "youthfulness"; so that if a passage from the quantity estimate of "youths" to the quality estimate of their common youth is not fully made, nevertheless the phrase hangs in some fashion in balance between the two.

Finally it may be remarked that Hemingway is not without a sense of humor—one which, I imagine, is quite frankly playing with the word's possibilities in such "translation" as old Anselmo's "One must move with much precautions" (p. 47).[3]

The use of the Spanish word itself is another thing, generally constituting a recognition in this or that object of a quality not inherent in the English equivalent; or of an objective quality attached to an object in the mind of one of the characters of the novel which can be conveyed to the English reader through the use of a term objective and more or less unfamiliar to him. Typical of this latter case is the word *máquina* which the gypsy Rafael uses almost exclusively in his recital of the dynamiting of

[3] Cf. *A Farewell to Arms*, p. 256: "When did she go?"—"She went two days ago with the other lady English." *Coll'altra signora inglese*. True, there is something in the word order of "she-mule" or "lady-poet," a minor differentiation in the great general class of the English. But there is chiefly the simple amusement to be found in the literal translation.

the train (p. 29). His earlier remarks have shown that the machine gun is a thing of relative mystery to Rafael, a thing with "a very rare name"; and the Spanish term provides the English reader something of the almost animate quality which the gun may be supposed to have had for the gypsy.

Frequently, however, Spanish and English equivalent are given together because the English is *not* an equivalent in any true sense. During the massacre of the Fascists a voice cries; "*Que salga el toro.* Let the bull out!" (p. 109). Roughly an equivalent, but only roughly so. While the English here provides guidance to a literal meaning, the Spanish provides the emotional connotation. For there is nothing inherent in the English word adequate to fill the image behind this cry. This is the fighting bull with his evocation of cruelty and blood, about to break from the *toril.* The attitude of the shouting drunk holds the intensity of that moment; and what is to emerge into the sunlight is, and is only, *toro.*

But perhaps the finest example of this is found in the passage between Pablo and Pilar on p. 90:

> "Yes," he said. "God and the *Virgen*."
> "*Qué va*, God and the *Virgen*," I said to him. "Is that any way to talk?"
> "I am afraid to die, Pilar," he said. "*Tengo miedo de morir*. Dost thou understand?"

Why *Virgen* rather than an English "Virgin" to match the English "God"? Because here again the Spanish word sets off the idea in the ear and imagination of the English reader. It places before him another conception of the Virgin—one which, by the word and context, is severed from the too familiar prettiness of the Rossetti kind, and which finds emotional reflection in the rather terrible Spanish phrase which follows.

I believe that that phrase, "Tengo miedo de morir," has for the English ear a starkness lacking in our equivalent. The equivalent, "I am afraid to die," is given here for the literal sense; but more than that is suggested to an ear in which Spanish is less than completely familiar and where consequently the etymological sense, strengthened in this case by the maintenance of that sense in kindred tongues, remains alive. To such an ear *tengo* inevitably means something more than "have," and it is this etymological overtone with its implication of physical grasp which gives the idiom its peculiar intensity and justifies its appearance here. For the English ear it is not simply that Pablo "has" fear of death: he holds it, desperately, in his two hands.

To these instances of the Spanish word must be added the frequently interjected *Qué va!*—the total effect of which (and for this suggestion, and not for this alone, I am indebted to Dr. Leo Spitzer) may be felt to transcend its immediate function from passage to passage, and emerge finally as a kind of "motif," crystallizing a fundamental spiritual attitude. That attitude is one which dismisses secondary values before the unilinear action which drives through the tale, a dismissal which is the prerequisite to effective participation in action. This is particularly true of Jordan, in whom the need to dismiss values not immediately pertinent is explicit. The extended recollection of Gaylord's (p. 228 ff.) paints a background and a body of uncertainty which must be ignored if he is to act at all. Jordan does not say "*Qué va,* Gaylord's!" in so many words, but he implies it. "My mind," he thinks (and we are justified in adding "my evaluation of all the means involved, of everything except the final result"), "is in suspension until we win the war" (p. 245).

Parenthetically, in view of these functions of the Spanish word as such, it may be well to anticipate an inevitable question: to what extent knowledge of Spanish seems necessary to a full reading of Hemingway's tale. Obviously, the sensitivity of one's reaction will vary, here and there, according to one's knowledge of Spanish—but in no direct ratio. Complete familiarity no less than complete ignorance would presumably destroy the overtone of a *tengo*. On the other hand, in such cases as "much horse" and, in short, all phraseology which is not colloquial English and hence may be reflected Spanish, knowledge of that language is immaterial to the important thing—the tacit assumption that it *is*

Spanish, and, based upon this assumption, our acceptance of a non-colloquial English.

To this end of establishing the unfamiliar, a major part is played by the best-known linguistic convention of the novel, the use of the word "obscenity" and one or two like it. This is but one means, although the predominant one, whereby the more pungent passages of the text are conveyed. The rest may be listed briefly: 1) the Spanish itself; 2) the English "semi-obscenity" based upon the allusion—the self-"besmirching"s and "befouling"s for example; and 3) the pseudo-euphemism of such English as "muck them," etc. (pp. 241, 369-370).

The interesting thing here is the very slight use made of this pseudo-euphemism which is adequately established in contemporary fiction and sets the reference beyond question of doubt. But Hemingway employs it only twice and then as English—for instance in R. J.'s mental discourse upon the discovery that Pablo has made off with the dynamite exploder. The explanation of this narrow use of the precisely-valued English, and on the other hand the wide use of the amorphous "obscenity" is in reality one. As observers of Jordan as thinker and speaker of English, we are on familiar ground. We share reflex and vocabulary: his speech is immediate and precise to us. But this is not so for the Spanish world in which he moves, and the true value of the word "obscenity" is that it fixes nothing. It writes a blank check which we fill out according to the nature of our imagination and (though this is wholly incidental) our knowledge of Spanish. The word is not, in short, a disguise; and although we feel more or less vaguely what is meant, to define the word too precisely is to destroy its function. To substitute the arbitrary English word is to shatter to this degree the whole frame of suggested unfamiliarity of the world of the novel, and make concrete what Hemingway has made formless not necessarily with an eye to the censor, but for the sake of the atmospheric consistency of his work.

Generalizing from this and what has preceded, we may say that as much of the novel is visually concrete, so is it linguistically aswarm with overtone and suggestion. It is against this linguistic ground of which we do not clearly grasp the frontiers that character and action are set, and from it they draw much of their epic quality. Like the *toro* and the *Virgen*, the phonetico-semantic translation and the verbal forms which are yet to be discussed, the word "obscenity" as used here is essentially a springboard into the undefined or the unfamiliar and foreign.

The term "literal translation" has been widely used in discussion of Hemingway's book, its users understanding thereby especially his "thee"s and "thou"s, his subjunctive imperatives and such. The significant thing is that this translation is completely irregular. Dialogue, that is, passes from purely colloquial English to the most Biblical style, with use of the second singular outstandingly variable. For instance on p. 92:

> "Where the hell are you going?" Augustin asked the grave little man as he came up.
> "To my duty," Fernando said with dignity.
> "Thy duty," said Augustin mockingly. "I besmirch the milk of thy duty . . ."

I assume that in a Spanish equivalent of this the singular would be constantly used. But the English second singular has all the peculiar sensitivity of an artificial and always consciously employed form. Here it is not made to carry the wholly idiomatic first sentence; but the dignity of the answer "my duty" opens the way to the mock dignity of Augustin's "thy duty" and the use of "thou" in the passage of formalized obscenity which follows in the text. Yet a page or so farther on, persons who have previously used the singular consistently employ "you" in dialogue of less personal intensity.

No less irregular is the verbal form of the singular. We have Pilar saying (p. 93): "Thou never had one." A dozen lines later: "Thou hast caught fear from them like all the others." The difference between "thou hast" and "thou hadst" is too slight to explain the ungrammatical "thou had" by awkwardness in the proper form—and especially so since "shouldst," "wouldst," "didst" etc. are not uncommonly employed (e.g. pp. 83, 390). If, then, "thou hast" appears in this last sentence, it is simply because the emotional gravity of the sentence itself calls out the dignity of the correct verbal form.

The two following passages are interesting. In the first, Pilar says (p. 68): "Thee would do well to go to bed now . . . Thou hast had a long journey." This is most indicative of the dependence of verbal form upon emotional tone. In the first sentence the Quakerish nominative "thee" holds much of the intimacy of a suddenly maternal and protective tone. By contrast, the second sentence broadens its connotation to epic dimensions. Substitute "thee" and the breadth is gone. "Thee has had a long journey" is, I feel, essentially intimate. "Thou hast had a long journey" is monumental and not without its heroism.

Secondly, this snatch of dialogue between Jordan and Maria from p. 269:

> "Kiss me," she said, "if thou goest."
> "Thou art shameless," he said.
> "Yes," she said. "Totally."
> "Get thee back now. There is much work to do . . ."
> "Thou," she said. "Didst thee see what he wore on his chest?"
>
> . . . . . .
>
> "Yes. All the people of Navarre wear it."
> "And thou shot for that?"
>
> . . . . . .
>
> "Thou saw nothing. One man . . . *Vete*. Get thee back."
> "Say that you love me."

This has at first glance the air of a perfectly wilful corruption of grammatical form—correct pronoun, in a full third of the cases. Actually it is an extremely subtle profiting by the fact that the second singular is so lost to us that nothing can really shock unpleasantly, that whereas the incorrect plural, for instance, smacks of crudity, the incorrect singular suggests something intimate and diminutive as in the Quaker usage. "Thou" with its proper verb is, in a context which does not force it to extreme artificiality, essentially dignified. But this scene is a very tender and moving one, and its quality is dependent upon the breaking down of the austerity of the verb form. Note that where the form is correct, it is forced into intimacy by the companion phrase. "Kiss me if thou goest," pleads Maria. The dominant effect is in the first verb—while, obviously, the second adds enormously to the total value.[4] So in the case of "Thou art"—noble words but drawn into the intimate by the adjective "shameless." Likewise the archaic "Get thee back" is affected by the preceding or following phrases and by the *Vete*, which justifies this archaism at its second appearance and recalls it to the assumed Spanish. Where, on the other hand, the tone of the dignified verb form is not thus broken by immediately associated words, the intimate is attained through a deliberate shattering of the verbal form itself—"didst thee," "thou shot," "thou saw," and finally the drop into the plural with "Say that you love me," because, I should imagine, the phrase as it stands is so familiar and so fixed in the language that it will not readily bear touching without loss of its emotional burden.

But now consider the following passage from p. 408 where the dignity of verbal form, with other elements, is played on to the fullest:

> "After the explosion when the people of Pablo come around that corner, thou must fire over their heads if others come after them. Thou must fire high above them when they appear in any event that others must not come. Understandest thou?"
> "Why not? It is as thou saidst last night."
> "Hast any questions?"
> "Nay . . ."

This is the dawn of the last day and on the verge of the final drama of the tale. That austerity of verb which in the previous passage it was necessary to break down, is here essential to the

[4] The verbal forms are not, of course, the whole of these lines, but I am concerned only with what they do contribute and the fact that were they other, the change would greatly alter the total effect. Consequently I deliberately omit the references to the Sacred Heart of the Navarrese uniform, for instance—an image which colors the whole passage.

desired effect. To the purity of this emotion there responds a purity of phrase—as, before, a many-threaded emotion is enwrapped in a complexity of verbal form. Further elements may be picked out. "The people of Pablo" echos of course *la gente de Pablo* of an assumed Spanish. But its contribution here is not in the Spanish it suggests, but in the dignity generally inherent in the prepositional possessive. So too, the "nay" of the last answer—a word necessarily independent of a Spanish original. It is justified not by the Spanish but by the "lofty style" of verb and possessive, these latter based on the Spanish but significant through their English formality.

Another instance of this introduction of terms which have no equivalent in Spanish but are additions to a tone established by elements which do reflect the Spanish, is in the line (p. 268): "Do you, Andres, saddle and hold the horses in readiness"—an imperative wholly English, and English in the grand manner, found here because it is called out by a context in which all possible dignity is desirable, and because the reader has from the beginning in view of the unfamiliarity and somehow "ancient" quality of the world of the novel, accepted a linguistic convention as remote as the scene and characters—one which finds its best chords in just such archaic forms.

There is a constant carrying over of tone from dialogue to narrative which tends to bear out this assertion. On p. 20, for instance:

> The gypsy said. "How do they call thee?"
> "Roberto. And thee?"
>
> . . . . . .
>
> Anselmo came out of the mouth of the cave with a deep stone basin full of red wine, and with his fingers through the handles of three cups. "Look," he said. "They have cups and all."
>
> . . . . . .
>
> "Here is the wine." Anselmo dipped a cup out of the bowl and handed it to Robert Jordan, then dipped for himself and the gypsy.
>
> The wine was good, tasting faintly resinous from the

> wineskin, but excellent, light and clean on his tongue. Robert Jordan drank it slowly, feeling it spread slowly through his tiredness.
>
> "The food comes shortly," Pablo said. "And this foreigner with the rare name, how did he die?"

It is not actually possible to say that here narrative shapes dialogue, or dialogue narrative. What is evident is their perfect harmony. The theme is that of the "stone basin full of red wine," "from the wineskin," of the mere presence of the gypsy. In an atmosphere of such images colloquial speech would destroy the suggestion of the narrative phrases. Where one dips from a bowl of wine, one man can ask another only "How do they call thee?" —quite frankly poetic. So it is with such scenes as those in which a robbers-cave setting seems literally to compel a language form befitting it (e.g. p. 49 ff.). There is a necessary identity of tone between such narrative phrases as "The wife of Pablo was standing over a charcoal fire on the open hearth in the corner of the cave," and such dialogue phrases as "One called Augustin says he dies of boredom above."

It is of course only proper to observe that perception of such inter-relationships and of the atmosphere of the second person singular cannot but be subjective to a certain extent. The singular especially, with its range of suggestion from Genesis to paper roses, will not permit analysis which fixes its value immutably for every reader. But common to all reactions (and that is its fundamental value as used here) will be the sense of its relative unfamiliarity, its role in lifting dialogue out of the frame of colloquial speech and into that of a speech which is something else.

To sum up briefly: this "something else" of the dialogue of the novel is not shaped by the nature of a Spanish assumed beneath it. The Spanish serves rather as a justification for breaking down the forms of colloquial English, thus opening up the way for a kind of reconstruction in which, although the Spanish is never wholly forgotten, the essential is the recapture of the varying tones inherent in a more or less unfamiliar, frequently artificial, but also vigorously poetic English. This English is controlled by contextual tone and image and by the emotional intensity of the given scene.

Several paragraphs above, I mentioned the Elizabethan tone of certain phrases.[5] That such a tone should haunt Hemingway's pages is inevitable. His tale has much of the epic in its breadth, in the plain fact that his characters mean more than themselves alone, the action they are engaged upon unmistakably a culminating point pushed up by profound national or, if we accept the implication of his title, universal forces. In the Elizabethan, the English possesses an epic language, and it is into the forms of this language that Hemingway, through the very nature of the world he is creating and the artistic intention in the light of which the inhabitants of this world are conceived, constantly passes. Or, more strictly, that artistic intention, the establishment of the epic spirit, requires and is dependent upon for its achievement, a dialogue actively contributing to this end. However the epic may be defined, it would seem to imply the element of remoteness in time or space. Hemingway's novel is an epic of our time, yet it is no paradox to say that essential to its epic quality is this speech which is not of our time. The temporal location of the novel is determined, but there remains the possibility of remoteness in space to throw characters and action into the epic frame. Something of this is of course attained through the geographical distance of three thousand miles, and the emotional distance which cannot be gauged, that separate us from Spain. That, however, is a distance which can be bridged. We could, were they so presented, identify ourselves completely with Hemingway's people. But artistically (and I may be allowed the reminder that I am not concerned with any other value of the book) it is absolutely necessary that we do no such thing—that,

[5] Occasionally this "Elizabethanism" draws out an echo of familiar quotation. For example, El Sordo says (p. 152): "But now with this we must go. We must think much about the manner of our going"—a spark, I should judge, struck from Lady Macbeth's: "Stand not upon the order of your going, But go at once."

on the contrary, we feel the reality of their remoteness on every page. And we do feel it—and in that lies their epic nature—in the one all-pervading quality of language. It is a language remote in time which, since the novel binds us to the present, lends its energies to establish a scene remote in space.

The nature of this language is not, however, entirely in its forms. It contains strong rhythmic qualities which are pertinent to this discussion because they too contribute largely to what we accept as the "Spanish" of the dialogue. Most immediately perceptible in that dialogue are brevity of construction (even when short elements are bound by conjunctions to form longer sentences) and repetition.

I take at random this passage from p. 205:

> "Roberto," Maria said . . . "Are you ready to eat?"
> "Is it ready?"
> "It is ready when you wish it."
> "Have the others eaten?"
> "All except you, Fernando and Anselmo."
> "Let us eat then," he told her. "And thou?"
> "Afterwards with Pilar."
> "Eat now with us."
> "No. It would not be well."
> "Come on and eat. In my country a man does not eat before his woman."

With the exception of the solitary "thou" there is nothing here which is not relatively colloquial English. Yet as we read it we feel it "Spanish," I think, for it carries out what might be termed the essentially unilinear psychology of the speakers, a concentration upon the solitary fact which is completely harmonious with the primitive tone. It is Spanish in the sense that as readers we tacitly assume the primitive, in common with all the unfamiliar, to be necessarily Spanish. Yet no more here than elsewhere does Spanish shape this prose. On the contrary, it is much rather Hemingway's familiar rhythmic patterns that contribute to what we accept as Spanish.

A few comparative passages may not be out of place. Here, for instance, is old Anselmo on watch in the snow, meditating in his native tongue and in a manner, we incline to feel, shaped by his simple and direct spirit (p. 196):

> It may be that in the younger people it does not have an importance. It may be that in foreigners, or in those who have not had our religion, there is not the same attitude. But I think everyone doing it will be brutalized in time and I think that even though necessary, it is a great sin and that afterwards we must do something very strong to atone for it.

It is unnecessary to point out the verbal and constructional repetitions of this, and especially the marked culminating rhythm of the last.

But now Robert Jordan meditates, presumably in English, at El Sordo's camp (p. 135):

> Of course they turned on you. They turned on you often but they always turned on everyone. They turned on themselves, too. If you had three together, two would unite against one, and then the two would start to betray each other. Not always, but often enough for you to take enough cases and start to draw it as a conclusion.

And finally we can step wholly outside this tale and find the very quality of Anselmo's inner speech and Jordan's speech, in the much admired paragraph from *A Farewell to Arms* written some ten years ago (p. 267):

> If people bring so much courage to this world the world has to kill them to break them, so of course it kills them. The world breaks everyone and afterwards many are strong at the broken places. But those that will not break it kills. It kills the very good and the very brave and the very gentle impartially. If you are none of these you can be sure it will kill you too but there will be no special hurry.

The pattern common to these three passages is evident. I want to suggest first that such patterns, underlying all of Hemingway, play an immeasurable role in creating the direct and, in a sense, primitive atmosphere of language which, in the context of *For Whom the Bell Tolls* is accepted as Spanish. But their significance transcends this. In their relentless heaping up of a given observation and the drum-beat of a word or words, they are patterns of the inescapable fatality so explicit in this novel. It is not only with the snowfall which will betray El Sordo that Jordan realizes the inevitable failure of his mission at the bridge. From his first sense of treason latent in Pablo, his first thought of the tragic flaws in the Loyalist forces, there is in the novel a deepening sense of inevitable defeat finally expressed in Golz's quiet "Nous sommes foutus. Oui. Comme toujours. Oui. C'est dommage" (p. 428).

In these passages we catch the audible march of force against which stands the individual—Jordan or any individual—and by which he will be crushed. "Of course they turned on you . . . they turned on themselves . . . to unite against one . . . to betray each other." *They* are not only the Spaniards. *They* are the tools of that "world" which kills and breaks with an inevitability that becomes concrete in the movement of this intensely personal prose.

In the light of this, there appears a further value in the abrupt dialogue. Not only has it value as "Spanish." It is also the expression of men before the inescapable force, in its word repetition a concentration upon the solitary fact which alone can be mastered and held to and made a kind of anchor against this destroying power.

It is with this moment of individual destruction that Hemingway is constantly concerned. It is worth recalling that in *For Whom the Bell Tolls* and *A Farewell to Arms* the same facile means are employed to get a Henry or a Jordan into the dramatic scene—a student of architecture or a student of Spanish who happens incidentally to be there when the forces move. The how and the why are unimportant. Any path to the crisis will do, for in a world which kills and breaks, any path may, sooner or later, bring the individual to the point from which no escape is possible.

JAMES T. FARRELL

The Sun Also Rises

1943

Ernest Hemingway's first novel, *The Sun Also Rises*, has been generally heralded as the definitive account of a war-wearied lost generation. In the light of this interpretation it is interesting to note that this novel was published in 1927, and that the time of its action is 1925. For these years fall within the most hopeful period of the post-Versailles world.

At that time there were many signs (at least in the eyes of superficial observers) to suggest that the world was returning to normalcy. After 1923, European capitalism seemed to have been restabilized, following the shocks of war, revolution, and dangers of revolution. At least to some, Germany looked like a going concern: the Weimar Republic was considered firmly secure. Hope was being revived in cartels as the means of achieving peaceable allocation of markets and equitable access to sources of raw materials. The epoch of disarmament talks, peace pacts,

---

From *The League of Frightened Philistines* by James T. Farrell.

peace conferences had begun. America was in the full sweep of a tremendous economic boom, leading many to believe that this country was paving the way toward a new era of unprecedented world prosperity.

It may seem paradoxical that in such a period a novel of war disillusionment, nihilistic in outlook, should have become an international success.

However, this paradox is only superficial. With signs of a return to world prosperity there were growing evidences of pacifism. In particular, the youth which had been too young to have been in the trenches was deeply pacifistic. Disillusionment with the war was more or less accepted. In addition, a re-examination of the character of disillusionment portrayed in *The Sun Also Rises* suggests that this mood had become a way of feeling and acting; in fact, a social habit. By 1925 those who had been morally unhinged or physically maimed during the war had had a number of years in which to make some kind of adjustment to the postwar world. This period of the first difficult readjustment had passed. Such, for instance, is the case of the chief protagonist in *The Sun Also Rises*. Jake Barnes, impotent as a result of wounds suffered on the Italian front, has more or less reconciled himself to his condition.

Whenever there is a widespread mood of disillusionment caused by an event as catastrophic as a world war, that mood is bound to be nihilistic and rather adolescent in character unless it serves as the basis for a radical and progressive political orientation that aims to change and better the world. This is illustrated in *The Sun Also Rises*.

The characters express their bitterness, their feelings of disenchantment, with calculated bravado. Their conversation is reduced to enthusiastic small talk about their escapades. And this talk, as well as their actions, is largely a matter of pose and gesture. They act like people who have not fully grown up and who lack the self-awareness to realize this; in fact, they possess no desire to grow up.

The Sun Also Rises influenced younger persons more widely

than it did members of Hemingway's own generation. He may have reflected the feelings of many who fought in the war; but most of these men were finding some way of settling down and adjusting themselves in the nineteen-twenties. Some were doing creative writing, some finding editorial jobs, some launching themselves in careers that later won them Pulitzer prizes in poetry and so on. This novel struck deeper chords in the youth of the Twenties.

Hemingway's first books had hardly been published when he had imitators all over America; furthermore, boys and girls on campus after campus began to talk like Hemingway characters. One need not go into detail to describe certain features of the Twenties; these are too fresh in our minds. Suffice it to say that by and large younger people were revolting against the standards and conventions of their elders, against the accepted notions of middle-class society. At the same time they were nonpolitical in their revolt. Add to this the deep pacifism of the decade, and one can easily understand why this novel struck such chords of response among young people, why Hemingway suddenly became the influence he did become at the time.

His influence was not merely superficial. It played a liberating and salutary role on those who would become the next generation of writers, and more so, numerically, on readers. The hopes of those days have now been proved a snare by history. The nihilistic character of Hemingway's writing helped to free younger people from these false hopes. And although this novel (and many of his early stories as well) is set against a European background, Hemingway helped focus the eyes of younger people sharply on American life.

His writing was exciting and possessed of an extraordinary power of suggestiveness; it won over the reader to the feeling that he was actually participating in the lives of very real men and women. His use of dialogue helped enormously to create this impression. Others, notably Ring Lardner, preceded Hemingway in exploring and revealing the literary possibilities of the use of American vernacular, but he used it with amazing skill and originality. Both his suggestiveness in conveying a sense of life and his use of dialogue tended to turn the attention of youth toward common American experiences and to the speech expressing them on city streets and farms.

But Hemingway's influence, though so widespread, at the same time has been one that seems quickly to have exhausted itself. For Hemingway is a writer of limited vision, one who has no broad and fertile perspective on life. Younger writers were influenced—even seduced—by his moods; and they could grasp from him a sense of the great possibilities to be discovered in the true and simple treatment of common subject matter and in the use of ordinary speech. But once they had learned these lessons, they could gain little more from Hemingway.

The Europe described in *The Sun Also Rises* is a tourist's Europe of the Twenties. Cafés, restaurants, hotels, particularly of the Left Bank, are the setting. When the action shifts to Spain, it is to permit a magnificent description of bull fights and a fiesta. The mood and attitude of the main characters is that of people on a vacation. They set out to do what people want to do on a vacation: they have love affairs, they drink, go fishing, and see new spectacles. Written in the first person, the book unfolds from the standpoint of a spectator's attitude. Jake, the narrator, is a newspaper man; his is an occupation that naturally tends to develop the point of view of the spectator. Jake is constantly looking at the other characters, at himself, at the scenery of Spain, at the bull fight, at everything that occurs or comes within his view.

The main characters have only a meager past. They are escaping from their past and usually do not wish even to talk or to think of it. They live for the present, constantly searching for new and fresh sensations. They do not really think; even Jake scarcely thinks about himself or about his own impotence. These people feel quite alike. They form a small clique stoically accepting the ills of their life.

Robert Cohn, however, is an outsider. He is with them because of his doglike love for Lady Brett Ashley. Unlike the others, he is unable to drown his feelings in banalities, small talk, and new spectacles. Cohn's difference from the others is one of the central points of the novel. This contrast is stated overtly when Lady Brett says that Cohn is "not one of us," and when Jake thinks that Cohn has behaved badly by pursuing Lady Brett. Focused against Cohn, Jake's simple, stoical attitude is enforced more strongly. The attitude of Jake is one of the basic attitudes in Hemingway's writings.

Hemingway's realism is, by and large, one which deals with sensations—with shocks to the senses. He has tended to reduce life to the effect that sights, scenes, and experiences make upon the nervous system; and he has avoided complicated types of response. Herein we find one of the major factors revealing his limitations as a writer.

In his most representative work he has saved himself from the crudities of simple behaviorism because of his gift of suggestiveness and his developed skill of understatement. The moral outlook in his work is on a plane of equal simplicity with his characters and subject matter. It amounts to the attitude that an action is good if it makes one feel good. Such an outlook on characters and events suggests that a development of greater understanding—broader range of feeling and sympathy, greater depth of imagination—is practically precluded.

This has been the case in Hemingway's career. He arrived on the literary scene absolute master of the style he has made his own; his attitudes were firmly fixed at that time. And he said pretty much what he had to say with his first stories and his first two novels.

As a novelist, it is my opinion that the best of Ernest Hemingway is still to be found in *The Sun Also Rises*. Its freshness has not faded with time. It remains one of the very best American novels of the Twenties.

JAMES GRAY

Tenderly Tolls the Bell

1946

They were products of the midwestern tradition, these three soldiers (Fitzgerald, Hemingway and Dos Passos); one of them lived his youth in St. Paul, the others theirs in the environs of Chicago. In their late teens or early twenties they closed their schoolbooks with a mixture of relief, impatience, resentment, and curiosity to go away to war. They did not like what they encountered in the midst of the military experience. They were, however, attracted by the freedom from parochialism they found in the European world.

Each in his different way was a glittering example of the psychology of the "sad young men" about whom F. Scott Fitzgerald wrote, of the despairloving expatriates about whom Ernest Hemingway wrote, of the thwarted intellectuals about whom John Dos Passos wrote. They might have been the originals of the *Three Soldiers* of the title of Dos Passos' first important

---

novel. They were the most conspicuous representatives of that "lost generation," fragments of which Gertrude Stein was forever stumbling upon in the byways of Paris.

The concept of a lost generation now seems an almost mawkishly sentimental one. Since 1918 another American generation has gone to war. It fought longer, harder, and in the face of a far more bitter challenge than did the generation of the First World War. Yet it has not become professionally "lost." Its psychoneurotics have been isolated from the healthy mass, which has survived with all its basic values whole and with perhaps a few worthy ones added as the gift of experience.

But there were extenuating circumstances to account for the intense self-consciousness of the lost generation. If cultures tend to pass through the cycle of birth, growth, and decay as individuals do, then American culture was in its adolescence when the First World War began. Its representatives had not been exposed to the shocks of conflict or to the discipline of comradeship as their French, English, and German contemporaries had been. They were the products of a tradition that worshiped individual initiative, success, and a very narrow interpretation of what constituted virtuous social behavior. Circumstances required them to learn a very great deal in a very short time as they were rushed into a hastily improvised and badly organized seminar of the human spirit. The young men who had a similar experience a quarter of a century later had something of cultural memory to draw upon. They met the experience of war with much more of sobriety, stability, and maturity; they have, apparently, felt no inclination at all to hide away in the dark alcoves of the mind and to devote themselves to feeling lost.

The effort of these lost angels to find their way back to an intelligible and endurable world can be traced out in their books. Each took a different route; each wandered in ways that seemed sometimes both hopeless and aimless. Yet the progress of all of them was marked by such brilliant qualities of eagerness and dread that a very large American public followed their movements with sympathy, curiosity, and absorption. Fitzgerald, Hemingway, and Dos Passos burned all along the way with fear and hope, with hatred and a never quite extinguished aspiration.

The drama of their association as representatives of aspects of American culture was made the neater by the fact that their personal association was intimate. Fitzgerald and Hemingway frequently linked their own names in considering the problems of the creative mind; they had a kind of joint egotism based on the idea that they were the two most important writers of their day. Dos Passos took a fraternal interest in the crises of Fitzgerald's life and, toward the close of that crowded chapter of human tragedy, an almost paternal attitude toward the perplexities of a genius who was, even at the end of his life, an immature spirit.

Both as artists and as human beings these three men shared the problems of adjustment to the complexities of times that were out of joint. Among them they divided up the virtues and the limitations of Hamlet, and their several responses to the "cursed spite" of being obliged to try to remake their world are recorded in the most absorbing, original, and tragic documents of the literature of our time.

Ernest Hemingway plunged into the foreground of the American literary scene with so pugnacious an air of dramatizing his own vitality that both the suspicious and the fastidious have been inclined to deny his pretensions to serious consideration as an author. In his early books it was clear that he was exploiting his own individuality, and in all his pantomime of muscle-rippling and shadow-boxing a naive exhibitionism was the most striking feature.

His every utterance, too, was characterized by a naive passion for the idiom of ruggedness. Like a very young boy who has just been initiated into manhood and who is not quite certain that his position is secure, Hemingway noisily paraded his interest in all kinds of sporting matters . . . piscatorial, taurian, and sexual.

He seemed determined to use literature for the purpose of advertising himself as a completely healthy male whose digestion was sound, whose metabolism offered a model of functioning, and whose general sense of well-being was greatly to be envied.

To be sure, he had the sane mind that belongs to a sound body, and that mind harbored certain resentments against the folly and viciousness of society. But in the early books this resentment did not run deep. Hemingway deliberately and consciously rejected the soft, narcissistic egotism that made the neurotics of the war generation regard themselves as lost. Indeed, in *The Sun Also Rises* he was careful to choose a war victim whose wound was clearly, devastatingly, physical. What mental maiming the character suffered was a direct result of an injury that made it impossible for him to enjoy the euphoria which the typical Hemingway character has always experienced so abundantly. Hemingway interpreted the tragedy of war in his first novel in terms of the sufferings endured by a frustrated sexual athlete.

He continued to be a kind of glorification of the post-graduate 4-H lad in each of the next few books. (The four H's of the improving organization of young farmers are hands, head, heart, and health.) He was a somewhat garrulous and insistent celebrant of the joys of sex in *A Farewell to Arms*. In the critical discussions in *Death in the Afternoon*, he mixed the interests of sport with those of the more rugged aspects of the literary sensibilities. In *To Have and Have Not* sport and sex supported the slightly uncertain structure of a new social consciousness. But all the while Hemingway was still conspicuously healthy and manfully devoted to the somewhat primitive ethics of doing "what made him feel good afterward."

We live in so sophisticated a day that such blatant exuberance as Hemingway's seems to us suspect. The man who must be forever talking about his capacity for love is probably overcompensating, and the one who thumps his chest and calls attention to the marvel of its capacity for expansion no doubt has nervous inner promptings that all is not well in the empire of the body.

But the surprising, perhaps unique, thing about Hemingway seems now to be that he has always been quite as healthy as he has declared. There has been no weakening of his stamina, but rather a steady growth. There has been no sudden breakdown of his claim to euphoria in the midst of shattering external experiences, but rather a constantly expanding warmth of graciousness and mellowness. *For Whom the Bell Tolls* justified his essential belief in himself and reconciled his readers to all the lapses from taste into tedium that had characterized earlier celebrations of his temperament.

His theme has always been man against war. But the earlier wars, actual or figurative, were ones into which his heroes had blundered, just for the hell of it, as they themselves would be sure to say, or which they did not understand. Robert Jordan's war in *For Whom the Bell Tolls* is one that he understands very well indeed. It is fought by a man of disciplined sensibility, for a completely altruistic and idealistic purpose.

Though Hemingway's most recent work was needed to justify his effort as an artist, his first novel spoke attractively and divertingly to his contemporaries because it had an original and audacious accent. This thin and largely uncritical comment of the young reviewer that once was I may serve to suggest what qualities in Hemingway's early work took the fancy of America. Recent graduates from college were looking for a literary tradition they could have all to themselves, one they need not share with the stuffy, censorious Victorians, the commonplace Edwardians, or the very nearly featureless Georgians.

A novel that quotes from Gertrude Stein and the Bible on its flyleaf ought to be an extraordinary novel. Not, of course, because it is so impossible to imagine the two having any sentiments in common, but because it is a little startling that anyone who knows very much about Gertrude Stein should have also heard of the Bible.

The sentences quoted by Ernest Hemingway to suggest the theme of his first novel, *The Sun Also Rises*, are not in the least incompatible. Gertrude Stein said in conversation, "You are all a lost generation," and Ecclesiastes says, "Vanity of vanities . . . all is vanity. . . . One generation passeth and another generation cometh; but the earth abideth forever. The sun also riseth, and the sun goeth down, and hasteth to the place where he arose."

Miss Stein's lost generation and Mr. Hemingway's is the one which came out of the war, shocked and full of mockery for most of the things which had been believed before. Mr. Hemingway has chosen to write about the most unfortunate of the war's victims, and the tragedy of his story is not in the least minimized by the fact that his characters are not at all "like Patience on a monument smiling at grief." Rather they thumb their noses at grief and then go out to the nearest cafe and get drunk. . . .

Hemingway writes in the first person and he does not touch up the idiom of the people he is presenting. His characters salute each other as "gents." they say "those sort." "Swell" is their favorite adjective. . . .

The significant thing for anyone who interests himself in matters of style is that, perhaps in spite of, but more likely because of, this refusal to be literary, Hemingway achieves a very real literary distinction. Artfully and shrewdly he makes his effects, and they include, though he would grimace at being told so, not a little of the irony and pity about which he allows one of his characters to amuse himself.

This is not a story to be put into the hands of book lovers who say they do not see the necessity of writing about this and that aspect of the human tragedy; that there is enough unhappiness in the world without insisting upon it in books; that, after all, there are such things as music and flowers and happy laughter. Such readers would discover in *The Sun Also Rises* a sensationalism which it does not in the least contain. They would think it horrid and bitter and they would go about making themselves and a great many others miserable by complaining of present-day tendencies in fiction. To others this novel will seem a fine and touching examination of the futility and purposelessness which the war imposed on those marked for its malign attention. They will realize that Ernest Hemingway has suggested with finished art the desperate gallantry with which such men have had to arm themselves.

With *A Farewell to Arms* Hemingway established himself as dean of the tough-tender school of fiction, which presently had matriculants not only from all the English-speaking countries, including Australia.

When he sat down to write this new novel, he undoubtedly told himself that it was time someone wrote the simple and sordid, tragic and touching truth about the war. Books had been written with elegance and books had been written with passion. He wanted to use his bluff, forthright, unadorned technique to tell what actually happened to men and women in the war, instead of what would have been theatrical and ethically improving if it had happened.

It was, of course, a fine idea. But unfortunately for Hemingway, an accident had entirely changed the face of the literary world before his book could get into print. The accident was the publication of *All Quiet on the Western Front*. The superlatives Hemingway might have had if *A Farewell to Arms* had preceded *All Quiet on the Western Front* he simply cannot have now. The adjectives great and vivid and impressive retreat just a little haughtily in the face of this book and leave words like good and suggestive and dignified standing their ground.

It is only, of course, in the approach to the subject of war as a human experience that there is any similarity between these books. Both authors are obviously bored and disgusted with the half-truths and evasions, the artificialities and manipulations which have made the previous war books seem trifling and frivolous even in the midst of their agonizings.

Hemingway like Remarque has refused contemptuously to heighten and exaggerate for literary effect. He means to reflect the war scene with literal accuracy. As in *All Quiet on the Western Front*, there is in the newer novel an unembarrassed and unself-conscious willingness to consider the grotesque and squalid impulse of the human animal at war. He has not been nonplused by the physical, nor is he morbidly concerned with it. The balance of values is sane and true.

But Remarque was able to blend into this treatment a vast and overwhelming sense of pity. He looked at the war through the eyes of a narrator who was acutely conscious of the world's folly in tearing itself to pieces. Hemingway has chosen instead a decent, intelligent, honest, comprehending person whose sensibility is on a distinctly lower and less interesting level. He has done what he intended to do, but what he intended was less important in the first place.

In his succeeding books Hemingway, never at a loss for words, was occasionally at a loss for a theme appropriate to fiction. At such times he indulged in curious extensions of the ego which exploited his audacity in snatches of criticism, fantasy, and nature lore. His audience followed him in these excursions with varying degrees of sympathy, not always sure that his work would be strong and enduring. His unsteady development introduced a sporting element into the effort to appraise his work, so that one felt like laying a bet on each book, hazarding a judgement in advance as to whether it would be one of the good ones or one of the bad ones.

It is, however, no longer possible to make a guessing game of Hemingway's place in American literature. Now at forty-odd he has produced a novel of unquestionable importance. *For Whom the Bell Tolls* is not merely Hemingway's best book; it is one of the finest books written by an American in our time.

The scene is Spain; the theme is war. But to say so gives little idea of the universality of the book's interest or of the high quality of the interpretive gift that it reveals. Hemingway has chosen a moment of tension when the spirit of man becomes quickened by a challenging crisis to an intensification of itself. Aware of the significance of its struggle, our human nature declares its character with dramatic emphasis. The contradictions are still there: the cruelty matched by tenderness, the cowardice by courage, the treachery by loyalty. But each is brilliantly defined in the light of a flaming disaster.

This long novel covers only four days in actual time. It begins with the appearance in the mountains of a young American intellectual who has gone to Spain to fight with the Loyalists. He is on a mission to blow up a bridge, which will be the signal for the attack on Segovia. There behind the Fascist lines he must seek the help of the guerrillas of the mountains . . . peasants, gypsies, women refugees from other battles . . . and among them he finds a microcosm of the Loyalist world in which all its attitudes, its loyalties, its fears are vividly dramatized.

Each figure is strikingly individualized. Pablo, once the dominating leader of the guerrillas, has become their potential enemy because his peasant shrewdness predicts the collapse of the cause and his impulse is to take to safety. But there is still his admiration of personal courage to control his wavering faith. In the end it saves him from treachery. Pilar, woman of the earth, lover of its pleasures, helps to bully her man, Pablo, back into loyalty with her mystical awareness of the unimportance of personal failure. Anselmo, the gentle old man who cannot kill animals, kills men unwaveringly because it is necessary. Maria, pitiful victim of Fascist violence, finds herself healed of all the scars left upon her mind by the act of rape when the enveloping generosity of an honest love is offered by the young American. Robert Jordan himself, warm in blood but cool in head, becomes for the reader the interpreter of the struggle as he feels growing within him the "deep, sound, and selfless pride" of complete identification with these people and with the impulse that makes them fight.

The scope of the book, deliberately compressed in time for purposes of drama, is widened again by several retrospective glimpses of other scenes. Robert Jordan's reflections call into being the strange Russian intellectuals who direct the war from Madrid; Pilar remembers the slaughter of the Fascists when Loyalists take an embattled town; Maria describes the cruel perversity of the revenge when the Fascists have their turn at violence.

Hemingway, evidently determined to be innocent of any special pleading for the Loyalists, scrupulously reveals in the peasant temperament a curious, contradictory, and fascinating combination of elements. A droll formality in speech is balanced by a rugged gift for obscenity; a gift for idealistic self-sacrifice goes hand in hand with an inclination toward primitive savagery. Yet through the whole character of each there blows a gusty, invigorating love of life. The relations of such people toward one another and toward their cause produce that finest kind of drama in which sensibility, thought, and humor reveal themselves against the background of man's tragic plight.

All the Hemingway themes are restated here: the courage of which human nature is capable when it has managed to identify itself with a moral issue; the humor that is ever present in the story of the appetites; the tenderness that declares itself in honest passion. But of none of these things has he ever written so well as he does now. With a new maturity of insight and a new subtlety of emphasis, he communicates his admiration for the simple profundity of faith that moved and occasionally inspired the Loyalists.

EDMUND WILSON

Hemingway: Gauge of Morale

1947

1

Ernest Hemingway's *In Our Time* was an odd and original book. It had the appearance of a miscellany of stories and fragments; but actually the parts hung together and produced a definite effect. There were two distinct series of pieces which alternated with one another: one a set of brief and brutal sketches of police shootings, bullfight crises, hangings of criminals, and incidents of the war; and the other a set of short stories dealing in its principal sequence with the growing-up of an American boy against a landscape of idyllic Michigan, but interspersed also with glimpses of American soldiers returning home. It seems to have been Hemingway's intention—'*In Our Time*'—that the war should set the key for the whole. The cold-bloodedness of the battles and executions strikes a discord with the sensitiveness and candor of the boy at home in the States; and presently the boy turns up in Europe in one of

From *The Wound and the Bow* by Edmund Wilson. Published by Oxford University Press.

the intermediate vignettes as a soldier in the Italian Army, hit in the spine by machine-gun fire and trying to talk to a dying Italian: '*Senta*, Rinaldi. *Senta*,' he says, 'you and me, we've made a separate peace.'

But there is a more fundamental relationship between the pieces of the two series. The shooting of Nick in the war does not really connect two different worlds: has he not found in the butchery abroad the same world that he knew back in Michigan? Was not life in the Michigan woods equally destructive and cruel? He had gone once with his father, the doctor, when he had performed a Caesarean operation on an Indian squaw with a jacknife and no anaesthetic and had sewed her up with fishing leaders, while the Indian hadn't been able to bear it and had cut his throat in his bunk. Another time, when the doctor had saved the life of a squaw, her Indian had picked a quarrel with him rather than pay him in work. And Nick himself had sent his girl about her business when he had found out how terrible her mother was. Even fishing in Big Two-Hearted River—away and free in the woods—he had been conscious in a curious way of the cruelty inflicted on the fish, even of the silent agonies endured by the live bait, the grasshoppers kicking on the hook.

Not that life isn't enjoyable. Talking and drinking with one's friends is great fun; fishing in Big Two-Hearted River is a tranquil exhilaration. But the brutality of life is always there, and it is somehow bound up with the enjoyment. Bullfights are especially enjoyable. It is even exhilarating to build a simply priceless barricade and pot the enemy as they are trying to get over it. The condition of life is pain; and the joys of the most innocent surface are somehow tied to its stifled pangs.

The resolution of this dissonance in art made the beauty of Hemingway's stories. He had in the process tuned a marvelous prose. Out of the colloquial American speech, with its simple declarative sentences and its strings of Nordic monosyllables, he got effects of the utmost subtlety. F. M. Ford has found the perfect simile for the impression produced by this writing:

'Hemingway's words strike you, each one, as if they were pebbles fetched fresh from a brook. They live and shine, each in its place. So one of his pages has the effect of a brook-bottom into which you look down through the flowing water. The words form a tessellation, each in order beside the other.'

Looking back, we can see how this style was already being refined and developed at a time—fifty years before—when it was regarded in most literary quarters as hopelessly non-literary and vulgar. Had there not been the nineteenth chapter of *Huckleberry Finn?*—'Two or three nights went by; I reckon I might say they swum by; they slid along so quick and smooth and lovely. Here is the way we put in the time. It was a monstrous big river down there—sometimes a mile and a half wide,' and so forth. These pages, when we happen to meet them in Carl Van Doren's anthology of world literature, stand up in a striking way beside a passage of description from Turgenev; and the pages which Hemingway was later to write about American wood and water are equivalents to the transcriptions by Turgenev—the *Sportsman's Notebook* is much admired by Hemingway—of Russian forests and fields. Each has brought to an immense and wild country the freshness of a new speech and a sensibility not yet conventionalized by literary associations. Yet it *is* the European sensibility which has come to Big Two-Hearted River, where the Indians are now obsolescent; in those solitudes it feels for the first time the cold current, the hot morning sun, sees the pine stumps, smells the sweet fern. And along with the mottled trout, with its 'clear water-over-gravel color,' the boy from the American Middle West fishes up a nice little masterpiece.

In the meantime there had been also Ring Lardner, Sherwood Anderson, Gertrude Stein, using this American language for irony, lyric poetry or psychological insight. Hemingway seems to have learned from them all. But he is now able to charge this naïve accent with a new complexity of emotion, a new shade of emotion: a malaise. The wholesale shattering of human beings in which he has taken part has given the boy a touch of panic.

2

The next fishing trip is strikingly different. Perhaps the first had been an idealization. Is it possible to attain to such sensuous bliss merely through going alone into the woods: smoking, fishing, and eating, with no thought about anyone else or about anything one has ever done or will ever be obliged to do? At any rate, today, in *The Sun Also Rises*, all the things that are wrong with human life are there on the holiday, too—though one tries to keep them back out of the foreground and to occupy one's mind with the trout, caught now in a stream of the Pyrenees, and with the kidding of the friend from the States. The feeling of insecurity has deepened. The young American now appears in a seriously damaged condition: he has somehow been incapacitated sexually through wounds received in the war. He is in love with one of those international sirens who flourished in the cafés of the post-war period and whose ruthless and uncontrollable infidelities, in such a circle as that depicted by Hemingway, have made any sort of security impossible for the relations between women and men. The lovers of such a woman turn upon and rend one another because they are powerless to make themselves felt by *her*. The casualties of the bullfight at Pamplona, to which these young people have gone for the *fiesta*, only reflect the blows and betrayals of demoralized human beings out of hand. What is the tiresome lover with whom the lady has just been off on a casual escapade, and who is unable to understand that he has been discarded, but the man who, on his way to the bull ring, has been accidentally gored by the bull? The young American who tells the story is the only character who keeps up standards of conduct, and he is prevented by his disability from dominating and directing the woman, who otherwise, it is intimated, might love him. Here the membrane of the style has been stretched taut to convey the vibrations of these qualms. The dry sunlight and the green summer landscapes have been invested with a sinister quality which must be new in literature. One enjoys the sun and the green as one enjoys suckling pigs and Spanish wine, but the uneasiness and apprehension are undruggable.

Yet one can catch hold of a code in all the drunkenness and the social chaos. 'Perhaps as you went along you did learn something,' Jake, the hero, reflects at one point. 'I did not care what it was all about. All I wanted to know was how to live in it. Maybe if you found out how to live in it you learned from that what it was all about.' 'Everybody behaves badly. Give them the proper chance,' he says later to Lady Brett.

' "You wouldn't behave badly." Brett looked at me.' In the end, she sends for Jake, who finds her alone in a hotel. She has left her regular lover for a young bullfighter, and this boy has for the first time inspired her with a respect which has restrained her from 'ruining' him: 'You know it makes one feel rather good deciding not to be a bitch.' We suffer and we make suffer, and everybody loses out in the long run; but in the meantime we can lose with honor.

This code still markedly figures, still supplies a dependable moral backbone, in Hemingway's next book of short stories, *Men Without Women*. Here Hemingway has mastered his method of economy in apparent casualness and relevance in apparent indirection, and has turned his sense of what happens and the way in which it happens into something as hard and clear as a crystal but as disturbing as a great lyric. Yet it is usually some principle of courage, of honor, of pity—that is, some principle of sportsmanship in its largest human sense—upon which the drama hinges. The old bullfighter in *The Undefeated* is defeated in everything except the spirit which will not accept defeat. You get the bull or he gets you: if you die, you can die game; there are certain things you cannot do. The burlesque show manager in *A Pursuit Race* refrains from waking his advance publicity agent when he overtakes him and realizes that the man has just lost a long struggle against whatever anguish it is that has driven him to drink and dope. 'They got a cure for that,' the manager had said to him before he went to sleep; ' "No,"

William Campbell said, "they haven't got a cure for anything."' The burned major in *A Simple Enquiry*—that strange picture of the bedrock stoicism compatible with the abasement of war—has the decency not to dismiss the orderly who has rejected his proposition. The brutalized Alpine peasant who has been in the habit of hanging a lantern in the jaws of the stiffened corpse of his wife, stood in the corner of the woodshed till the spring will make it possible to bury her, is ashamed to drink with the sexton after the latter has found out what he has done. And there is a little sketch of Roman soldiers just after the Crucifixion: 'You see me slip the old spear into him?—You'll get into trouble doing that some day.—It was the least I could do for him. I'll tell you he looked pretty good to me in there today.'

This Hemingway of the middle twenties—*The Sun Also Rises* came out in '26—expressed the romantic disillusion and set the favorite pose for the period. It was the moment of gallantry in heartbreak, grim and nonchalant banter, and heroic dissipation. The great watchword was 'Have a drink'; and in the bars of New York and Paris the young people were getting to talk like Hemingway.

3

The novel, *A Farewell to Arms*, which followed *Men Without Women*, is in a sense not so serious an affair. Beautifully written and quite moving of course it is. Probably no other book has caught so well the strangeness of life in the army for an American in Europe during the war. The new places to which one was sent of which one had never heard, and the things that turned out to be in them; the ordinary people of foreign countries as one saw them when one was quartered among them or obliged to perform some common work with them; the pleasures of which one managed to cheat the war, intensified by the uncertainty and horror—and the uncertainty, nevertheless, almost become a constant, the horror almost taken for granted; the love affairs, always subject to being suddenly broken up and yet carried on while they lasted in a spirit of irresponsible freedom which derived from one's having forfeited control of all one's other actions—this Hemingway got into his book, written long enough after the events for them to present themselves under an aspect fully idyllic.

But *A Farewell to Arms* is a tragedy, and the lovers are shown as innocent victims with no relation to the forces that torment them. They themselves are not tormented within by that dissonance between personal satisfaction and the suffering one shares with others which it has been Hemingway's triumph to handle. *A Farewell to Arms*, as the author once said, is a *Romeo and Juliet*. And when Catherine and her lover emerge from the stream of action—the account of the Caporetto retreat is Hemingway's best sustained piece of narrative—when they escape from the alien necessities of which their romance has been merely an accident, which have been writing their story for them, then we see that they are not in themselves convincing as human personalities. And we are confronted with the paradox that Hemingway, who possesses so remarkable a mimetic gift in catching the tone of social and national types and in making his people talk appropriately, has not shown any very solid sense of character, or indeed, any real interest in it. The people in his short stories are satisfactory because he has only to hit them off: the point of the story does not lie in personalities, but in the emotion to which a situation gives rise. This is true even in *The Sun Also Rises*, where the characters are sketched with wonderful cleverness. But in *A Farewell to Arms*, as soon as we are brought into real intimacy with the lovers, as soon as the author is obliged to see them through a searching personal experience, we find merely an idealized relationship, the abstractions of a lyric emotion.

With *Death in the Afternoon*, three years later, a new development for Hemingway commences. He writes a book not merely in the first person, but in the first person in his own character as Hemingway, and the results are unexpected and disconcerting.

Death in the Afternoon has its value as an exposition of bullfighting; and Hemingway is able to use the subject as a text for an explicit statement of his conception of man eternally pitting himself—he thinks the bullfight a ritual of this—against animal force and the odds of death. But the book is partly infected by a queer kind of maudlin emotion, which sounds at once neurotic and drunken. He overdoes his glorification of the bravery and martyrdom of the bullfighter. No doubt the professional expert at risking his life single-handed is impressive in contrast to the flatness and unreality of much of the business of the modern world; but this admirable miniaturist in prose has already made the point perhaps more tellingly in the little prose poem called *Banal Story*. Now he offsets the virility of the bullfighters by anecdotes of the male homosexuals that frequent the Paris cafés, at the same time that he puts his chief celebration of the voluptuous excitement of the spectacle into the mouth of an imaginary old lady. The whole thing becomes a little hysterical.

The master of that precise and clean style now indulges in purple patches which go on spreading for pages. I am not one of those who admire the last chapter of *Death in the Afternoon*, with its rich, all too rich, unrollings of memories of good times in Spain, and with its what seem to me irrelevant reminiscences of the soliloquy of Mrs. Bloom in *Ulysses*. Also, there are interludes of kidding of a kind which Hemingway handles with skill when he assigns them to characters in his stories, but in connection with which he seems to become incapable of exercising good sense or good taste as soon as he undertakes them in his own person (the burlesque *Torrents of Spring* was an early omen of this). In short, we are compelled to recognize that, as soon as Hemingway drops the burning-glass of the disciplined and objective art with which he has learned to concentrate in a story the light of the emotions that flood in on him, he straightway becomes befuddled, slops over.

This befuddlement is later to go further, but in the meantime he publishes another volume of stories—*Winner Take Nothing*—

which is almost up to its predecessor. In this collection he deals much more effectively than in *Death in the Afternoon* with that theme of contemporary decadence which is implied in his panegyric of the bullfighter. The first of these stories, *After the Storm*, is another of his variations—and one of the finest—on the theme of keeping up a code of decency among the hazards and pains of life. A fisherman goes out to plunder a wreck: he dives down to break in through a porthole, but inside he sees a woman with rings on her hands and her hair floating loose in the water, and he thinks about the passengers and crew being suddenly plunged to their deaths (he has almost been killed himself in a drunken fight the night before). He sees the cloud of sea birds screaming around, and he finds that he is unable to break the glass with his wrench and that he loses the anchor grapple with which he next tries to attack it. So he finally goes away and leaves the job to the Greeks, who blow the boat open and clean her out.

But in general the emotions of insecurity here obtrude themselves and dominate the book. Two of the stories deal with the hysteria of soldiers falling off the brink of their nerves under the strain of the experiences of the war, which here no longer presents an idyllic aspect; another deals with a group of patients in a hospital, at the same time crippled and hopeless; still another (a five-page masterpiece) with a waiter, who, both on his own and on his customers' account, is reluctant to go home at night, because he feels the importance of a 'clean well-lighted cafe' as a refuge from the 'nothing' that people fear. *God Rest You Merry Gentlemen* repeats the theme of castration of *The Sun Also Rises*; and four of the stories are concerned more or less with male or female homosexuality. In the last story, *Fathers and Sons*, Hemingway reverts to the Michigan forest, as if to take the curse off the rest: young Nick had once enjoyed a nice Indian girl with plump legs and hard little breasts on the needles of the hemlock woods.

These stories and the interludes in *Death in the Afternoon* must have been written during the years that followed the stock-market crash. They are full of the apprehension of losing control of oneself which is aroused by the getting out of hand of a social-economic system, as well as of the fear of impotence which seems to accompany the loss of social mastery. And there is in such a story as *A Clean Well-Lighted Place* the feeling of having got to the end of everything, of having given up heroic attitudes and wanting only the illusion of peace.

4

And now, in proportion as the characters in his stories run out of fortitude and bravado, he passes into a phase where he is occupied with building up his public personality. He has already now become a legend, as Mencken was in the twenties; he is the Hemingway of the handsome photographs with the sportsmen's tan and the outdoor grin, with the ominous resemblance to Clark Gable, who poses with a giant marlin which he has just hauled in off Key West. And unluckily—but for an American inevitably—the opportunity soon presents itself to exploit this personality for profit: he turns up delivering Hemingway monologues in well-paying and trashy magazines; and the Hemingway of these loose disquisitions, arrogant, belligerent and boastful, is certainly the worst-invented character to be found in the author's work. If he is obnoxious, the effect is somewhat mitigated by the fact that he is intrinsically incredible.

There would be no point in mentioning this journalism at all, if it did not seem somewhat to have contributed to the writing of certain unsatisfactory books. *Green Hills of Africa* (1935) owes its failure to falling between the two genres of personal exhibitionism and fiction. 'The writer has attempted,' says Hemingway, 'to write an absolutely true book to see whether the shape of a country and the pattern of a month's action can, if truly presented, compete with a work of the imagination.' He does try to present his own rôle objectively, and there is a genuine Hemingway theme—the connection between success at big-game hunting and sexual self-respect—involved in his adventures as he presents them. But the sophisticated technique of the fiction writer comes to look artificial when it is applied to a series of real happenings; and the necessity of sticking to what really happened makes impossible the typical characters and incidents which give point to a work of fiction. The monologues by the false, the publicity, Hemingway with which the narrative is interspersed are almost as bad as the ones that he has been writing for the magazines. He inveighs with much scorn against the literary life and against the professional literary man of the cities; and then manages to give the impression that he himself is a professional literary man of the touchiest and most self-conscious kind. He delivers a self-confident lecture on the high possibilities of prose writing; and then produces such a sentence as the following: 'Going downhill steeply made these Spanish shooting boots too short in the toe and there was an old argument, about this length of boot and whether the bootmaker, whose part I had taken, unwittingly first, only as interpreter, and finally embraced his theory patriotically as a whole and, I believed, by logic, had overcome it by adding onto the heel.' As soon as Hemingway begins speaking in the first person, he seems to lose his bearings, not merely as a critic of life, but even as a craftsman.

In another significant way, *Green Hills of Africa* is disappointing. *Death in the Afternoon* did provide a lot of data on bullfighting and build up for us the bullfighting world; but its successor tells us little about Africa. Hemingway keeps affirming —as if in accents of defiance against those who would engage his attention for social problems—his passionate enthusiasm for the African country and his perfect satisfaction with the hunter's life; but he has produced what must be one of the only books ever written which make Africa and its animals seem dull. Almost the only thing we learn about the animals is that Hemingway wants to kill them. And as for the natives, though there is one fine description of a tribe of marvelous trained runners, the principal impression we get of them is that they were simple and inferior people who enormously admired Hemingway.

It is not only that, as his critics of the Left have been complaining, he shows no interest in political issues, but that his interest in his fellow beings seems actually to be drying up. It is as if he were throwing himself on African hunting as something to live for and believe in, as something through which to realize himself; and as if, expecting of it too much, he had got out of it abnormally little, less than he is willing to admit. The disquiet of the Hemingway of the twenties had been, as I have said, undruggable —that is, in his books themselves, he had tried to express it, not drug it, had given it an appeasement in art; but now there sets in, in the Hemingway of the thirties, what seems to be a deliberate self-drugging. The situation is indicated objectively in *The Gambler, the Nun and the Radio*, one of the short stories of 1933, in which everything from daily bread to 'a belief in any new form of government' is characterized as 'the opium of the people' by an empty-hearted patient in a hospital.

But at last there did rush into this vacuum the blast of the social issue, which had been roaring in the wind like a forest fire.

Out of a series of short stories that Hemingway had written about a Florida waterside character he decided to make a little epic. The result was *To Have and Have Not*, which seems to me the poorest of all his stories. Certainly some deep agitation is working upon Hemingway the artist. Craftsmanship and style, taste and sense, have all alike gone by the board. The negative attitude toward human beings has here become definitely malignant: the hero is like a wooden-headed Punch, always knocking people on the head (inferiors—Chinamen or Cubans); or, rather, he combines the characteristics of Punch with those of Popeye the Sailor in the animated cartoon in the movies. As the climax to a series of prodigies, this stupendous pirate-smuggler named Harry Morgan succeeds, alone, unarmed, and with only a hook for one hand—though at the cost of a mortal wound—in outwitting and destroying with their own weapons four men carrying revolvers and a machine gun, by whom he has been shanghaied in a launch. The only way in which Hemingway's outlaw suffers by comparison with Popeye is that his creator has not tried to make him plausible by explaining that he does it all on spinach.

The impotence of a decadent society has here been exploited deliberately, but less successfully than in the earlier short stories. Against a background of homosexuality, impotence and masturbation among the wealthy holiday-makers in Florida, Popeye-Morgan is shown gratifying his wife with the same indefatigable dexterity which he has displayed in his other feats; and there is a choral refrain of praise of his *cojones*, which wells up in the last pages of the book when the abandoned Mrs. Popeye regurgitates Molly Bloom's soliloquy.

To be a man in such a world of maggots is noble, but it is not enough. Besides the maggots, there are double-crossing rats, who will get you if they are given the slightest chance. What is most valid in *To Have and Have Not* is the idea—conveyed better, perhaps, in the first of the series of episodes than in the final scenes of massacre and agony—that in an atmosphere (here revolutionary Cuba) in which man has been set against man, in which it is always a question whether your companion is not preparing to cut your throat, the most sturdy and straightforward American will turn suspicious and cruel. Harry Morgan is made to realize as he dies that to fight this bad world alone is hopeless. Again Hemingway, with his barometric accuracy, has rendered a moral atmosphere that was prevalent at the moment he was writing—a moment when social relations were subjected to severe tensions, when they seemed sometimes already disintegrating. But the heroic Hemingway legend has at this point invaded his fiction and, inflaming and inflating his symbols, has produced an implausible hybrid, half Hemingway character, half nature myth.

Hemingway had not himself particularly labored this moral of individualism *versus* solidarity, but the critics of the Left labored it for him and received his least creditable piece of fiction as the delivery of a new revelation. The progress of the Communist faith among our writers since the beginning of the depression has followed a peculiar course. That the aims and beliefs of Marx and Lenin should have come through to the minds of intellectuals who had been educated in the bourgeois tradition as great awakeners of conscience, a great light, was quite natural and entirely desirable. But the conception of the dynamic Marxist will, the exaltation of the Marxist religion, seized the members of the professional classes like a capricious contagion or hurricane, which shakes one and leaves his neighbor standing, then returns to lay hold on the second after the first has become quiet again. In the moment of seizure, each one of them saw a scroll unrolled from the heavens, on which Marx and Lenin and Stalin, the Bolsheviks of 1917, the Soviets of the Five-Year Plan, and the GPU of the Moscow trials were all a part of the same great purpose. Later the convert, if he were capable of it, would get over his first phase of snow blindness and learn to see real people and conditions, would study the development of Marxism in terms of nations, periods, personalities, instead of logical deductions from abstract propositions or—as in the case of the more naïve or dishonest—of simple incantatory slogans. But for many there was at least a moment when the key to all the mysteries of human history seemed suddenly to have been placed in their hands, when an infallible guide to thought and behavior seemed to have been given them in a few easy formulas.

Hemingway was hit pretty late. He was still in *Death in the Afternoon* telling the 'world-savers,' sensibly enough, that they should 'get to see' the world 'clear and as a whole. Then any part you make will represent the whole, if it's made truly. The thing to do is work and learn to make it.' Later he jibed at the literary radicals, who talked but couldn't take it; and one finds even in *To Have and Have Not* a crack about a 'highly paid Hollywood director, whose brain is in the process of outlasting his liver so that he will end up calling himself a Communist, to save his soul.' Then the challenge of the fight itself—Hemingway never could resist a physical challenge—the natural impulse to dedicate oneself to something bigger than big-game hunting and bullfighting, and the fact that the class war had broken out in a country to which he was romantically attached, seem to have combined to make him align himself with the Communists as well as the Spanish Loyalists at a time when the Marxist philosophy had been pretty completely shelved by the Kremlin, now reactionary as well as corrupt, and when the Russians were lending the Loyalists only help enough to preserve, as they imagined would be possible, the balance of power against Fascism while they acted at the same time as a police force to beat down the real social revolution.

Hemingway raised money for the Loyalists, reported the battle fronts. He even went so far as to make a speech at a congress of the League of American Writers, an organization rigged by the supporters of the Stalinist régime in Russia and full of precisely the type of literary revolutionists that he had been ridiculing a little while before. Soon the Stalinists had taken him in tow, and he was feverishly denouncing as Fascists other writers who criticized the Kremlin. It has been one of the expedients of the Stalin administration in maintaining its power and covering up its crimes to condemn on trumped-up charges of Fascist conspiracy, and even to kidnap and murder, its political opponents of the Left; and, along with food and munitions, the Russians had brought to the war in Spain what the Austrian journalist Willi Schlamm called that diversion of doubtful value for the working class: 'Herr Vyshinsky's Grand Guignol.'

The result of this was a play, *The Fifth Column*, which, though it is good reading for the way the characters talk, is an exceedingly silly production. The hero, though an Anglo-American, is an agent of the Communist secret police, engaged in catching Fascist spies in Spain; and his principal exploit in the course of the play is clearing out, with the aid of a single Communist, an artillery post manned by seven Fascists. The scene is like a push-over and getaway from one of the cruder Hollywood Westerns. It is in the nature of a small boy's fantasy, and would probably be considered extravagant by most writers of books for boys.

The tendency on Hemingway's part to indulge himself in these boyish day-dreams seems to begin to get the better of his realism at the end of *A Farewell to Arms*, where the hero, after many adventures of fighting, escaping, love-making and drinking, rows his lady thirty-five kilometers on a cold and rainy night; and we have seen what it could do for Harry Morgan. Now, as if with the conviction that the cause and the efficiency of the GPU have added several cubits to his stature, he has let this tendency loose; and he has also found in the GPU's grim duty a pretext to give rein to the appetite for describing scenes of killing which has always been a feature of his work. He has progressed from grasshoppers and trout through bulls and lions and kudus to Chinamen and Cubans, and now to Fascists. Hitherto the act of destruction has given rise for him to complex emotions: he has identified himself not merely with the injurer but also with the injured; there has been a masochistic complement to the sadism. But now this paradox which splits our natures, and which has instigated some of Hemingway's best stories, need no longer present perplexities to his mind. The Fascists are dirty bastards, and to kill them is a righteous act. He who had made a separate peace, who had said farewell to arms, has found a reason for taking them up again in a spirit of rabietic fury unpleasantly reminiscent of the spy mania and the sacred anti-German rage which took possession of so many civilians and staff officers under the stimulus of the last war.

Not that the compensatory trauma of the typical Hemingway protagonist is totally absent even here. The main episode is the hero's brief love affair and voluntary breaking-off with a beautiful and adoring girl whose acquaintance he has made in Spain. As a member of the Junior League and a graduate of Vassar, she represents for him—it seems a little hard on her—that leisure-class playworld from which he is trying to get away. But in view of the fact that from the very first scenes he treats her with more or less open contempt, the action is rather lacking in suspense as the sacrifice is rather feeble in moral value. One takes no stock at all in the intimation that Mr. Philip may later be sent to mortify himself in a camp for training Young Pioneers. And in the meantime he has fun killing Fascists.

In *The Fifth Column*, the drugging process has been carried further still: the hero, who has become finally indistinguishable from the false or publicity Hemingway, has here dosed himself not only with whiskey, but with a seductive and desirous woman, for whom he has the most admirable reasons for not taking any responsibility, with sacred rage, with the excitement of a bombardment, and with indulgence in that headiest of sports, for which he has now the same excellent reasons: the bagging of human beings.

5

You may fear, after reading *The Fifth Column*, that Hemingway will never sober up; but as you go on to his short stories of this period, you find that your apprehensions were unfounded. Three of these stories have a great deal more body—they are longer and more complex—than the comparatively meager anecdotes collected in *Winner Take Nothing*. And here are his real artistic successes with the material of his adventures in Africa, which make up for the miscarried *Green Hills*: *The Short Happy Life of Francis Macomber* and *The Snows of Kilimanjaro*, which disengage, by dramatizing them objectively, the themes he had attempted in the earlier book but that had never really got themselves presented. And here is at least a beginning of a real artistic utilization of Hemingway's experience in Spain: an incident of the war in two pages which outweighs the whole of *The Fifth Column* and all his Spanish dispatches, a glimpse of an old man, 'without politics,' who has so far occupied his life in taking care of eight pigeons, two goats and a cat, but who has now been dislodged and separated from his pets by the advance of the Fascist armies. It is a story which takes its place among the war prints of Callot and Goya, artists whose union of elegance with sharpness has already been recalled by Hemingway in his earlier battle pieces: a story which might have been written about almost any war.

And here—what is very remarkable—is a story, *The Capital of the World*, which finds an objective symbol for, precisely, what is wrong with *The Fifth Column.* A young boy who has come up from the country and waits on table in a pension in Madrid gets accidentally stabbed with a meat knife while playing at bullfighting with the dishwasher. This is the simple anecdote, but Hemingway has built in behind it all the life of the pension and the city: the priesthood, the working-class movement, the grown-up bullfighters who have broken down or missed out. 'The boy Paco,' Hemingway concludes, 'had never known about any of this nor about what all these people would be doing on the next day and on other days to come. He had no idea how they really lived nor how they ended. He did not realize they ended. He died, as the Spanish phrase has it, full of illusions. He had not had time in his life to lose any of them, or even, at the end, to complete an act of contrition.' So he registers in this very fine piece the discrepancy between the fantasies of boyhood and the realities of the grown-up world. Hemingway the artist, who feels things truly and cannot help recording what he feels, has actually said good-bye to these fantasies at a time when the war correspondent is making himself ridiculous by attempting to hang on to them still.

The emotion which principally comes through in *Francis Macomber* and *The Snows of Kilimanjaro*—as it figures also in *The Fifth Column*—is a growing antagonism to women. Looking back, one can see at this point that the tendency has been there all along. In *The Doctor and the Doctor's Wife*, the boy Nick goes out squirrel-hunting with his father instead of obeying the summons of his mother; in *Cross Country Snow*, he regretfully says farewell to male companionship on a skiing expedition in Switzerland, when he is obliged to go back to the States so that his wife can have her baby. The young man in *Hills Like White Elephants* compels his girl to have an abortion contrary to her wish; another story, *A Canary for One* bites almost unbearably but exquisitely on the loneliness to be endured by a wife after she and her husband shall have separated; the peasant of *An Alpine Idyll* abuses the corpse of his wife (these last three appear under the general title *Men Without Women*). Brett in *The Sun Also Rises* is an exclusively destructive force: she might be a better woman if she were mated with Jake, the American; but actually he is protected against her and is in a sense revenging his own sex through being unable to do anything for her sexually. Even the hero of *A Farewell to Arms* eventually destroys Catherine—after enjoying her abject devotion—by giving her a baby, itself born dead. The only women with whom Nick Adams' relations are perfectly satisfactory are the little Indian girls of his boyhood who are in a position of hopeless social disadvantage and have no power over the behavior of the white male—so that he can get rid of them the moment he has done with them. Thus in *The Fifth Column* Mr. Philip brutally breaks off with Dorothy—he has been rescued from her demoralizing influence by his enlistment in the Communist crusade, just as the hero of *The Sun Also Rises* has been saved by his physical disability—to revert to a little Moorish whore. Even Harry Morgan, who is represented as satisfying his wife on the scale of a Paul Bunyan, deserts her in the end by dying and leaves her racked by the cruelest desire.[1]

And now this instinct to get the woman down presents itself

[1] There would probably be a chapter to write on the relation between Hemingway and Kipling, and certain assumptions about society which they share. They have much the same split attitude toward women. Kipling anticipates Hemingway in his beliefs that "he travels the fastest that travels alone" and that "the female of the species is more deadly than the male"; and Hemingway seems to reflect Kipling in the submissive infra-Anglo-Saxon women that make his heroes such perfect mistresses. The most striking example of this is the amoeba-like little Spanish girl, Maria, in *For Whom the Bell Tolls*. Like the docile native "wives" of English officials in the early stories of Kipling, she lives only to serve her lord and to merge her identity with his; and this love affair with a woman in a sleeping-bag, lacking completely the kind of give and take that goes on between real men and women, has the all-too-perfect felicity of a youthful erotic dream. One suspects that *Without Benefit of Clergy* was read very early by Hemingway and that it made on him a lasting impression. The pathetic conclusion of this story of Kipling's seems unmistakably to be echoed at the end of *A Farewell to Arms*.

frankly as a fear that the woman will get the man down. The men in both these African stories are married to American bitches of the most soul-destroying sort. The hero of *The Snows of Kilimanjaro* loses his soul and dies of futility on a hunting expedition in Africa, out of which he has failed to get what he had hoped. The story is not quite stripped clean of the trashy moral attitudes which have been coming to disfigure the author's work: the hero, a seriously intentioned and apparently promising writer, goes on a little sloppily over the dear early days in Paris when he was earnest, happy and poor, and blames a little hysterically the rich woman whom he has married and who has debased him. Yet it is one of Hemingway's remarkable stories. There is a wonderful piece of writing at the end when the reader is made to realize that what has seemed to be an escape by plane, with the sick man looking down on Africa, is only the dream of a dying man. The other story, *Francis Macomber*, perfectly realizes its purpose. Here the male saves his soul at the last minute, and then is actually shot down by his woman, who does not want him to have a soul. Here Hemingway has at last got what Thurber calls the war between men and women right out into the open and has written a terrific fable of the impossible civilized woman who despises the civilized man for his failure in initiative and nerve and then jealously tries to break him down as soon as he begins to exhibit any. (It ought to be noted, also, that whereas in *Green Hills of Africa* the descriptions tended to weigh down the narrative with their excessive circumstantiality, the landscapes and animals of *Francis Macomber* are alive and unfalteringly proportioned.)

Going back over Hemingway's books today, we can see clearly what an error of the politicos it was to accuse him of an indifference to society. His whole work is a criticism of society: he has responded to every pressure of the moral atmosphere of the time, as it is felt at the roots of human relations, with a sensitivity almost unrivaled. Even his preoccupation with licking the gang in the next block and being known as the best basketball player in high school has its meaning in the present epoch. After all, whatever is done in the world, political as well as athletic, depends on personal courage and strength. With Hemingway, courage and strength are always thought of in physical terms, so that he tends to give the impression that the bullfighter who can take it and dish it out is more of a man than any other kind of man, and that the sole duty of the revolutionary socialist is to get the counter-revolutionary gang before they get him.

But ideas, however correct, will never prevail by themselves: there must be people who are prepared to stand or fall with them, and the ability to act on principle is still subject to the same competitive laws which operate in sporting contests and sexual relations. Hemingway has expressed with genius the terrors of the modern man at the danger of losing control of his world, and he has also, within his scope, provided his own kind of antidote. This antidote, paradoxically, is almost entirely moral. Despite Hemingway's preoccupation with physical contests, his heroes are almost always defeated physically, nervously, practically: their victories are moral ones. He himself, when he trained himself stubbornly in his unconventional unmarketable art in a Paris which had other fashions, gave the prime example of such a victory; and if he has sometimes, under the menace of the general panic, seemed on the point of going to pieces as an artist, he has always pulled himself together the next moment. The principle of the Bourdon gauge, which is used to measure the pressure of liquids, is that a tube which has been curved into a coil will tend to straighten out in proportion as the liquid inside it is subjected to an increasing pressure.

The appearance of *For Whom the Bell Tolls* since this essay was written in 1939 carries the straightening process further. Here Hemingway has largely sloughed off his Stalinism and has reverted to seeing events in terms of individuals pitted against specific odds. His hero, an American teacher of Spanish who has enlisted on the side of the Loyalists, gives his life to what he regards as the cause of human liberation; but he is frustrated in the task that has been assigned him by the confusion of forces at cross-purposes that are throttling the Loyalist campaign. By the time that he comes to die, he has little to sustain him but the memory of his grandfather's record as a soldier in the American Civil War. The psychology of this young man is presented with a certain sobriety and detachment in comparison with Hemingway's other full-length heroes; and the author has here succeeded as in none of his earlier books in externalizing in plausible characters the elements of his own complex personality. With all this, there is an historical point of view which he has learned from his political adventures: he has aimed to reflect in this episode the whole course of the Spanish War and the tangle of tendencies involved in it.

The weaknesses of the book are its diffuseness—a shape that lacks the concision of his short stories, that sometimes sags and sometimes bulges; and a romanticizing of some of the material, an infusion of the operatic, that lends itself all too readily to the movies.

LEO GURKO

Hemingway in Spain

1947

As befits a period that lifted foreign correspondence into a form of literary art, the war in Spain attracted creative writers from nearly every country, some of whom, like André Malraux, came to fight with the International Brigade, while others went simply as reporters whose personal sympathies were more or less on the side of the besieged government. Among those in this second classification was one of America's most distinguished and influential novelists, a writer who had always been attracted by the smell of death, the stronger and more dramatic the better, to whose imagination the bloodshed in Spain was a high and passionate stimulant. Ernest Hemingway came to Spain on assignment as a reporter; he left with plans for a play, *The Fifth Column*, and a novel, *For Whom the Bell Tolls.* The civil war might have been made to order for him; it embodied most of the salient features of the script Hem-

---

ingway had been working with for fifteen years: two sides fighting with unbridled ferocity, every known variety of cowardice and heroism, characters who were aficionado and characters who were not, and a backdrop of great events against which the fortunes of selected individuals could be projected in dimensions somewhat larger than life.

It was the act of dying that bound these several elements together, and made them centrally attractive to Hemingway. He had already studied men dying in every kind of situation he could lay hands on: the Swede lying in bed waiting for the gunmen in "The Killers" to get him; Jake, in *The Sun Also Rises*, consigned to a living death by his sexual impotence, drinking himself into an actual one, while Lady Brett follows the same course along the road of sexual dissipation; Catherine Barkley in *A Farewell to Arms* dying in childbirth for no particular reason at all, against the canvas of the retreat at Caporetto in which thousands of Italian soldiers were slaughtered; Manuel, the bullfighter in *The Undefeated*, being killed by the bull; Morgan, the smuggler in *To Have and Have Not*, living a hard jungle existence in the dangerous waters off the Florida Keys, and dying bloodily in the pursuit of his profession. When Hemingway ran out of human death, he fell back on animals, took to big game hunting, and described in *The Green Hills of Africa* the supreme thrill of drawing his rifle sights on a buck and despatching it with an accuracy and released tension beautiful to behold.

In Spain, however, he found men dying in a slightly different context, no longer out of mere resignation or boredom, or for purely occupational reasons or purely accidental ones. They were now dying for a political cause, for an idealism greater than their own egos. It was a new kind of dying for Hemingway, and it drew him; it inflamed his creative ardor, and inspired the longest and most grandiose of his novels. *For Whom the Bell Tolls* has little of the tight, clipped, underaccented style which made Hemingway famous. For him, indeed, it sprawls and rambles, goes off on frequent digressions, and even pries the author out of his traditional impersonality. He begins it in what appears to be a new vein. After all the cynical disillusioned heroes, Robert Jordan is a refreshing type. He has gone to fight with the Loyalists partly because his grandfather had fought for freedom in the Civil War and he wants to do the same in his time. But Hemingway whittles away at his idealism until pretty soon it begins to look a little threadbare. First, there are André Marty and the Communists who, according to Hemingway, seek to organize the Loyalists' cause for their own purposes, and come in for some savage blasting outside the framework of the plot. Then the Loyalists themselves turn out to be pretty brutal, and the one massacre described at length in the novel is a massacre of the fascists by the government forces. There are even stinging comments on the Spaniards as a people. They are characterized as treacherous.

"Of course they turned on you. They turned on you often but they always turned on every one. They turned on themselves, too. If you had three together, two would unite against one, and then the two would start to betray each other. Not always, but often enough for you to take enough cases and start to draw it as a conclusion."

And as callous, too:

"He (Lister, a Loyalist leader) was a true fanatic and he had the complete Spanish lack of respect for life. . . .

"But they (the Spanish) did that on purpose and deliberately. Those who did that are the last flowering of what their education has produced. Those are the flowers of Spanish chivalry. What a people they have been. What sons of bitches from Cortez, Pizarro, Menendez de Avila all down through Enrique Lister to Pablo. And what wonderful people. There is no finer and no worse people in the world. No kinder people and no crueler."

After a few hundred pages of this, Jordan and his idealism are a pretty sickly looking pair. He clings to it to the end, however, and gives up his life to save his comrades, but by that time our feeling is, "What a damn fool! What an admirable damn fool!"

Having battered away at the one redeeming motive that has

ever animated his heroes, Hemingway succeeded in preserving the continuity of his nihilism. Death as a form of art has been his abiding theme, and made him one of the inevitable writers of the era of global wars. He encompassed the postwar 20's even more than the 30's, and now, in the atomic age, he seems more than ever destined to be nourished with a fresh supply of variations on his major theme, and to articulate in fiction the destructive forces of the century.

W. M. FROHOCK

Violence and Discipline

1947

1

No one should write of Ernest Hemingway without asking himself first if he does not owe this man a particular debt. We all imitated him at one time or another. What he taught us was frequently so insidious that we never quite realized we were learning it. Even yet, after twenty years, the familiar contours of the Hemingway style keep turning up in the most unexpected places. The following sample was printed in March, 1946:

> There was this Frenchman who came up from Venezuela and he talked in the Palace d' Orient Armenian restaurant in New York about the recent revolution in Venezuela. Which is Venezuela, I said. It does not matter,

This essay originally appeared in the *Southwest Review*, Volume XXXII, Nos. 1 and 2, 1947. It has been reprinted in *The Novel of Violence in America: 1920-1950* published by University Press in Dallas. Copyright 1950. Reprinted by permission of the author and publisher.

> he said. The socialists made the revolution against the conservatives and the communists—the socialists and a part of the army, the part that is young and wants to be a colonel . . .

This is by C. G. Paulding, Literary Editor of the *Commonweal*, a Roman Catholic publication in which one would not regularly expect the influence of Hemingway to be visible. Yet the pace of the thing, the rapidity of the sentences, the corner-cutting, the suppression of unessentials, all suggest very compellingly where Mr. Paulding learned to write.

We imitated almost everything Hemingway did: the famous dialogue which sounds so much like transcribed talk precisely because it leaves out all the things we say but never hear ourselves say; the deceptive simplicity of description; the understatement, or seeming understatement, of the emotions; the delight in such elementary pastimes as fighting, fishing and sexual intercourse; the fascination with pain and violent death; the fine, irresponsible, free-associative spoofing. But in general we missed the fact that these things, new and shining as they were to us (with the added and somewhat false luster they also had through contrast with the great complexity of Joyce, Lawrence and Proust) were only ancillary.

It is a mystery now to us how we contrived to miss the existence, in the center of these things which we imitated, of a discipline which Hemingway had worked out for himself and which made the difference between him and his imitators. He loved and admired Flaubert, and he wanted to achieve an accuracy of statement like Flaubert's—the difference between them being that whereas Flaubert had aimed especially at accuracy of statement regarding the exterior world, trying to nail an object with the one word that fitted it, for Hemingway the great necessity was to be accurate in the statement of emotions. Critics have rarely said much about this, although Edmund Wilson, whose chapter on Hemingway in *The Wound and the Bow* I admire, mentions it in passing. Yet Hemingway's varying career can be summed up in reference to this discipline. He adheres to it in the early short stories and the first two novels, and they are admirable. In the nineteen thirties either he runs away from the discipline or it runs away with him; he preaches it, rather raucously, but has such great trouble with the practice that it is hard to admire much that he writes. And then, in a third stage, he returns to it again—not with complete success, because the job that he tackles is bigger than any of the earlier ones; but with enough success so that it is once more possible to regard him as a major novelist.

From the beginning the thing that stirred him most was violence, and the emotions of which he wrote were those stimulated by pain and killing—war, and bull-fighting, and big game-hunting, and fishing to kill rather than for sport, and love conceived as something in itself very akin to violence. Purposely he chose a material which was stronger stuff than that of Frank Norris, and wrote about it as Sherwood Anderson might have written, if Anderson, who was a great story-teller but a lazy artist, had not sloughed the job whenever a specific emotion was involved. The places where Anderson dodged, saying "that's another thing" or "but let that pass," are the ones in which by instinct Hemingway saw his major goal.

The discipline is present and fullgrown in *The Sun Also Rises*, and becomes explicitly visible when the Paris episode is over and the characters have got into Spain. Jake and Bill are now on top of the bus from Pamplona to Burguete:

> The bus climbed steadily up the road. The country was barren and rocks stuck up through the clay. There was no grass beside the road. Looking back we could see the country spread out below. Far back the fields were squares of green and brown on the hillsides. Making the horizon were the brown mountains. They were strangely shaped. As we climbed higher the horizon kept changing. As the bus ground slowly up the road we could see other mountains coming up in the south. Then the road came over the crest, flattened out, and went into a forest. It was a forest of cork oaks, and the sun came through the trees in patches, and there were cattle graz-

> ing back in the trees. We went through the forest and the road came out and turned along a rise of land, and out ahead of us was a rolling green plain, with dark mountains beyond it. These were not like the brown, heat-baked mountains we had left behind. These were wooded and there were clouds coming down from them. The green plain stretched off. It was cut by fences and the white of the road showed through the trunks of a double line of trees that crossed the plain toward the north. As we came to the edge of the rise we saw the red roofs and white houses of Burguete ahead strung out on the plain, and away off on the shoulder of the first dark mountain was the gray metal-sheathed roof of the monastery on Roncesvalles.*

This comes extremely close to being a classic example of getting a maximum of effect from the least expenditure of materials. Twelve of the eighteen adjectives are color references, and remarkably unspecific; of the rest four are relatively empty—"barren, heat-baked, rolling, spread out"—and of the other two, one tells you only that the shape of the mountains on the horizon was strange. This leaves only the metal-sheathed roof, and even here again, except in relation to the others, there is nothing arresting. The adverbs—"slowly, steadily, higher"—contribute no more. This is also true of the verbs: "was-were" turn up thirteen times; most of the others are simple statements about the movement of the bus and changes in the countryside resulting from it. Only one, "ground," makes much of a sense impression, taken by itself, and the sense impression is one which we are too used to. Out of the others I find that I can get images as follows—rocks sticking up out of the ground, a flattened road, cows grazing, sunlight through trees, a road stretching away, fields cut by lines of trees. And there is nothing in all of this, except the mention of cork oaks and the monastery at the very end, to identify the scene as specifically Spanish. You can find most of the rest of it, even the red roofs, in the American West.

At first glance the sentence structure presents the same sim-

* Passages from Hemingway's novels are quoted by permission of his publisher, Charles Scribner's Sons.

plicity. But attempt complicating it and you see what Hemingway is doing: change the three sentences from "Making the horizon . . ." as far as ". . . the horizon kept changing," into "the brown, strangely shaped mountains that made the horizon kept changing as we climbed higher," and you discover that in doing it you have interfered with a procession which has a characteristic orderliness and pace of its own. Up to the moment when the bus comes over the crest, Hemingway has been setting out straight statements each containing one sense impression, with a full pause after each, as the eye wanders farther from the grassless shoulder of the road to the mountainous horizon; but slowly, with recognizable purposelessness. But presently the impressions become somewhat more specific. This forest above the crest is identifiable as cork oak; there are patterns of light and shadow; those are cows you see through the trees. And as he does this, the sentences become relatively more complicated, there is less pause between the impressions, and they are coming thick and fast when you at last see the monastery roof and know that it is Roncesvalles and wake up to being in Spain.

In other words, the procession and pace here are essentially emotional. We now remember how the ride started. The two men are on the bus with a number of Basque country people, among whom Jake feels especially at home. We get the feeling that to Hemingway, unspoiled people of this sort are always good. (See his treatment of the African tribe in *Green Hills of Africa* for the type of primitive he likes particularly.) Wineskins have passed around. Jake and Bill are happy and full of good fellowship, completely relaxed and certainly mellowed by the wine. They are watching the view without paying any special attention to it until the bus nears its destination, where they have the right to expect a great deal of pleasure which they have come a long distance to get. Taken this way, the description makes particularly good sense; and a substitute job, full of color and precise detail and sharp, striking imagery, would be phoney. Jake and Bill are in no mood for distinguishing between colors, or for looking closely at particular parts of the landscape, and their minds are too comfortable for them to be making any particularly acute associations which might produce metaphor. From this point of view, anything but what Hemingway has produced would be emotionally faked, unnatural, a sort of impurity. Certainly there would be nothing hard or clean about it. This constant checking of the writing against the emotion involved is what I mean by discipline. It should be the central element in any discussion of Hemingway.

In the light of the discipline, the emotional pattern of the book as a whole becomes important; and we had better reconstruct it, since the passing of time is obscuring it more and more, at least to the new reader. The whole job of reading this book has changed from what it was twenty years ago. The Lost Generation has already achieved the dignity—and unreality—of a Historical Concept. It is increasingly hard to remember that the American expatriates of two decades back were serious artists and not spoiled brats; it may be too much to expect that a group which fled America because it did not feel emotionally secure and at home there should seem anything other than trivial to another generation which, after another war, is compellingly impressed by the insecurity of mere *physical* life anywhere on the planet.

Certainly Hemingway's despair, like that of Eliot in "The Waste Land," is the kind which can be contemplated with leisure and some ease; it is despair without terror. As a matter of fact, the years of the great depression had already blunted its point; too many people discovered that it is even more important to eat regularly than to feel out of place among one's contemporaries. And consequently it is easy to miss the essential datum, that the emotional mood of the first part of *The Sun Also Rises* is a ceaseless, dull ache. The reader is supposed to know that Jake's physical disability is in large part a symbol for the general feeling of frustration and pointlessness of life, that if Jake were physically qualified to possess Brett it would make very little difference, that Brett's nymphomania is really unimportant because if she ever managed to overcome it she would be accomplishing the eradication of a symptom without doing anything for the sickness of the soul. I should think that it might be impossible for anyone opening the book now to find anything much, other than irrelevant digression, in the pages about the self-made Greek Count whose fantastic wine-parties, of course, used to have so much to do with the reader's getting into the mood of the whole first part, since Jake so palpably feels that while such things are not a very profitable occupation they are certainly as profitable as anything else.

Yet only if we understand the essential emotional mood of the first part of the book can we appreciate the careful balance between the emotions and the writing—otherwise there is no reasonable explanation for Hemingway's writing so completely under wraps. We risk seeing much more of the snaffle and the bit than we do of the bloody horse. Either we feel the appropriateness of the constant toning down of the whole Paris episode or it will seem like a somewhat stagey preparation for the Spanish part, designed to make the latter look brilliant by contrast. We have to know that we get a scant and referential treatment of the Paris scene because Jake is so used to it, and it is so much a part of his dull ache that he does not really see it. We get some of the free-associative spoofing that Hemingway loves to do, about taxidermy and the possibility of stuffed dogs as gifts, but this, as compared with the lovely examples of the same stuff in the Burguete episode, is carefully restrained. The characters do not yet appear as particularly interesting people; we know that Cohn is an importunate romantic oaf, that Mike Campbell is a drunken chronic bankrupt, that Brett is a drunk with a tendency toward promiscuity—and even of her we get something short of a full picture until the Paris episode is over and we discover that she has been sleeping with Cohn, for whom she cares absolutely nothing. Of them all we know just enough so that nothing they do later in the story will catch us by surprise.

Hemingway's whole method in this first part is pretty well summed up in his description of Brett as she is riding with Jake in a taxi. It is night. Illumination is provided by an occasional shop window and by the flares of workmen who are repairing trolley tracks. All that you actually get of Brett (and here again Hemingway is sticking to his purpose of giving you what the character actually sees, not what he should see) is the whiteness of her face and the long line of her neck—even though these people are alone and they are as much in love as their personal disabilities will permit. Substitute in this instance the idea of emotion for light and you have Hemingway's guiding motive throughout the first part: he sees and says only what the abomination-of-desolation mood permits. Obviously, if the emotional mood is misunderstood by the reader, the whole point is lost.

For the structure of *The Sun Also Rises* starts with the low-pitch of the Paris episode, and begins to rise when the people approach the Pyrenees. There is a general increase of awareness and a livening of the senses—the impressions we get from the page and a quarter describing the ride from San Sebastian to Pamplona are more intense than anything similar in the preceding ninety-five pages. The old ache remains, but emotions become more vivid and sense perceptions flow faster all the way through to the last day of the Pamplona fiesta; characters round out—as far as Hemingway's characters ever round out—and the clashes toward which they all have been heading take place. Then there is the magnificent account of the performance of Romero and Belmonte in the Pamplona ring; the party breaks up; Brett goes off with the bullfighter; and from here on to the end the emotions scale down into the old dull ache again.

I hope that this does not constitute an unorthodox reading of the book. What Hemingway does, having established the fundamental lack of integrity of Jake's friends Brett, Mike and Cohn, is to take them on the last brilliant days of the fiesta to witness a display—even though none of them seems qualified to recognize it or to profit by it—of the closest approach that he knows to perfect integrity.

> Romero never made any contortions, always it was straight and pure and natural in line. The others twisted themselves like corkscrews . . . Afterward, all that was

> faked turned bad . . . Romero's bull fighting gave real emotion, because he kept the absolute purity of line . . . Since the death of Joselito all the bull-fighters had been developing a technic which simulated this appearance of danger in order to give a fake emotional feeling, while the bull-fighter was really safe. Romero had the old thing, the holding of his purity of line . . .

The fact of the great beauty of integrity is what, if I am right, makes the last day of the fights the climax of *The Sun Also Rises*. After this the story works down into the emotional doldrums of the dull ache in which it began, and the demonstration is completed that there is no new thing under the sun. In this interpretation of the novel, of course, Romero becomes even more than a man who pursues a dangerous trade with great integrity; he becomes a symbol for general integrity itself. When Brett runs away with him after the fights, she is messing up something more important than the life of a promising young artist.

What Romero accomplishes with the sword and *muleta* is precisely what Hemingway wants to accomplish with words. In connection with the ride up from Pamplona to Burguete, we identified as his discipline a determined effort to be emotionally honest, to render the emotions pure, straight, real and unfaked; and we applied to his writing in that instance adjectives just now applied by Hemingway to Romero's performance with the bulls. We now have to emphasize the way in which Hemingway's ideal of integrity is connected with the act of violence and how, as a corollary, being able to write well about violence becomes the test of the writer's discipline.

For this purpose it is important that the spectacle of integrity in bull-fighting is double: beside Romero and his artistic perfection we have Juan Belmonte, who can not match Romero even when unhandicapped and who, on this day, is fighting in spite of the paralyzing pain of a fistula. He is significant to this argument because in his case as in Romero's, Hemingway, who, we say, has accepted a discipline of writing which forbids anything but the completely unfaked feeling, lets his emotions run.

> . . . Belmonte's jaw came further out in contempt, and his face turned yellower, and he moved with greater difficulty as his pain increased, and finally the crowd were actively against him, and he was utterly contemptuous and indifferent. He had meant to have a great afternoon, and instead it was an afternoon of sneers, shouted insults, and finally a volley of cushions and pieces of bread and vegetables, thrown down at him in the plaza where he had had his greatest triumphs. His jaw only went further out. Sometimes he turned to smile that toothed, long-jawed, lipless smile when he was called something particularly insulting, and always the pain that any movement produced grew stronger and stronger, until finally his yellow face was parchment color, and after his second bull was dead and the throwing of the bread and cushions was over, after he had saluted the President with the same wolf-jawed smile and contemptuous eyes, and handed his sword over the barrera to be wiped, and put back in its case, he passed through into the callejon and leaned on the barrera below us, his head on his arms, not seeing, not hearing anything, only going through his pain.

Particular attention is invited to the last sentence of this passage—which is actually half the quotation in length—to the rushing summary of all the indignity and all the suffering, to the intuition of the defiant spirit of the man as long as defiance is called for, to the eye of the writer following the minor detail of the sword wiping, and to the final overwhelming mastery of the pain. I do not know of any other place in Hemingway where he has reached such tension as this.

The figure of the bull-fighter who for money, and for his own integrity, faces death with nothing but his courage left to carry him, comes up at least four times in Hemingway's work—here, and again in *Death in the Afternoon* with Manuel García Maera, who ruins his wrist by hitting bone with his sword but still goes on, try after try, until he has killed his bull, even though he has to use his left hand to pick up his sword each time it flies out of the grasp of his right; and in the case of the bull-fighter in "The Undefeated" who returns to the ring when he is too old to fight; and in "Banal Story," which consists entirely of a bitter antithesis between the phoney contents of the *Forum Magazine* and the honest death of the Maera above mentioned, who dies in Madrid of pneumonia. This comes near to being a listing, to be put with the retreat from Caporetto in *A Farewell to Arms* and the story of the boxer in "Fifty Grand," of Hemingway's most effective writing.

The quality which makes men do these things Hemingway will later refer to as the quality of having *cojones;* I take it there is thus a connection between having *cojones* and having integrity, and am consequently willing to put up somewhat with the protracted demonstrations of sexual stamina which make Hemingway's later novels at times sophomoric if not simply offensive. How plainly *cojones* symbolize the kind of integrity Hemingway admires, and was setting as a rule of discipline for himself in his early writing, becomes apparent even in the lamentable *To Have and Have Not*, in which Harry Morgan's lusty bed sessions are set up against the masturbations of the rich woman on the yacht and the adultery-for-profit of the aspiring writer. This discussion could even be extended to include speculations on the meaning of Jake's particular disability and the recurrent talk of steers in the middle part of *The Sun Also Rises.*

Meanwhile, the literary value of this sort of integrity comes home with all its force as soon as you pick up *A Farewell to Arms.* Strictly speaking, this book is hardly a novel at all, at least if the word novel is used in the traditional sense of a story which develops through the interactions of a group of characters one upon the other. For Hemingway's story has really but one major character, Frederic Henry, and is in the last analysis nothing more than the account of how falling in love feels to a young man who is sick of a war. Few books are made of less material. Hemingway depends almost entirely on the trained and disciplined eye, and the carefully accurate report on the emotions. The end product may be—and I believe it is—closer to a good movie script than to a conventional novel: but it is still one of the few books of our time that stands entirely by itself.

I do not mean exactly that Hemingway was working on this book, as I believe he was working on *For Whom the Bell Tolls*, with Hollywood production and even possibly a specific Hollywood actor in mind. I do mean that in large portions of the book his eye is working as the camera works when it is responsible to a good director. Time is relentlessly foreshortened: chapter one takes you through a whole fall and part of a winter of the war, in a series of rapid impressions briefly sketched, one flowing into another, by a sort of selection very much like that of the narrating lens. Then you narrow into the village and move into the officers' mess, to a table, and to a conversation which is significant only in that you know that this sort of thing goes on eternally. By the end of chapter three you have Henry back from his winter leave and spring coming on; what has intervened amounts to nothing —you know this from the stream-of-memory stuff, the familiar flashback technique which was probably an even more common device in the day of the silent film than it is now. The ambulance trips in the mountain are handled as if the camera were mounted on the truck.

> We were in the foot-hills on the near side of the river and as the road mounted there were the high mountains off to the north with snow still on the tops. I looked back and saw the three cars all climbing, spaced by the interval of their dust. We passed a long column of loaded mules, the drivers walking along beside the mules wearing red fezzes. They were bersaglieri.
>
> Beyond the mule train the road was empty and we climbed through the hills and then went down over the shoulder of a long hill into a river-valley. There were trees along both sides of the road and through the right line of trees I saw the river, the water clear, fast and shallow. The river was low and there were stretches of sand and pebbles with a narrow channel of water and sometimes the water spread like a sheen over the pebbly bed.

This is straight movie, complete with everything but the shooting directions, the lens being permitted to pick up more or less, and to hold it longer or shorter times, according to the mood of Frederic Henry. The technique is basically the same for the moment when the shell hits his dugout, for the Caporetto episode, for the row up the lake, for Catherine's death in the Swiss hospital. For the reader it all amounts to a remarkable feeling, at times almost painful, of the immediacy of the sensations.

Henry's mood, of course, is compounded of his disgust with the war and his love for Catherine Barkley. Just how scrupulously Hemingway reports this mood can be picked out of a comparison between two passages, superficially similar, which at first look like identical handlings of the stream-of-consciousness. One is the summary, mentioned above, of Henry's late-winter leave; the other the account of what runs through his head later on the same day, as he lies stretched on his bed waiting for supper. The first is a stream of jumbled memories of the one-night cheap hotels and the drinking and the whores, which added together make the story of his meaningless furlough. In the second he is becoming aware that he is really in love with Catherine; his fantasy fastens on taking her with him back to Milan, where he has just been, and each detail stands out alone in spite of the way they flood in on him.

> Because we would not wear any clothes because it was so hot and the window open and the swallows flying over the roofs of the houses and when it was dark afterward and you went to the window very small bats hunting over the houses and close down over the trees and we would drink the capri and the door locked and it hot and only a sheet and the whole night and we would both love each other all night in the hot night in Milan.

The difference between the two passages lies of course in their representing two sides of a romantic antithesis which is not at all original with Hemingway, a variation on the As-in-the-midst-of-battle-there-is-room-for-thoughts-of-love theme, i.e., the bravest are the tenderest; but the antithesis is stated here through a change in the manner of reporting sensations which has to be attributed to the essential discipline of the man and merits the adjectives we applied to the Burguete episode of *The Sun Also Rises*. This is the stuff *A Farewell to Arms* is made of.

Plus, to be sure, the inevitably deft dialogue and the unobtrusive insertion of a minor symbol here and there—for example, the rain. At the beginning of the book, the rain is only the misery of the soldier, a part of the ineluctable boredom of war. But after Catherine becomes pregnant we learn that she is afraid of "being dead in the rain." When the idyll is broken off and Henry has to go up to the front before Caporetto, they separate in the rain after the bleak experience in the station-side hotel. Rain falls on the whole Caporetto debacle, and Henry has to escape both the Italian battle-police and the rain-filled river; and finally, after everything is over and Catherine is dead, he walks away from the hospital in the rain. This sort of thing does not, of course, impede the book's value as a movie script.

Neither does the eroticism which is the constant companion of violence in almost everything that Hemingway has written and which sooner or later has to be evaluated by any critic who writes seriously about him. The Hemingway who had always been preoccupied with catching and reporting the most intense sensations has, from the earliest short stories on to the present, been bewitched by the problem of writing about the emotional obbligati of the most exclusively physical act the human animal can contrive. This is not, at least not in the Bostonian sense, pornography. It is obscene in the same sense that Hemingway's descriptions of violent death are obscene. In death and in procreation and possibly in several other necessary human activities a man has a right to a certain amount of privacy, because what takes place simply does not happen on a vocal level: the reader invades these privacies only with a sense of intrusion and as likely as not comes away with, more than anything else, a keen feeling of disbelief. Probably he does not want to believe.

In any case, from the short story in which the owl goes flapping off through the forest, to the long tale of how Robert Jordan in his sleeping bag feels the earth move, I have to report that Hemingway leaves me entirely unconvinced. From another angle, however, this matter probably reveals the essential weakness of Hemingway's basic interpretation of life. As Edmund Wilson has pointed out, Hemingway has never succeeded in making love a two-way enterprise: the women are silently submissive instruments, not autonomous personalities. Similarly the matter of violence seems to become more and more a personal concern of Hemingway's, rather than a part of the general predicament of the race. Out of such a view, no adequate explanation of human suffering, or of human love, is likely to come.

But the meaning of this is less apparent in *A Farewell to Arms* than it will be later, after this first period in Hemingway's career —the period of the successfully disciplined vision—is past and done.

2

Hemingway's position at the turn of the twenties was admirable. He had behind him two good novels, one of them (*The Sun Also Rises*) hailed more or less accurately as "speaking for a whole generation" and the other (*A Farewell to Arms*) destined to certain success in Hollywood; and the whole list of his early short stories, which critics might deny were stories in the accepted sense at all, but which succeeded time after time in nailing the emotional mood Hemingway was after, and were consequently things of beauty. Writers all over Europe and America would have been glad to have Hemingway's past for their future —and he was still a young man, with power to burn, and to develop.

But at this point a change came. Up to now there had always been, along with the other things, a perceptible moral aspect in Hemingway's work: what attitude should a man take toward a world in which, for reasons of the world's making and not of his own, he is fundamentally out of place? What personal happiness can he expect to find in a world seething with violence, endurable only at the cost of tolerating an abundance of pain which, unless one adopts a religious explanation, is meaningless? What values could one respect when ethical values as a whole seemed universally disrespected?

In a way, Hemingway may have been right in his conclusions—or at least in what he took to be his conclusions. Probably a world in which honesty turns out to be the only certain virtue a man can cling to, instead of one of the permanent data of human character of which one need not speak because it is assumed to be universally present, is in literal fact a hell of a world. America had been a slough of materialism—shortly the material benefits would disappear, and we would all learn that we had spent a decade kidding ourselves. Certainly this world wherein the identifiable goods were few—friendship, nature, the thrill of action, and love of woman, and all of them very transient and always under tribute to war, pain, and death—could not be said to be much better after three thousand years than the world of the *Iliad*. In such circumstances honesty, integrity, or whatever one calls the ability to face the truth and tell it, was almost bound to become disproportionately important.

Now the need for integrity, out of which Hemingway had made a discipline and subjected himself to it, became for him a sort of refuge. His work had always displayed—as critics never tire pointing out—a tendency toward such withdrawal. Jake in *The Sun Also Rises* has had a sort of retirement forced upon him; Lieutenant Henry's farewell to arms is a personal withdrawal from the war. Now in the thirties Hemingway begins to maintain that when you have served your time defending Democracy and all that sort of thing, you have a right to go away afterward and do what is important to you. (One can only conclude that the defense of democracy and the other things whose defense is a constant concern to men of good will is, in this view, unimportant.) "The great thing," he writes in *Death in the Afternoon*, "is to last and get your work done and see and hear and learn and understand; and write when there is something that you know; and not before; and not too damned much after. Let those who want to save the world, if you can get to see it clear and as a whole. Then any part you make will represent the whole if it's made truly."

This new emphasis is dramatic enough to invite any amount of amateur psychiatry and psychiatry is dangerous as a critical tool. I can not help pausing, however, over the note of world-weariness here; it is as if we had a belated expression of the mood of "The Waste Land" and of *Ash Wednesday*. This sounds somewhat like another Aged Eagle reluctant to stretch his wings because they are no longer wings to fly but merely fans to beat the air. Actually Hemingway was only a ripe thirty-two in 1930. Actually the life he retired to was the least retiring sort of retirement the world has yet seen in a man of letters: hunting mountain sheep, fishing for marlin, attending bullfights, and shooting big and dangerous game, always and everywhere in his goings and comings attended by the flashbulbs of publicity. All in all there may be nothing rarer, psychologically, in his case than that he was another young man who had succeeded in something too early in life for the success not to go to his head.

Hemingway had taken to reading the critics and they now infuriated him. The letter he wrote to *Hound and Horn* in reply to a thoughtful and perfectly sincere article by Lawrence Leighton was insulting to the point of libel. Max Eastman had the misfortune to meet him in a publisher's office, and got a physical beating, the seriousness of which depended on what newspaper you read. In *Death in the Afternoon* he lashed out at Margaret Anderson, who, he says, called him yellow; at Aldous Huxley, for accusing him of intellectual innocence; and at the New Humanists, for insisting on dignity and decorum in spite of the fact that he, Hemingway, knew of several fundamental aspects of life—death and procreation among them—which were not fundamentally decorous. It was all very immature and brash, and probably symptomatic. But after all, he was no more intolerant of criticism than Flaubert was before him: the difference was that the Aged Eagle was young enough to let it get on paper and into the papers.

By retirement Hemingway meant mainly a change of attitude. He had never been one of those objective novelists who delight in the creation of character. In all three of the books of the retirement period, the central character is Hemingway; the other figures are there as a supporting cast. He appears as himself in *Death in the Afternoon* and in *Green Hills of Africa*, and in *To Have and Have Not* as Harry Morgan, the man who does everything (Freud would say "including die") that Hemingway would like to do. In the first two he is contemplating violence in the most striking forms he can find, at a time when, as he says somewhat regretfully, war is not available; and he is striving to report, still with the greatest possible accuracy, the emotions this violence inspires in him. Between the first book and the second, a further complicating factor intrudes itself. Hemingway now changes from the spectator, central and important, that he is in the bullfighting book; he becomes the participant—in the last two books, it is he who runs the danger and does the killing. It is as if he had come to final dissatisfaction along the line: to watch killing and to experience the associated aesthetic emotion is no longer enough; he must have the actual feel of the kill and the feel of the danger that attends it. On this subject, a passage on hunting is extremely revealing. The hunters have wounded a buffalo which has taken cover, and are waiting for it to charge them:

> This was different, this was no rapid fire, no pouring it on him as he comes groggy out into the open, if he comes now I must be quiet inside and put it down his nose as he comes with the head out. He will have the head down to hook, like any bull, and that will uncover the place where the boys wet their knuckles on and I will get one in there and then must go sideways into the grass and he would be Pop's from then on unless I could keep the rifle when I jumped.

This grows more suggestive the more one studies it. Here is Hemingway, reporting with scruple the emotions he experiences at one of those moments of tension which fascinate him so much. He is waiting to be charged by a dangerous animal, and suddenly his imagination changes him from the hunter, which he is, to a bullfighter, which he isn't. He thinks of shooting down into the buffalo's chest, through between the shoulder blades where the matadors drive their swords, as he has just thought of the other buffalo he has killed in terms of a boxing image, and he has mastered his opponent to the extent that he can walk in and "pour on" punishment for the inevitable knockout. But now suddenly he realizes that this wouldn't work (the verb shifts into the conditional) and that if he goes through with his fantasy, not he but the white hunter with him will kill the buffalo. If Hemingway is telling the truth about his emotions here, the strange confusion of sports involved constitutes a most startling account of a man's wanting to identify himself with three figures of the killer. His wilful placing of himself in the way of violence will turn out later to be the chief reason—among a number—for the failure of *To Have and Have Not*, because it is related to the feeling one has, in reading this novel, that none of its happenings is in any way inevitable.

Meanwhile, we have here also a symptom of the giddy loss of perspective which overcomes Hemingway in the thirties. Almost everything he does is exaggerated. The fine spoofing which is so natural a part of *The Sun Also Rises* and *A Farewell to Arms* now becomes the garrulous joking with the Old Lady interlocutor in *Death in the Afternoon*. The characters, already given to understatement and averse to intellection in the earlier novels, now descend to communication almost on the level of grunting. The tendency to reduce people to the animal level, always present in Hemingway, now results in a situation such as that in *Death in the Afternoon*, wherein the brave, integrity-filled bulls are almost superior, in Hemingway's own scale of human values, to the men who kill them. And the gift for semi-involuntary memory which gave us the page in *The Sun Also Rises* where Jake, light-headed from being knocked out by Cohn, comes back to the hotel feeling as he used to feel coming home after a football game in which he had been kicked in the head—with his feet hardly seeming to touch the dead leaves along the gutter—now enters into the last chapter of *Death in the Afternoon*, from which you learn that Hemingway likes bullfighting in large part because of all the good times he has had in connection with it. Obviously, Hemingway is exploiting himself.

To what extent he is doing so is apparent when even the careful gearing of the report of emotions to the intensity of the emotions themselves, so excellently done in the Burguete incident in *The Sun Also Rises*, now becomes almost a set technique. In the following, watch the emotions rise as Hemingway takes in the whole grace and beauty of the animal he has shot:

> I looked at him, big, long-legged, a smooth gray with the white stripes and the great, curling, sweeping horns, brown as walnut meats, and ivory pointed, at the big ears and the great, lovely maned neck the white chevron between his eyes and the white of his muzzle and I stooped over and touched him to try to believe it . . .

Here the trick is done by the sudden removal of the punctuation, but the total effect is familiar. In *Death in the Afternoon*, the same trick is being used to give you the emotions of a man who shouts at a bull:

> If the bull in the pen below raises his great head with the wide horns, solid-looking and smoothly pointed and the hump of muscle on his neck and shoulders, heavy and wide in repose, rises in a great swelling crest under the black, hairy sheen of his hide and his nostrils widen and he lifts and jerks his horns as he looks toward the spectator then the amateur speaker of bull talk has had a success.

With all this, there remains a determination to tell the truth, to discern faking wherever it may be, that becomes almost pathological. Perhaps more of Hemingway's explanation of bullfighting is devoted to how to tell the fake stuff than to how to recognize the real. The same desire to get at true feeling, and true things, and how for example to kill in the honest and true way, runs through *Green Hills of Africa* and is always linked with the problems of writing: Hemingway's criterion of judgment becomes almost exclusively whether the writing is faked or real, and whether it is written simply enough so that any faking is discernible.

Ironically, for the first time in his career Hemingway himself begins to sound precious. In his earlier writing he mainly prefers direct statement to metaphors, and the rare metaphors the reader notices ring entirely true. For example, the figure in *The Sun Also Rises* which refers the slow, impeded movement of the crowd from the bull ring to the movement of a glacier. Now we get many more figures, some good like the one which refers the smell of sweat to the taste of a brass coin in the mouth, some less striking, like those repeated ones which refer animal's horns to wood, and some as labored as the facetious one in *Death in the Afternoon* which makes "the morning glory . . . a floral monument of lasting endurance." The need for such ornamentation is something new and a little ominous: what worries us is less the presence of the ornaments than the fact that Hemingway should feel he needed them.

The actual shift from the novel to another form of writing had much less in it to worry us. *The Sun Also Rises* and *A Farewell to Arms* are novels only in a very loose sense of the word. Neither of them depends for its effect on the interactions of a group of characters. Jake's emotions are the center of *The Sun Also Rises*, and what happens in the book makes sense only when interpreted by—perhaps rather through—Jake's personality. *A Farewell to Arms* is even more strictly the story of one man; here, even more than in *The Sun Also Rises*, the reader feels the cleft between the primary and secondary figures. Both books have the foreshortening of time which is more properly the privilege of the drama than of the traditional novel—a technique toward which, since Hemingway demonstrated its immense value, American fiction has been striving with remarkable persistence. Back in the nineteenth century, when people like Henry James and Paul Bourget were taking such distinctions seriously, books like these would have been classified as *novelas*. I have some difficulty in feeling any wide gap between books in which Hemingway is reporting upon young men who are in character—tastes, occupations, age—very much like himself, and books in which he drops the pretense of fiction in order to discuss the same materials in definite reference to himself.

And why, to come directly to the main question, do we have to consider *Death in the Afternoon* and *Green Hills of Africa* such failures, anyway? One may not be particularly interested in bullfighting and still find that the considered statement, by an accomplished artist, regarding the effect on his own personality of the study of the world's most stylized form of violence is a document of extraordinary interest, particularly if the artist is making a special effort to see himself clearly at the time. We can also agree with Edmund Wilson that as a book about animals *Green Hills of Africa* is dull, as we can agree with Max Eastman that as a manual of tauromachy *Death in the Afternoon* is silly, and still be passionately interested in Hemingway's report on himself as a killer. I imagine the answer is that we were concerned by the apparent disappearance of a novelist who seemed to be losing his grip. Hemingway himself was aware of the danger and discoursed upon it for the benefit of the German traveler in the beginning of *Green Hills of Africa*. He also seemed to feel the danger of losing his memory for sharply characterized sensations, so essential to his kind of writing. In the books after 1930 he seems disproportionately intent on catching things before he forgets them. Where most of the sensations recorded in the earlier books are sights, he is now noting smells: smells, for example, of the horns of dead animals, of the native villages, of the trail where the buffalo have passed, of trees where baboons have been sitting, of a new shot sable. He tries repeatedly to register the sensation of mixed exhaustion-satisfaction that follows a kill. He studies out each element in the series of sensations that follow the killing of a big antelope: from the spreading in him of the alcohol from the celebrative drink, to the eating of the fresh-killed meat, to all the smells rising around the fire, to the growing relaxation, to wondering whether one of the natives perhaps does not have an available sister. And repeatedly there is the expressed concern lest the sensation be lost before it can be set on paper. All this suggested, as did the various forms of exploitation of himself in which Hemingway was indulging, that still another novelist of promise even greater than his achievement was embarked toward a sterile middle age.

I am much more concerned about these books than about *To Have and Have Not*. I trust that it is possible to qualify as an admirer of Hemingway without having to admire this poor excuse for a novel. Fundamentally it consists of two long short stories, obviously written separately and with only the personality of the hero to hold them together. As short stories, they may or may not belong with Hemingway's best; what is certain is that they do not belong in special proximity to each other. But Hemingway, like so many others in the middle thirties, had seen the Communist vision: *To Have and Have Not* marks his emergence from the let-the-other-people-save-the-world mood into one of class consciousness, and the two stories, poorly glued together, become a class-conscious novel. Thus we get, sandwiched between the story of swordfishing and the story of the Cuban revolutionaries, all the business about the rotten rich, with their masturbations and homosexualities and promiscuities, who haunt the same waters as Hemingway's hero. The great trouble with it all is that nothing Harry Morgan has done had to be done that way. There is no clear connection between the social-economic background and whatever it is that forces Morgan to kill Chinamen and Cubans for a living. He is a buccaneer (not that he is the namesake of two very brilliant characters, Morgan the pirate and Morgan the raider). The book is best read, if it must be read at all, as an adventure story. I do not want to spend much time on it here. Occasionally there are flashes of authentic Hemingway, as for instance in the part where Mr. Johnson hooks, fights and by his own carelessness loses the big marlin; but they are only flashes.

Those of us who really admired Hemingway had reason to be

glad that *To Have and Have Not* was as feeble as it was, and so obviously an improvisation. It really proved nothing that we did not already know about him, and it left still open the great question, whether he really could write another novel as good as the two he already had written.

I hold that *For Whom the Bell Tolls*, which some seem to consider Hemingway's masterpiece, falls short of his best work, and for reasons which justify our earlier concern about the books just discussed.

The subject is ambitious enough in scope to make one mention Tolstoy and Stendhal and the much neglected Zola of *The Debacle*, even though it is focused on one local incident and takes its unity from its interest in the fortunes of one individual. The technical problem involved is the one Stendhal discovered when he had to write about Waterloo: that while the individual sees little, understands less and knows almost nothing of a battle, the only other alternative is to postulate a more or less omniscient observer, with all this implies in the way of calling in post facto and inevitably false-ringing history to complete the panorama. But still, the subject was of the kind Hemingway needed. We know that he felt the challenge, that he felt that writing about war is one of the great tests, if not the greatest test, of a writer. In the sense that Flaubert said "Madame Bovary is me," Robert Jordan is Hemingway; *For Whom the Bell Tolls* is his chance to write on a subject he has lived in his full maturity, and it may be regarded as a full-dress performance.

Like Hemingway's other novels, this story grows out of an initial situation rather than out of the conflict of characters. Jordan has to die, from the start, because the stupid inefficiency and political maundering of the people on his side have to kill him. Golz is a good and intelligent soldier, and Golz has good reasons for putting Jordan in this fix, but Golz is not good enough to defeat the Fascists and his own side also; the irreparable lack of cohesion, the insubordinate and loose-tongued individualism, and the treachery of comrades in arms must throttle the offensive as surely as Jordan must blow the bridge. And if the offensive fails, Jordan will die.

In contrast with the mood of the earlier novels, however, the essential mood of the book is tragic. The characters are caught in a box from which there is no exit except through the inevitable violent catastrophe. We, the readers, know from the start what Robert Jordan suspects but hopes is not true, what he must as long as possible refuse to believe: that this is the last bridge he can ever destroy, that the role in which he has cast himself leads straight to the final and complete solution. The atmosphere—maintained by Hemingway at times through such an illegitimate device as the business of what Pilar sees in Robert's palm—is one of rapidly gathering storm, heightened and driven home by the destruction of El Sordo's group, the defection of Pablo, the threatened defection of Pilar.

Admittedly the tragedy of the book is, in William Empson's sense, pastoral. The characters, Jordan included, are all simpler personalities than is the reader, and fail for this reason to give the reader any feeling that these are people entirely like himself. I suppose that this makes them swains—but certainly not completely creatures of an imaginative convention. Like Steinbeck's Joads they all understand, at least in part, that a Force is driving them to the catastrophe. Jordan has the rich understanding of his plight that marks the tragic hero, even though he is unable to put in words—he is a writer who like Hemingway becomes completely tongue-tied at times—his whole conception of why it is basically right for him to be where he is. And at the end, his understanding of the story becomes one with the reader's, so that the tragic irony—the discrepancy between the hero's understanding of his misfortune and the audience's understanding of it—is resolved. The reader has no trouble in identifying himself satisfactorily with Jordan through their common humanity; he admits that, in true fact, this man's death diminishes him; pity and terror are legitimatized. Thus our emphasis falls less on pastoral than on tragedy.

Meanwhile, the treatment of time is dramatic, and lends itself to the building of the tragedy. I have no doubt that Hemingway was "writing for Hollywood," and that one reason for keeping everything in this book within the scope of four highly-packed days was his wish to be sure the action of the script would not drag. It still remains that this is a way of securing a maximum of dramatic impact on the reader. What the American novel has done to time since 1930 is matter for special study. Faulkner, for example, has managed a telescoping of time which removes him almost from the same world in which Dos Passos and Tom Wolfe did their writing. The reader is focused, in Hemingway here as in Faulkner, on the actual moment of the story, almost on the line at which the future joins the present; his apprehensions center always on what is going to happen in the moment next to come. What is past is handled by movie flashbacks; it is not significant for itself but only for the meaning which it adds to the present action. This is *significant*, rather than *astronomical*, time. We have to accept the fiction, as Robert Jordan wants to accept it when he is with Maria, that a man can live out the meaning of his lifetime in a few revolutions of the hour-hand. It is a fiction, a time-concept, by the way, which we accept unquestioningly in any number of American short stories, including some of Hemingway's own like "The Short and Happy Life of Francis Macomber." Hemingway has not used it in his earlier novels. In fact, the argument that time is fundamentally insignificant is basic to *The Sun Also Rises*, and the only importance of time in *A Farewell to Arms* is related to the cycle of human gestation. But these novels were written before American novelists—Steinbeck, Faulkner, sometimes Caldwell—moved into such close alliance with the drama, including the movie.

So, basically, *For Whom the Bell Tolls* is something akin to tragedy, with an exterior force driving the characters through a swift rush of events to a catastrophic conclusion. But what a mess of extraneous material one has to accept along with the tragedy!

I have more than a mere suspicion that Hemingway's fundamental discipline in writing—which still holds for this book (Robert Jordan has been engaged in writing a "true" book about Spain; the ambition echoes all that Hemingway has said first and last about writing only what one knows, reporting what is seen instead of what one by convention ought to see, feeling only what one actually feels)—stands in basic conflict with the necessities involved in writing a long novel in which there are other important characters than the hero. It is not natural, or lifelike, or "realistic" for Pilar to describe the violent opening of the revolution and the murder of the local Fascists as she does.

> . . . Then the two lines fell back and let him lay the dust over the center of the plaza; the hose sweeping in wide arcs and the water glistening in the sun and the men leaning on their flails or the clubs or the white wood pitchforks and watching the sweep of the stream of water. And then, when the plaza was nicely moistened and the dust settled, the lines formed up again and a peasant shouted, 'When do we get the first Fascist?'

Take this out of quotes and it is straight Hemingway, not Hemingway seeing the thing through his character's eye, but the character seeing it through Hemingway's. As one follows the whole story of the uprising, the feeling grows that it is always Hemingway talking, rather than Pilar, and eventually one comes to wonder what all this is doing in the present story anyway, since it has nothing to do with Robert Jordan's story nor very much to do in revealing the character of Pilar, and is much too much to prove that the sadly shrunken Pablo was at one time a whole man. The fact of the matter is that the uprising is a wonderful invitation to write about particularly shocking violence for its own sake, and one which Hemingway can not resist. I am not here questioning its quality as a detached piece of writing; the point is that it should have been physically detached from *For Whom the Bell Tolls* and included in an appendix. But this would not obviate the whole difficulty. Pilar has not only Hemingway's way of seeing things; she also has his *afición*, has like him frequented bullfights, and we get all the long pages about the declining weeks of the life of Finito, a somewhat latter day version of Juan Maera except that instead of pneumonia Finito has tuberculosis.

There is also a chance that Pablo, like Pilar, is at times merely an aspect of the character of Hemingway. Pablo is the man who can see too clearly how things are going to come out, who loses any fervor he has left and decamps, only to return at the last moment for reasons which he cannot explain very well and to participate in the attack on the bridge. This so clearly sketches the outlines of Hemingway's own career in political liberalism over the years—his participation in making the world safe for Democracy, his subsequent withdrawal (let those who want to save the world), his eventual angry return—as to make it seem that in Pablo Hemingway is expressing a side of himself that he could not well put into Robert Jordan.

Meanwhile the multitudinous garrulity which annoys readers of the Hemingway books of the 1930's now turns up in the interior monologues of Hemingway's hero. Robert Jordan's preoccupation with his family, particularly with the bravery of his Civil War veteran grandfather and the suicide of his father, runs on interminably. He probes the reasons and relives the events, fascinated with the problem of his father's cowardice now that he the son runs such fearless risk of death. Suicide, of course, is a violation of what we have seen as Hemingway's notion of integrity, being a failure either to live with courage against the odds of life or to die with *cojones*, as Jordan himself will die. To this extent Jordan's interior monologue is a continuation of the longer discussion of courage that has always bemused Hemingway, and the subject has grown on him just as boyhood reminiscence has grown on him—compare Jordan's verbose flashbacks to American boyhood with the brief one in *The Sun Also Rises* where Jake remembers how he felt after the high school football game. The fact of the matter seems to be that over the years Hemingway, whose earlier work had been extremely reticent even when the basic material—especially in the early short stories—was palpably autobiographical, has given way to the romantic need for confession, has become an *homme qui se raconte.*

This is too bad, because all this is just another way of saying that Hemingway's personality, his basic exhibitionism, foils his intent as artist. Obviously the great departure of this book from his earlier ones is that here he is attempting a work with scope enough to hold important characters other than himself. He has not tried this before. Nick Adams in the short stories, Jake, Frederic Henry, and Harry Morgan are, as I have already pointed out, in one way or another facets of Hemingway's public personality; but this does not seem particularly illegitimate in the respective situations in which they appear. In *For Whom the Bell Tolls*, on the other hand, there is a feeling almost of frustration as the author peeks in turn out of each of his major characters. The people who stand alone are the minor ones: Sordo, Anselmo, Augustin, Karkov. The less we see the character, the less he looks like Hemingway.

Except, of course, Maria. The obsession to write about sex has grown in proportion to the size of Hemingway's books, and less appropriate to the stories as it has grown. What there is of sex in *The Sun Also Rises* is entirely necessary to the story and thus appropriate; in *A Farewell to Arms* it is basic to the plot and thus unobjectionable as matter, even though the manner has at times been criticized as adolescent. By the time we get to *To Have and Have Not*, however, the bed passages come in because the author wants them rather than from any necessity of his art; and finally in the latest novel Hemingway simply lets the war go hang during the intervals of the sleeping bag. I do not deny that there is some poignance in Jordan's experience. He has waited until the eve of death to discover a good thing, and having found it, must now lose it. But these entr'actes of the tragedy use up very nearly a quarter of the book. Here again, Hemingway's personal interests intrude upon the story; personality and basic discipline clash.

One regrets these things because otherwise the book is so good. The chapter relating how Sordo and his companions make their last stand is one of the clean, hard, sharp-focused jobs that Hemingway does at his best. The actual blowing up of the bridge is as successful as the Burguete episode in *The Sun Also Rises.*

The testimony of the book points not to a decline, but to the failure of certain powers to develop. The long list of reasons why American novelists peter out after brilliant beginnings, which Hemingway compiled at the behest of the German admirer in the first pages of *Green Hills of Africa*, contains nothing especially applicable to his own case. From the beginning he has been concerned less with the relations between human beings than with the relations between himself—or some projection of himself—and a harsh and mainly alien universe, in which violence, suffering and death are the rule, and which, in terms of what the human being expects of it, stubbornly refuses to make sense. This preoccupation could and did make for the writing of good books, but *For Whom the Bell Tolls* is not of their number.

Thus we are brought finally to conclude that the best Hemingway was the Hemingway we imitated for a generation, even though we imitated him for the wrong reasons. The sad corollary is that this forces us to class the later Hemingway as one of the more successful imitators of the Hemingway who contrived the ride to Burguete and Frederic Henry's retreat from war to love.

JOHN PEALE BISHOP

The Missing All

1948

Allen Tate in the first of his recent "Reactionary Essays," speaking of the tradition of Puritan theocracy as it was finally reflected in the poetry of Emily Dickinson, has this to say: "Socially, we may not like the New England idea. Yet it had an immense, incalculable value for literature: it dramatized the human soul."

This is quite true. In those allegories which we call his novels, Hawthorne is concerned only with spiritual conflicts. But Hawthorne came late; before the Civil War his New England was already on the decline. Salem harbor was not empty: the clipper ships, still increasing in speed, scudded, all whiteness, on the farthest oceans; brigantines called with a Yankee twang among the Malayan islands; and captains from Bristol still occasionally caught a profitable black cargo on the Gold Coast of Africa. But

From *The Collected Essays of John Peale Bishop*. Copyright 1948 by Charles Scribner's Sons. Reprinted by permission of the publisher. This essay originally appeared in *The Virginia Quarterly Review*, Winter, 1937. Vol. 13, No. 1.

the land, once neglected for the sea, was being abandoned for a western promise. The mercantile class was destined to go down before the mill-owners, for they, no more than the farmers, could withstand the necessities of the time. "The Scarlet Letter" is fine, intense, austere, but already a little strangely so. Hawthorne is at his best looking backward.

The great seventeenth-century certitude of God is gone. Emily Dickinson seldom came down to the parlor when there were guests in the house at Amherst.

> The missing All prevented me
> From missing minor things.
> If nothing larger than a World's
> Departure from a hinge,
> Or Sun's extinction be observed,
> 'Twas not so large that I
> Could lift my forehead from my work
> For curiosity.

This is magnificent. And it is New England. There the summer is brief, and after, the bedrooms are chilly. They admitted, however, "a polar privacy." Upstairs, in New England, the soul was still intact.

But already Ohio had been settled with white villages dominated by a spire. New England moved westward; men and women followed the course of the rivers into Illinois, and mounted the currents, flooded yellow in spring, into the forests of Michigan. With them went the New England idea.

2

In the summer of 1922, in Paris, Ezra Pound told me about a young newspaper correspondent who had written some stories. Pound had not then renounced discovery; he had a restless passion for literature which led him to seek it out wherever it might be. And presently he took me to the rue Cardinal Lemoine, where I followed him up five flights of narrow winding stairs. At the top, answering the poet's knock against a door under the roof, came a stalwart, smiling, good-looking young man. It was he, Pound said, who had written the stories. His name was Ernest Hemingway. As he led us into his apartment, I saw that he limped badly.

We did not stay long. On the way back across the Left Bank, Pound told me that the limping young man had been with the Italians during the war and, when his trench was blown up, wounded and, covered by falling dirt, left four days for dead.

3

Just how old Scott Fitzgerald was when I first met him is a question. He afterwards said that he had lied so often about his age that he had to bring his old nurse on from Saint Paul in order himself to know in just what year he had been born. He was, as nearly as I can make out, seventeen; but even then he was determined to be a genius, and since one of the most obvious characteristics of genius was precocity, he must produce from an early age. He did, but wanted through vanity to make it even earlier.

Long afterwards, I complained to him that I thought he took seventeen as his norm, making everything later a falling off. For a moment he demurred, then said, "If you make it fifteen, I will agree with you."

He had, like myself, only arrived in Princeton; the Commons for Freshmen was not yet open; we sat side by side at a large round table in a corner at the Peacock Inn. It was the first time I had gone out alone, for in those opening days we stuck very close to the boys who had come down from school with us. It was by chance that I sat next to this youth so quick to conversation; we stayed on when the others had gone. In the leafy street outside the September twilight faded; the lights came on against the paper walls, where tiny peacocks strode and trailed their tails among the gayer foliations. I learned that Fitzgerald had written a play which had been performed at school. Places were cleared; other students sat down at the tables around us. We talked of books: those I had read, which were not many, those Fitzgerald had read, which were even less, those he said he had read, which were many, many more. It was the age at which we were discovering Meredith and the writers of the Yellow Book. Wells had not yet come, but to the youth from Saint Paul it was soon clear that Compton Mackenzie had.

Fitzgerald was pert and fresh and blond, and looked, as some one said, like a jonquil. He scribbled in class, or sat in an apparent dreaming drowse, from which he was startled from time to time by a question which he had only half heard. Though he arrived at what seemed a clever way of stalling until he could at least guess what had been asked him ("It all depends on how you look at it. There is the subjective and the objective point of view."), it did not prevent his being dropped from the class. He had an ailment, which served as excuse for his departure. Like so many precocious literary talents, he had, I believe, a tendency to tuberculosis. When he returned, it was, so far as the registrar of Princeton was concerned, to take his place in another class. I saw as much of him as ever, perhaps more, for his ambitious political career on the campus had been damaged by his absence.

He left Princeton without a degree and without much of an education; but he had with him the material for two novels. The first, "The Romantic Egoist," not many have seen in its entirety beside myself, a few old school friends who appeared in it, and the unwilling publishers. It was written on Saturday nights and Sunday afternoons at the Officers' Club at Fort Leavenworth, Kansas, where he was stationed during a period of training as Second Lieutenant in the regular Army. Scraps of it were saved, trimmed, and refurbished to appear here and there as patches in "This Side of Paradise," a book which, when it appeared, was reviewed by one of the author's Princeton friends, T. K. Whipple, as The Collected Works of F. Scott Fitzgerald. So it was, for the time being, for not a line from any of those poems scribbled in lecture halls, if it chanced to be good, had been wasted.

4

Some of his earliest stories Hemingway wrote lying on a bed in a roof-sharpened room which once had provided shelter for Verlaine in his last decrepit and drunken years. After the war, which Hemingway had seen fought, with terrible retreats, on the Italian front, he passed as newspaper correspondent from line to line of the Turkish-Greek War; talked to the Greek King; heard at the Quai d'Orsay what the French Foreign Office wanted the reporters to hear; saw in the Ruhr a good deal that Poincaré did not want him to see. Between times, he drank with the other reporters in the bars of the rue Daunou. He ranged from Pamplona to Kansas City, but always came back to Paris. Much of his writing was done there, and perhaps only there could he have developed a perfect consciousness of his craft. From Pound, he learned the lesson of Flaubert, profiting by it only because of his innate honesty, his incorruptible subjection to his art. He dislikes, with strange intensity for a writer who has successfully surmounted every one he has undergone, to admit influence. Mark Twain apart, there is none that he freely owns. Yet in those years he read Turgeniev and Defoe, masters both of straight narrative, and Marryat, and showed his sound instinct by learning from the Joyce of "Dubliners" and discarding, with immense admiration, the Joyce of "Ulysses." Yet it was Sherwood Anderson of the Ohio Valley, and Gertrude Stein, who sat among the Picassos like a monument of home, who taught the young Hemingway to write as an American. It was from his own speech that he made his admirable prose.

Fitzgerald came over for the second time in 1924. We had a late and confused lunch at Armenonville in the Bois, the green of early summer making a calm background for the disturbed waiters. His wife and child were with him, and it was very hard to order satisfactorily for a little girl in so expensive a restaurant. Fitzgerald, to quiet her, took out his shoestring and gave it to her with a handful of French coins to play with on the gravel under the tables.

He was on his way to the Riviera, which was not then, as it soon became, a summer resort. "The Great Gatsby" was written at Saint Raphael, and that other novel, which was to consume nine years in the writing and accumulate as a trunkful of manuscript before he called it "Tender is the Night," was started at Juan-les-Pins. It is an uneven and at times unnecessary romantic book; yet, crowded with incident, it is as complete a record as any yet written of the discordant doings of Americans abroad in that decade.

5

"All modern American literature comes out of one book by Mark Twain called 'Huckleberry Finn,'" Hemingway allows himself to say in a conversation in "The Green Hills of Africa." And to insist upon it he adds: "All American writing comes from that. There was nothing before. There has been nothing as good since."

And Fitzgerald, toward the end of "The Great Gatsby," has his narrator meditate on the tragedy which has just occurred and remark that all the principals have come out of the Middle West. The body of Gatsby, after the bullet, floats on the bathing mattress around the artificial pool on his Long Island estate. But all that had made the life of Gatsby had come out of the Midwest. This return toward the East was one of the factors that made the time. The Midwesterner had become the American. He was ready to deny the authenticity of any compatriot not of his kind. Sinclair Lewis's Babbitt had superseded an older conception which Henry James had dared call "The American."

Fitzgerald and Hemingway belong to what was in its day the Younger Generation. It was certainly not the first to be called so, but it was the first to gain capitals from the press. And, as Malcolm Cowley has pointed out, it was really the first literary generation in America. There had been groups before, but they were not united by a communion of youth, a sense of experiences shared and enemies encountered simply because they happened to have been born within certain years. They were those who were of an age to be combatant when America declared war on the Central Powers.

Not all of them fought; but most of them had of their own choice supported a uniform of some sort. When they returned from arms, it was in revolt. What they protested against was called Puritanism, which is a fairer name than it deserves; for the enemy was the New England idea, not in its original purity, but in that corrupt state to which it had arrived through the hundred and more years in which the West was settled.

The pioneer had not gone into the wilderness empty-handed. For beyond those two instruments of the Puritan condemnation of nature, the rifle and the axe, he carried the New England idea. In the shadow of the forest, something of his intellectual toughness was shed. When at last the pioneer strode out on the prairies, his skin was toughened by the sun and the rain; he was hardened to the bone; his distrust of nature had not lessened. That hatred of death which is behind the Puritan hatred of life was still with him, but through varying vicissitudes was lost. The meaning of Puritanism is a contempt for mortality; in the Midwest it was forgotten.

The New England idea had never provided the new country with a particularly satisfactory morality. Along the seaboard, it was counterbalanced by other forces, inherited decencies, values transmitted and transmuted, some brought by sailing vessels, all altered by these shores. There was, in brief, a culture, rather cold, but flowering nevertheless in a lovely and inclement air. But across the Appalachians, New England began to go bad. It needed the strictness of the village, it demanded the sense of the community. Else it was disembodied. Beyond the mountains, in the limitless expanse of the West, it was not all wrong. But it certainly was not so good.

Mark Twain has shown its shortcomings. To him, it was all meanness and hypocrisy, so that his serious work is one long protest against a morality that neither aided goodness nor sustained honesty. Huckleberry Finn, who is his creator's exponent of natural morality, becomes in Missouri a notoriously bad boy. All is reversed, so that Huck himself is almost convinced that he is lost.

So long ago did the Midwesterner decide that New England morality was inadequate. But with what could he oppose it, unless with conceptions which had been shaped for him, as for all Americans, in Concord and by Walden Pond? The Midwesterner was self-reliant, he had a profound trust in the natural goodness, the sanctity almost, of unrestricted man. If we look closely, we shall see his beliefs return, altered but recognizable, not only in the "Green Hills of Africa," but in all of Hemingway. We shall find them as well in Fitzgerald.

They came from all over, those who made up the Younger Generation, but it is scarcely an accident that those I consider here as its spokesmen had their origin in the Middle West. There were others, no doubt, who equalled them in talent. But the time was favorable to Hemingway and Fitzgerald. They had, as Hemingway was to say later of the garbage men of Havana, the viewpoint. And more than any others who wrote in prose, they succeeded in communicating their emotional attitudes to their contemporaries. They were never consciously regional, as a somewhat older lot of Middle Western writers were: Masters, Sandburg, and the Anderson of those years when Mr. Mencken was proclaiming that Chicago was the literary capital of America. They had no need to be. They could, as Middle Westerners, assume that they were the country. And in many ways they were right. "Wait and see," Masters had written, not all ironically, in 1918, "Spoon River shall be Americee." And now Middletown was spreading from coast to coast its monstrous and monotonous regimentation of mediocrity. Besides, the Younger Generation were conscious of belonging nowhere. How could they have a place in space, whose roots, whether deliberately or through the uncontrolled accident of war, had been destroyed in time?

They converged on Chicago, and one or two, I believe, stayed there. They came to New York, and once so far, found it as simple to cross the Atlantic as to survive in that costly city. From Land's End to the Golden Horn they scattered; carried, as it were a knapsack, their childhood through the Alps; saw girls with print dresses over their starving nakedness throw themselves from bridges of Vienna; saw the hungry eyes of boys, ready for depravity, in the underworld of Berlin; saw the collapse of empires. Some sought the more than sunny warmth of the Mediterranean; some reached Persia; a few, even in those years, penetrated Russia. The world was in throes, but, like the Magi in Eliot's poem, when they had come to the end of their journey, they did not know whether it was a birth or a death they had come for. But most Paris attracted them. In the international intellectual ferment there, they were variously aware of their century, increasingly conscious that they were creatures of its catastrophes. There it seemed possible to know what was happening: not that the event was likely to take place there—Paris was too old; but because it was old and sensitive with a very long memory, it seemed possible that the import of the event would be known there sooner than elsewhere. The collapse of the New England idea was only one more loss in the spiritual débâcle of the times. Meanwhile, one could eat on the sidewalks of Paris, drink at every corner, make love in the streets, under the trees.

6

In Fitzgerald the romantic will is strong, all its pursuits subject to disillusionment. In his novels, these pursuits are many, and love is among them, particularly the first loves of endowed youth, prolonging anticipation, delaying those satisfactions which are of the feelings rather than the senses. For his young men are assuaged by what stirs them, the scents, dresses, the slippers of silver and gold. He lingers with knowledge over these adolescent sentiments, confined, like those nostalgic dance tunes which recur through his pages, to the shortest of seasons. Obviously he prefers these young attachments, in which the emotion, part vanity, part desire, has been just felt and is not yet proved by performance. He has not, however, evaded his responsibilities as a novelist; he has seen his lovers through, to tell what becomes of them later. Afterwards come the broker's office, the bank, the racket; the sad young men take to drink; successful or failures, they know the discouragements of a predatory civilization. For let no one be mistaken: though love is always in the foreground in the sentimental world of Fitzgerald, no allure is so potent as money.

"The rich are not as we are." So he began one of his early stories. "No," Hemingway once said to him, "they have more money."

This belief, continually destroyed, constantly reasserted, underlies all that Fitzgerald has written. It made him peculiarly apt to be the historian of the period. Those who have wealth have an assurance that those without cannot hope to have; they dance, they play, they marry none but the loveliest girls; they beget their own kind. They dare where the others falter. Pretty much anything goes, so long as there is money. At their worst, the successful will still have the air "of having known the best of this world." They must have spiritual possessions to match their material accumulations.

That the rich are a race apart is a current and not always complimentary assumption. In the Midwest where Fitzgerald grew up, it was the common dream that riches made the superior person. To the acquisitive powers all others would be added. His America, at least in recollection, was that country which, with a sort of ignorant corruption, could profess its love for Lincoln, while completely satisfying the appetites of James K. Hill. And worse than Hill. The Great Gatsby is the Emersonian man brought to completion and eventually to failure; he has returned to the East; the conditions which could tolerate his self-reliant romanticism no longer exist.

Fitzgerald partakes of that dream and is too intelligent not to know it for what it is worth. One can scarcely say that he thinks; like the Rosemary in "Tender is the Night," his "real depths are Irish and romantic and illogical." He has an uncanny touch for probing his own or another's weakness; politically ignorant, he can see much that ails society. He gave as no other American writer the expensive charm, the sensational display of the post-war decade, but began counting the cost long before the bills came in. He made money, and like Gatsby remained an intruder in the moneyed world; he admired it and would have liked to be a part of it; and yet with every passing year it becomes more difficult for him to face it. He has learned the price of everything, and is not a cynic, but a moody sentimentalist who gives himself a very bad time. At heart, he is a prude and suffers from remorse. For Fitzgerald, brought up as a Catholic, cannot but recognize damnation when he sees it. His Nicole, irresponsible, heartless, beautiful, and mad, crosses herself reverently with Chanel Number 5.

7

The story that Ezra Pound told me in the taxicab was that Ernest Hemingway, at nineteen, had been dead and brought to life again. He had lain four days under the débris of the trench, which is one day longer underground than Lazarus. I do not doubt Pound's word, but I have never asked Hemingway to substantiate the story and it is not in his writings, as almost everything else from his youth is. Even if it should not conform to fact, it would still be true. It was true for a great part of Hemingway's generation.

It was his awareness of death that separated Hemingway from the Middle West. The West had never known what the war was about; Hemingway returned from it like Krebs in that story which is the best account written by an American of the returned soldier. Krebs found all communication with his family impossible. He sat on the front porch and saw the girls that walked on the other side of the street. "He liked the look of them much better than the French or the German girls. But the world they were in was not the world he was in." He could not talk to any of them. The Midwest had never, like the lady in Amherst, known what it was to die every day it lived. Behind the Puritan hatred of life was always the hatred of death. That alone gave it excuse and dignity.

It was in a Midwestern town that the old prizefighter of "The Killers" merely waited for death. Lying on a slovenly bed, he waits for nothing but the courage to get up and go downstairs to take what is coming to him in the street from the two men who also wait, with black gloves and hands in the bulging pockets of their tight black overcoats. It was the first of the gangster stories, and was never bettered. Hemingway concentrates not on the killing, but on the apprehension of the old double-crosser on the bed.

Presently, Hemingway was to be found in Spain, seeking to learn from the bullfighters how it is a man confronts death on the sunny sand with skill and beauty and discipline. For in the *corrida* he saw his own apprehension reduced to a ritual, publicly performed, more violent than any ritual of the Church, and more immediate, since it was concerned only with the body, its courage and control. It was because of their tragic sense that the bullfighters were utterly alive; Hemingway's famous remark about them has been misinterpreted as an admiration for mere toughness. But his real meaning is made clear if we see how, in "The Sun Also Rises," he plays his other characters—Americans, British, Jews—of the contemporary world against his Spaniards. Plenty of things can happen to his drunken expatriates, but nothing they do, nothing that is done to them, can have any significance. For they are all of them, amusing as they are, aimless and will-less; they are so completely devoid of spiritual life that neither stupefying drink nor the aware intelligence can save them. The Spanish Romero, young and courteous, is there for lively contrast. He is as far as anyone could be from a tough guy.

The most tragic thing about the war was not that it made so many dead men, but that it destroyed the tragedy of death. Not only did the young suffer in the war, but every abstraction that would have sustained and given dignity to their suffering. The war made the traditional morality inacceptable; it did not annihilate it; it revealed its immediate inadequacy. So that at its end, the survivors were left to face, as they could, a world without values.

Conscious of this as he is, Hemingway is, among his contemporaries, incomparably conscious of the art of prose. He seems to have known throughout what he had to do; and that was, as he discovered on the bed in Verlaine's old room, to find out in any given incident what really had happened. It is the mark of the true novelist that in searching the meaning of his own unsought experience, he comes on the moral history of his time. It is a hard task, and one that requires great scrupulousness; it is not one that can be generously undertaken while serving a cause.

Hemingway's accomplishment will, I think, stand. It has an historical, as it has a literary importance. It is idle to predict for posterity, but what he has done should give him a place in American literature as sure as that of—to name a writer he admires not at all—the New England Nathaniel Hawthorne. For it was given to Hawthorne to dramatize the human soul. In our time, Hemingway wrote the drama of its disappearance.

8

To those returning from the war, the New England idea appeared no more favorable than it had to Mark Twain. It showed as meanness and hypocrisy and repression; it had crossed the continent and was everywhere. So now, to every revolt that had been started against it, intensity was added. The war had removed young men from families and all the ordinary restraints of society, and had given them to the army which imposed strange new restrictions of its own. It left them impatient of all discipline and profoundly distrustful of the very words which had once been used to signify virtue. They returned from whatever danger they had been in to find the country made safe, remarkably safe, for complacency. Their lives had been salted by the taste of death. They thought they had now a right to lead them. Returning, they found an opposition in control decidedly prepared to deny this. For neither had their opponents come unchanged through the war. They had discovered, or so they thought, better means and more competent to prohibit, to cast out, our corruptible nature. Intolerance had new screws and they would twist them. Never had the old Puritanism looked so strong. It was about to collapse.

It was precisely because all spirit had gone out of it that Puritanism had now resorted to laws, depending on the police to enforce what the conscience would no longer command.

Against all this, then in his earliest twenties, Fitzgerald appeared, proclaiming anew the inalienable rights to liberty and the pursuit of happiness. Handsome, gifted, fortunate, he made himself for a time the embodiment of youth's protest against the inhibitions and conventions of an outworn morality. He had allies, and quickly found followers. Sincerity for hypocrisy, spontaneity in the place of control, freedom for repression—who could resist such a program? The response was prodigious. Success, as we know, was only less immediate. The faults in that program were not so soon apparent.

Only one of them can I comment on here. With all respect for the original author of the phrase, happiness cannot be pursued. At least not so rapidly as the Younger Generation demanded. Sensation can. No man can say, I will be happy at such an hour. He can perfectly well say, I intend to get drunk tonight, and if only he has money, or friends, to pay for his drinks, by midnight be as drunk as he pleases, in spite of all prohibitions. In this discrepancy between happiness and dissipation lies, I should say, something of the history of the 1920's in America.

The decade was over when Fitzgerald wrote an essay which was a sort of farewell to it.

"Contemporaries of mine," he wrote of those years, "had

begun to disappear into the dark maw of violence. A classmate killed his wife and himself on Long Island, another tumbled 'accidentally' from a skyscraper in Philadelphia, another purposely from a skyscraper in New York. One was killed in a speakeasy in Chicago; another was beaten to death in a speakeasy in New York and crawled home to the Princeton Club to die; still another had his skull crushed by a maniac in an asylum where he was confined. These are not catastrophes that I went out of my way to look for—these were my friends; moreover, these things happened not during the depression but during the boom."

This is not exaggerated: I could put names to most of these catastrophes and for every one I cannot name I could offer three out of my acquaintances. All these were excellent people, personable companions. Morally, they were, perhaps, the last romantics, and it may be that the worst enemy the romantic has to fear is time. Or it may be that like the earlier Romantics, they did not know enough. But at least they knew their own predicament.

9

This account may conclude with a short note on John O'Hara, for, though he is not properly speaking one of the Younger Generation (he was fifteen at the time of the Armistice), he shows in his novels something of the conclusion of its history.

O'Hara has been affected by both Hemingway and Fitzgerald, though the influence is not particularly literary. According to a passage in his writing which may be taken as autobiographical, he read them at that impressionable age when all reading tends to become an imaginary extension of experience. His world, as we see it in his novels, is that of the Younger Generation, no longer so young, but still sustaining a fiction of youth. It has been supplemented by those who were boys and girls when the soldier's pole had fallen and who, at bars, are level now with men.

It is a world of country clubs and speakeasies, manufactured in Detroit, where in the 1920's the frontier took its last stand and for a time paid tremendous dividends, for though there was less of nature to exploit, there was more of humankind. It runs, this world, as it has been said the motors of the future will do, on alcohol. We are in the prosperity of Mr. Coolidge, the depression of Mr. Hoover.

Here are the loves of Fitzgerald turned into quick adulteries on the seats of parked cars or in the apartments of Park Avenue, the freedoms that have run to perversions, lost happinesses, and lives mechanized out of all meaning. That consciousness of death which pervades so much of Hemingway's writing has here become that *goût du suicide* which gave a special savor to the decade. It is fitting that the Appointment in Samara should be kept in a garage: Death could not come more appropriately than in the fumes of a running motor. In Hemingway, the emotions that are not there are a silence underlying all sound, a lack which, once felt, constantly gives poignancy to the whole. But in the world of John O'Hara, these emotions are not even missed. His plots have a mechanical perfection, which well they may, for nothing from within moves these people. They merely react, like Behaviorists' dogs, to certain stimuli; they have appetites, they come into heat, they suffer from sex as from a last disagreement of nature. One imagines their emotional connections as having been put through by the telephone operator of Butterfield-8. It is a mere matter of putting in and taking out plugs. The rest is conversation. For when, as in his latest novel, O'Hara would give us a human emotion, the episode falls flat; any affair which involves love is nothing more than a schoolboy recollection. It does not, in this world cannot, exist.

It is the world of the Younger Generation played out to the doom. These are the lost people: they are below moral condemnation. The Missing All is no longer missed.

EDWIN BERRY BURGUM

Ernest Hemingway and the Psychology of the Lost Generation

1949

Ernest Hemingway's first published novel was *The Sun Also Rises*. But if chronology be determined by content, his second novel, *A Farewell to Arms*, has prior claim. It is the story of a soldier in love in the First World War. Hospitalized for a wound in the knee during the Italian campaign, this American officer falls in love with his nurse after the usual manner of soldiers. His intentions are not altogether honorable, since war leaves men no alternative but to gather rosebuds before they fall. The casualness of such friendships, bound to be ruptured as the furlough ends and death or distance calls, debases love into the sensuality of the moment; and youth, ardent for ever more varied experiences, responds. But before experience has accumulated into the cynicism of habit, there is a period of flexibility. If events permit the acquaintance to continue, acquaintance may make the heart grow fonder. So it chances with these two. The long convalescence encouraged a qualitative change. With each meeting, sensuality is further absorbed into a richer distillation of mutual interests. The crude barbarism of war, the disintegration of retreating armies, no longer holds the officer in its sinister spell. It fades into a background for the integration of love. The indifference to conventions induced by the war survives only in the rejection of the importance of the marriage tie, though the girl's initiative in this rejection is perhaps intended by Hemingway to suggest a fear that events may make the relation temporary after all. So, in fact, it turns out, to the soldier's consternation. Both woman and child die in childbirth; and he leaves the hospital for a world that has become empty of warmth and meaning.

On the whole this novel is written in a more awkward style than any other work of Hemingway's. Only in the scenes given over to the war does the writing reach his usual level. If the well-known scenes of the Italian retreat are better told than the love affair, the hindsight of the critic may now find in this discrepancy a prediction that Hemingway will never be able to express any profound and positive emotions. But the crude impulsiveness of the dialogue between the lovers, even the colorless banality of much of it, at least registers his determination to avoid the sentimental.

Despite these faults, *A Farewell to Arms* remains an outstanding example of good fiction of wartime in its freedom from the emotional meretriciousness which the hysteria of war often stimulates. Against a conviction that war, however necessary, is like racketeering, a dirty business in which one would prefer not to be involved, the narrative proceeds on an even keel, of facing the facts without turning either toward a specious idealism to cover them up or into an opposite reaction of pessimism, which would expose an incapacity to cope with them. Indeed, ideals of any validity are but an occasional echo in this novel amid the clamor of the egocentric. Enough that one is doing the job assigned at a great personal inconvenience and with no little show of manliness. But the spare time of the soldier is his own, and he will turn in it to the predilections he cherished at home. And though pursued at an increased tempo, they are not always vicious. The novel has become a classic statement of the psychology of the soldier of our generation both in his new profession and in his private life. It shows that the healthy attitudes of peace may survive the devastating attack that war makes upon our normal standards, holding before the reader this possibility in anticipation of its denial in the *Brick Fox-Holes* and *Shore Leaves* of the Second World War. At the end of the book it is not war but chance that plunges the soldier into gloom.

When, however, the book as a whole has been deposited in the memory, a shift of interpretation is likely to occur. And it is identical with our reaction in real life to the memory of such an experience. By involuntary association, the frustration in love, though not logically related to the war, is bound to become so psychologically, and we blame the war for personal consequences for which it was not responsible. The strangling of hope in love, which had in fact been a relief from despondency in war, not only in effect lands one where *Shore Leave* begins, but all the more bitterly since there is no escaping this false association. For these reasons this realistic novel, which shows no trace of symbolism or nuance of larger meanings, becomes a single sufficient symbol of the frame of mind in which modern wars leave the citizens of the democracies. What in the novel is the escape from the cynicism set up by the retreating armies into the awakening of love that dies to reduce the soldier to a more intense cynicism: this becomes the statement of an emotional pattern which some of those who fought in the First World War (and some of those in the Second) accepted as symbolic of a quite different content. What such men "loved," what afforded them hope in contradiction to the sordidness of the immediate task, was their belief in its social ideals. When, at its ending, they became aware that the settlement of the peace spelt the death of their hopes or, more selfishly, provided no opportunity to translate their abstract ideals into a job and security for themselves, then hope collapsed, became a vain memory, just as love died in the novel, and left men adrift in a world they had not made.

From this point of view, *A Farewell to Arms* gives the history of those basic emotional reactions which culminated in the maladies of the postwar generation, and marks Hemingway, from the outset of his career, as pre-eminently the novelist of the "lost generation" of the twenties. More specifically, he was the novelist of the expatriate Americans. For the "lost generation" as a whole did not know it was lost. Most of the American soldiers returned, concealing their dubieties under a show of recklessness. But, absorbed into the American Legion and fortified by the false hope of a revival of prosperity, they recovered from their discontent and lived in fantastic expectations until the Depression brought them to their senses. The expatriates had been in their senses all along, to the extent at least that their cynicism formed an emotional pattern which, though not consciously related to the real consequences of the peace, actually corresponded to them as they were disclosed after a time by the economic collapse of both Europe and the United States, the rise of fascism, and the outbreak of the Second World War. It would be idle to say that their frame of mind had any overt justification in so accurate an understanding of the international situation. Their freedom from illusion, nevertheless, was in conformity with the underlying facts, and provided them thus much of a sound basis for facing the ills of the world: that they were determined never again to be fooled by false promises.

Meanwhile the cynicism that was uppermost in this minority of veterans produced a new type of American personality, which it was Hemingway's distinction to translate into fiction. In a general sense this new personality was a variant of a change of attitude common to the postwar generation everywhere. Everywhere save in the United States, men felt restless, at cross purposes with themselves and the world. A grudge had grown in them because the war had disturbed their normal expectation from life at an age when these were keenest and most promising. Not knowing precisely who or what was to blame, they had an impulse to blame anybody or anything. But, sensing the folly of such petulance, they sought to control it by camaraderie with the like-minded. Many of them who were well educated sought relief also in a hectic pursuit of new theories, esthetic movements, any intellectual activity that offered the illusion of an aim in life. By such a show of activity they often succeeded in concealing their despondency both from themselves and others. Sometimes, indeed, they projected their inner conflict upon the world at large, and then took ironic cheer in the discovery that their projection conformed to the facts. Vaguely they craved the aid of some revolutionary movement which the perverse anarchism of their spirit would embrace only to reject, after their manner in personal friendship.

Such a personality is caught in a conflict between rebelliousness and a sense of its futility; and the American variant of the type, as seen in the difference between the characters of Hemingway and Aldous Huxley, was an emphasis upon rebelliousness which demolished class distinctions. The men in the English writer's novels for the most part have accepted their hopeless state. Typically, they submitted to the aggressiveness of women and were horrified at the fascist implications of aggressiveness in men. Their inner turmoil was less intense. They seemed to take a sad pleasure in awareness of their impotence, of their being borne this way and that by less reliable breezes than Shelley had in mind. When they acted, if it was not a fling to the opposite extreme of sadism in love and fascism in politics, it was a febrile splutter which soon burned out. Their normal state was to be as receptive to sin as a saint to virtue.

The American variant, on the contrary, is best defined as the degeneration of the frontier tradition. Indeed, Paris was to these expatriates the last frontier, where nothing counted but the assertion of the individual spirit. Since the American of those days always had money enough to pay, or friends who had, his ego could expand, find friendship everywhere, and meet no opposition except from his friends. Still fundamentally aggressive, he was involved in constant quarrels and reconciliations, and he accepted the equality of women by treating them as though they were men and expecting to be treated likewise. Unlike the Englishman who despised the poor because he was afraid of them, his American counterpart felt superior to distinctions of class or education. Where the Englishman satisfied his ego by the range of his ideas alone, the American demanded also range of friendship, and was therefore a more active person. But activity actually diminished the intensity of any single interest, whether an experiment in painting or the pursuit of love. It was a method by which he concealed both his inner conflicts and his hatred of them. Since he refused to play the passive role of the English sophisticate, his unhappiness was a more positive state, and apathy a sign of exhaustion rather than the consolation of self-pity. But both were fundamentally alike in the deeper apathy of distrust of their own abilities.

In either case, very few of these turmoils got through to the surface. These expatriate Americans, in particular, had learned one lesson from the aristocratic tradition which the frontier tradition could not provide. They had learned the use of manners, as an attempt at control of the disorderly emotions within. Proud of their sophistication, they refused to acknowledge the aimlessness of their lives. They imposed upon their random activities so rigid a control as to provide an illusion of purpose, even of heroism, since the façade of manners enabled them to confuse a sporadic impulse with a profound emotion. Thus they were proud never to wear their hearts upon their sleeves, forgetful that it was not the heart at all that sought the limelight but some whim whose suddenness they confused with intensity and which would as suddenly disappear. To keep a stiff upper lip was their most valid rule, affording them a specious unction of manhood, carrying over into their frivolous peacetime pursuits the stoicism of the soldier to grin and bear. Actually the inner turmoil broke through the purpose of the façade by becoming stylized as a part of it. For this code of manners had overtones of irony and indeed of hatefulness; so that there was always in it a contradiction between either the crisp assault of the phrase as sound and its careful understatement of meaning, or the pugnacity of meaning and its apparent check by the firm control of the utterance.

This façade of language, in fact, whose intonation seemed so aristocratic, was, when analyzed for more essential elements, actually derived from the other end of the social scale. It was only the typical speech of the proletariat, taken over and stylized, as the last step in a process long under way in the speech of the American collegian and his elder brother, the sportsman of the mature world. The underprivileged classes, both here and abroad, had long been in a frame of mind into which the war had driven these better educated and financed gentlemen from the best American colleges. They had long felt themselves without a future, at the mercy of forces beyond their control. No training in bourgeois mores, no seduction by bourgeois comforts, had purged away the pugnacious directness of their utterance. A mood of rebellion paralyzed by a deeper sense of insecurity spent itself in the short staccato sentence, in which the brevity of the utterance negated the intention of assault. The sentences in Hemingway are closer to the speech of workers in Lawrence than to that of Huxley's British sophisticates. They are American variants of the Lawrence cadence and interrogation, which reduces conversation to a verbal battle, but in them the restraint imposed by fear and helplessness is replaced by this conscious code of manners. Our expatriates found the atmosphere most congenial where rebelliousness was controlled by becoming convention in the ill-concealed cynical mood of revolt, the brusque grumbling, which still characterizes the language of the working class today.

Such is the type of personality and manner of speaking as presented with varying shades of emphasis in every piece of fiction

Hemingway ever wrote. Whether his characters be Americans of wealth or racketeers, artists or soldiers or college graduates, they follow the same pattern of speech and emotion. Hemingway's greatness lies not in the range of his characterization or the suppleness of his style but in the astonishing perfection of these limited objectives. And they never later got a more profound statement than in his first novel, *The Sun Also Rises.* In the simple plot of this novel, Lady Ashley runs away from Paris to enjoy an affair with a new lover. But as customary in her set, she is accompanied by other men: a young Jew from Princeton who cannot tear himself away from her though she has terminated his affair; and the interlocutor, who, disabled in the war, plays the role of disinterested observer. But in Spain she forces herself upon a young bullfighter, leaving all the Americans restless onlookers. After demoralizing his fight to satisfy her vanity by his attention, she has a change of heart, and, in a fit of remorse that she has ruined him, impetuously leaves to return to her fiancé in England and a second marriage.

This novel is important for other reasons than the verisimilitude of its dialogue or the typicalness of its plot. In the portrait of Lady Ashley, Hemingway goes deeper into analysis of personality than he was ever to do again. In the treatment of his heroine, he clarifies in the round the personality structure of the postwar generation. Perhaps since she is a woman, he feels more free to break through the façade she shares with his masculine characters and himself. In later stories he remains on the surface of his characters, and their real depth is to be deduced only from the development of the plot. But from his picture of Lady Ashley it is apparent that his characters are typically self-defeating and project this perversity upon their friends. Their *bonhommie* conceals a surly dislike of the very persons they pretend or desire to have as friends. And the differentiations among the stories is in the degree to which this conflict is carried and is permitted to show through. In most instances the action takes place within the limited democracy of the façade. But in *The Sun*

Also Rises the inner conflict is for once thoroughly exposed in this shift from an irresistible attraction, with its desire to dominate, to the remorse of a renunciation when the desire has been satisfied and the damage done. In other stories the conflict is concealed since they tend to confine our attention to the particularity of the action, to the plot, and at best to insinuate rather than elaborate the motivation. But this conflict within the personality nevertheless remains, to reduce any ideological belief in democracy to a precarious significance, since it is bound to be distorted by some interference from the anarchism of this inner discontent.

The only fiction of Hemingway's, therefore, which vies in quality with *The Sun Also Rises* is to be found in his short stories. This absorption in the façade, this need to live on the surface, is especially suited to the limited demand for meanings inherent in the shortness of the short story. For this reason, the technique of his stories is structurally similar to that of Katherine Mansfield, emotionally a masculine counterpart to her feminine quality. His material is more melodramatic, his conclusion more abrupt, his theme more bitter than those of the English writer. But these differences are deceptive, since in both writers intense emotion is either wanting or suppressed, and the theme is presented only by insinuation. "The Killers," for all the gruffness of the surface, is as casual in its indictment of American society at the moment when bootleggers were virtually in control of our local governments as the delicate shading of Mansfield's "The Garden Party" is subtle in indicting the well-to-do for their crass obtuseness regarding the emotions of the poor. Indeed, as the tone of the surface in a Hemingway story draws closer to that of Mansfield, even though the theme remains of a disparate intensity, the identity of technique becomes more apparent. "An Alpine Idyll" is in the restraint of its style closer to Mansfield than either of them is to the casual manner of their progenitor, Chekhov. In both writers the mastery of the art of the short story lies in this contrast between the nature of the surface, which reflects the consciousness of the characters, and the contradictory meaning of the theme, which is slowly gathering from the denouement of the action. Writers of good short stories of this type will seldom be good novelists. Not having very much to say, they do their best work in the shorter form. When they try to elaborate they go against the grain of their talent, and ruin their most carefully planned plots by the intrusion of elements of which they are unaware.

This is not to deny the sensitiveness of Hemingway's artistry but only to define the limits within which he must work. For his next book proved him sensitive to esthetic problems as American writers seldom are, even in our present sophistication. The most significant part of *Death in the Afternoon* from this point of view is its interpretation of the bullfight as a game that is also a form of art, the nature of which is conditioned by the economic circumstances of the country. Hemingway praises the bullfight as the only game that takes the form of tragedy instead of comedy. To clarify what he means: in our own country, baseball is obviously comedy on the verge of farce (when Babe Ruth is around); and football, though it has the intensity of the tragic action, does not intentionally achieve the plot of tragedy. Bullfighting alone can do so without the derogation of human values, such as took place, for instance, in the Roman gladiatorial combats, because it is the bull that is the victim of a situation potential with tragedy, and rarely the bullfighter. But this value of the form of the game is dependent upon the significance of its theme. What gave it continued importance in a barren country like Spain was that it kept before men's attention their struggle with the brute forces of nature, to control them to their own ends, in which their human ingenuity gave them the assumption of victory, if they spent their best effort. In comparison one can see in the rodeo the rudiments of a game, sketches toward the style of a game, which miserably failed to develop its form. But the perfected form decayed in Spain with the decline of a feudal economy in the face of an industrialized world. Ideologically, when machinery enabled man to achieve the victory over nature without effort, the bullfight became an anachronism; and under the Republic the art became a mark of the decadence of the aristocratic society with which it had long been associated. But what Hemingway is chiefly interested in is the relation between these social conditions and the art of the game. At its height, the performance of a good bullfighter was measured by his efficiency. So long as the game remained close to its thematic significance, close therefore to the everyday life of the functioning feudal estate, the good fighter was one who could measure the precise instant when the bull had been sufficiently weakened so that the thrust of the knife behind the neck could take place without unnecessary hazard to human life, but before the bull's weakness had removed the conflict of wills and made the killing mere slaughter. It should take place at such a time and in such a direct clean way as to give the most vivid spectacle of the authority of the human personality. When, however, the bulls declined in fierceness, since the raising of them had become a luxury the country was too poor to afford, this aim became a pretense. The fighter, no longer facing a hard problem, must make it appear hard; style became involved, unnecessary twists and flourishes entered; it had become style for style's sake; and Hemingway, like a sensitive artist, recognized the degeneration.

Hemingway's admiration was perforce for the past; and one wondered for a time which horn of the dilemma a writer of so much esthetic insight would choose; whether he would align himself with the past, choosing the perfect at the price of its having become illusion, or accept the reality of the present with its apparent imperfection. Doubtless the influence of many forces, including the leftism of foreign friends, had a hand in his decision. But a powerful factor must have been the very quality of his bohemianism as I have defined it. He would remain with the present not so much because he wished to improve it, but because it provided fuel for his contempt. Sympathy for the underdog was there. He liked his informality, the casual democracy of his mores. But unwittingly, he liked even better their common grudge against the powers that be. If he could not have the perfections of a feudal art, he could at least hate the imperfections of the social system that had done away with it. The times, also, were forcing a decision upon him. Rebuffed by prohibition in America, he turned to the wisdom of simple foreign-born farmers, who continued their old customs of wine making, unable to comprehend our divorce of law and tradition, even when it landed them in jail.

Suddenly he saw this oppression as but one aspect of a universal oppression of the free spirit, through which a handful of wealthy persons, who lived as they liked, were able to demoralize the poor. He turned against one part of his bohemianism, the pointless self-indulgence which it shared with the rich, and retained for the time only this genuine and spontaneous camaraderie, the equalitarianism which, by transcending class distinctions, actually put him with the majority, that is to say, with the poor. And he saw from his experience of all sorts of men, and perhaps from some hearsay of political talk, that society forms one great hierarchy, in which the idle rich live well, but all the others poorly in proportion to their distance from the top, until those at the bottom are crushed by the weight that bears indifferently down upon them. The spectacle stirred his emotions during the winter of the Depression, and the façade became rigid with contempt. The style of *To Have and Have Not* is almost ugly, as though he could fight privilege and its agent, racketeering, only in the temper of the racketeer. Conscious for the first time of social justice and the good intention of the common man, he could present their defeat in modern society only with the brutality of men of ill will. The owner of a motorboat seeks no more than to give his big blonde wife and little girl a stable home, but he is forced to loan his boat to rum runners, and is killed when he tries to kill them or turn them over to the law. But the reader's admiration for this heroism is overwhelmed by the cynicism of the plot. He gets an impression that the common man fights a stout but hopeless battle for abstract principles of justice he alone respects and fears. The definition of tragedy has become the impotence of his courage and the illusion of his faith to challenge the injustice that unfortunately rules the world.

From the sidelines where the reader stands, death is preferable to surrender. The tyranny of the powers that be, offering their permanent challenge to the individual spirit, gives to the sacrifice of life a mystic sanction, provided it is sought with all the violence of dedication to a valid and ideal goal that man is capable of. Such an analogue of anarchistic attitude lurks in the latter writing of Hemingway, and doubtless is partly responsible for his interest in the Spanish civil war. But it never became clear in his thinking or wholly acceptable to his feelings. The control of the façade had become habitual and prevented the resolution of conflicts in so definite a theory of self-sacrifice. The type of personality he shared with the bohemians of the twenties disdained the philosophy of politics as an un-American retreat from living and recoiled from the violence of anarchism as a Latin excess. Even in this single book, in which, stimulated by the Depression in America, Hemingway drove wilfully through a simple plot toward this stark conclusion, he pulls his punch at the end. A coastguard cutter in search of rum runners might have intervened in time, so that the state cannot be dismissed as altogether bad or always inefficient. The directness of anarchistic thinking dissolves in this unanarchistic but quite American retreat into equivocation, and the simplicity of our pity for the hero is qualified by the ironic insinuation that chance cannot altogether be eliminated, however rigid the predestination may appear to be. It may be no more than the pip-squeak of a chance, since we do not expect much help from the coastguard, but it is enough to confuse the philosophy of the action under the guise of a Hollywood device to increase the suspense.

Despite appearances to the contrary, Hemingway's confusion was increased rather than lessened by his attachment to the Loyalist cause in Spain. One doubts neither the sincerity nor the helpfulness of his public announcements of support. But novels are written from a deeper level of the personality than the rationale of pronunciamentoes. Indeed, what is fundamental to their orientation and its effect is governed by more complex (though not necessarily more creditable) factors than either reason or action. For action may be only a temporary solution of permanent conflicts, the existence of which fiction of any quality will expose. Such, I believe, was the case with Hemingway. From this point of view, his little play, *The Fifth Column*, is the prelude by the light of which *For Whom the Bell Tolls* should be read. It relates to the novel in a way somewhat analogous to the relationship I have pointed out between the portrait of Lady Ashley in *The Sun Also Rises* and the familiar Hemingway type. If it was easier for him there to give an adequate description of the bohemian of the twenties through the not altogether gallant device of the portrait of a lady, in *The Fifth Column* he similarly projects his fear of the meretriciousness of the bohemian support of the Spanish Republic by an attack upon a woman. The woman reporter is depicted as attracted by the sensations of danger rather than the ideals involved in the conflict, and as more interested in making a name for herself by her articles than in clarifying the issues. In proportion as this temptation may have existed in Hemingway also, his very determination to avoid it would increase the basic distortion set up by the bohemian habit of finding fault with one's friends. In addition there was the inescapable fact that his friends were losing the war and thereby causing him to do a great deal of rewriting. Under such circumstances his good intention was bound to capsize in an undertow of moody exasperation.

The result was that *For Whom the Bell Tolls* did not merely record the defeat of the Loyalists (as it had to), but turned into an indictment where an exoneration was intended. If the average American reader did not take it as such, it was because faulty reading habits encouraged a faulty political perspective. Approaching the book with an avowed political interest, accepting in advance Hemingway's adherence to the Loyalist side, predisposed to favor democracy but not having the slightest notion whether the Spanish Government was or was not democratic, the average reader found in the book the confirmation of a confusion analogous to Hemingway's, instead of the political guidance he had expected. Since the Loyalists aroused such contradictory reactions in him, he was inclined to leave the book with a feeling of relief that in such a doubtful case, our Government was probably right in holding aloof from aid. If, devoid of all political interest, he had approached the book solely as a good story, but with a capacity, rare in the casual American reader, to follow a text sensitively and interpret its meaning from the flow of the action, he would have found his confusion dispelled by a surprisingly definite conclusion. He would have perceived that it accomplishes precisely the opposite from what it intended, that it is derogatory to the cause of Spanish democracy, and therefore, by implication, sympathetic to Spanish fascism.

No reader can escape a certain awareness, to be sure, of the mood of despondency in which *For Whom the Bell Tolls* leaves him. But the significance of this mood is obscured by the sustained breathlessness of the action and especially by the interest in the personality of the hero. Robert Jordan's love affair distracts attention by the intensity of its description. Its passionate sensuality represents the very ideal of love according to the postwar generation (to which its accomplishment was in such shabby contrast), and those no longer trapped by its fetish of virility will dislike the histrionics of the masculine role. But if we are minded to analyze the cause of our melancholy, we find that it is not caused by Jordan's being killed, but by the fact that we are uncertain about the profitableness of his sacrifice.

Jordan is, indeed, the only character of Hemingway's creation whom he treats with unreserved affection and admiration. The qualification upon friendship in other instances is wanting here; there is no trace of detachment concealing an inward contempt. The old attitude once characteristic of his relationships with his fellow expatriates is now transferred to the Spanish characters (with the exception of course of his lover, who does not count in the essential action), to all of whom Jordan stands in contrast as a discreet representation of the ideal American. The distortion that characterizes his personality as lover disappears in his functioning as soldier; and, I think, it does so because Jordan as soldier and hero comes pretty close to being the accepted functioning American conception of the good soldier. He is one who doggedly does his duty, his not to reason why, sustained by the mystical belief (symbolized a little sadly in the title of the novel) that every individual is a part of a social whole, just as a peninsula is part of a vast continent. For this reason, even though Jordan realizes that the action of blowing up the bridge he has been sent to perform has become useless through changed events, when he cannot make contact and get permission from remote authority to change the order, he carries it through at the sacrifice of his life. He has not invoked his own powers to analyze a situation and act independently in an emergency, willing to accept responsibility for reversing the plan. Instead, he buttresses his rigid sense of duty with a mystical theory that any sacrifice of life that at all hinders the enemy, however ineffectually, must promote the good cause merely because it has behind it his wholehearted enthusiasm as a subjective potential. Perhaps fundamentally, on the subjective side, such an ideal approaches the anarchistic belief in the mystical value of self-sacrifice as an act in itself. But Jordan's ideal is conspicuously not anarchistic, in that this subjective state is made possible only by the sense of obedience to a higher authority. Doubtless such is the obligatory psychology of many a soldier in the ranks who must do as he is told because he cannot be in a position to understand the reasons justifying a command. But surely for an officer, and one on a special mission, where he has superior opportunities to gauge the overall situation, to act in such a way is only to conceal a dependency upon external authority for the very decision which affords the greatest sense of personal achievement through self-sacrifice. As such, the psychology of Robert Jordan is, I should say, strangely enough that typical of the authoritarianism of fascism.

But Hemingway does not stop here. Against such a picture of Jordan, with whom he identifies himself as with no other character in his fiction, he puts the clearest assemblage of evidence that the higher authority is not to be trusted. The Loyalists have neither the materials nor the co-ordination necessary for victory. Lack of communications makes co-ordination impossible. But Hemingway gives the impression that, even with material, the co-ordination would not have become any better. The anarchism in the Loyalist higher command is a matter of temperament, and is reflected in the philosophy of anarchism prevalent among Spanish liberals. This confusion and contradiction at the top betrays their lack of a sense of duty like Jordan's, which would have imposed at least a rigid assent to some common plan. But when it is a matter of direction from above, when it is a matter of imposing orders rather than obeying them, this obverse of the sense of duty, the obligation to exercise authority, is by no means palatable to Hemingway. If he objects to the laxity of the anarchistic temperament, his rejection of the surly attempts of the Communists to achieve discipline, as he describes them, is even more positive. He pictures their hysterical insistence upon action and obedience as offensive to the dignity of the individual and equally benighted as planning. Nowhere at the top is there the wisdom and firmness that can command respect. Hemingway's bohemian background leads him into a perverse enjoyment of the picture. His idealism is outraged; that is enough; for he makes no conscious effort to suggest what type of command will avoid the laxity of anarchism on the one hand and the rigidity of his Communists on the other. He wallows instead in the subjective pleasure (in itself a kind of anarchism) of denunciation. And to intensify this mood of fighting the windmills of futility, he chooses to put Jordan in a situation in which his immediate associates are worse than the men at headquarters, even less typical of the Loyalist fighters. Jordan has to deal with non-

Spanish gypsies in the mountains, who have withdrawn and ceased fighting when they have acquired for themselves booty in the form of mules and horses. It is exciting to follow Jordan's tact in winning back the support of these selfish dissident individuals, and it restores for the time being one's confidence in human nature. But the fact that the principal characters in the novel have to be wheedled and cajoled into a sense of duty by an American reinforces the gathering cynicism of the reader for the Loyalist cause.

One's cynicism is further intensified by the intensity of the spontaneous emotional reactions set up by episodes not directly concerned with Jordan's blowing up the bridge. These subtly accumulate to establish an emotional orientation of uneasy suspicion of the Loyalists and unconscious admiration for their fascist opponents. There are acts of horror on both sides. But those on the Loyalist side are made indelible by the manner in which they are treated; whereas those on the other are absorbed by the narrative and fade away. Jordan's lover, for instance, had been raped by the fascists. But since the memory is too painful for her recollection, it becomes a cold fact in the reader's mind, quite forgotten in the activity that enabled her to forget it, her ecstatic participation in her new and satisfactory love affair with Jordan. Utterly different is the reader's attitude toward Pablo's confession of his part in the murder of the anti-democratic officials of his village. His sense of guilt keeps the episode vivid to the reader, since it still preys on his own mind and forces him to recount most vividly the gruesome details. His weakness of character, as revealed in his later treachery to the Loyalists, not only lessens one's sympathy for his contrition, but makes one wonder how typical he is of the Loyalists in general. His present disloyalty toward the Republic comes to seem indicative of a tendency there toward disintegration that is stimulated not so much by the success of the enemy as by flaws in Spanish democracy itself.

Such a conclusion is strengthened when one realizes that there is no character on the fascist side who arouses as much detestation as Pablo, and no description of fascist brutality (when so many abounded in the actual events which Hemingway might have chosen) is inserted to palliate and compensate for our dislike of Pablo as a Loyalist. The fascists are not on the center of the stage, and Hemingway's bohemian personality, which seizes upon the flaws in any ideal he has grasped, by compensation tends to find a sentimental idealism in whatever is beyond contact. The fascists in the novel, who are not close at hand and therefore do not require to be described in any detail, approach the reader through an emotional haze which is not at all sinister but fundamentally agreeable. They are almost always depicted as gentle refined officers, who do what they must out of a sense of duty like Jordan's but under circumstances where they can have confidence in the integration both of their philosophy and their army. They are the men who are destined (as it turned out, at least for the time being) to win. Serene in their conviction, they soil their hands as little as possible; and such is the author's perversity in planning his book that by the time one has read it carefully, they seem to serve to win. Jordan's heroism, therefore, is put within a context of overwhelming detail that proves its folly as a practical code of action. In the larger context of the narrative, it is seen to be as futile as it seemed without qualification admirable as immediate subjective experience. And though it is given the emphasis of being the final action of the book, for any careful reader who cannot forget his accumulation of previous impressions, its position only makes its meaning the more melancholy.

Hemingway's attitude toward the Loyalists, therefore, is similar to that of the postwar bohemian toward his erstwhile friends. Any keen emotion of attachment carries its hidden counterpart of contempt. And any attitude toward persons like the fascists, whom one dislikes in theory but does not know, takes on a flavor of liking precisely because, free from this inner contradiction by not being known, they become vague and gentle images which seem not so much unreal as ideal. Indeed, to a person of Hemingway's type, unlike the anarchist, the ideal will always be delectable because it cannot be realized either through life or death, either through social or individual action. Once you come into any form of contact with it, it ceases to be ideal. The ideal, consequently, fails, just as friendship fails, and the failure of democratic societies is analogous to this failure of friendship. Goodness drifts and is as impotent in the world of practical affairs as these men sense themselves to be in their personal lives. They project their own failure upon the world at large.

Anyone as interested in the facts of the Spanish War as the abundant detail of Hemingway's novels show him to have been could not, unless blinded by some prejudice, have avoided the most pertinent facts of all. Inefficiency there was on the Loyalist side, but no greater than on the fascist; and in the course of the fighting, the co-ordination actually increased despite the tremendous handicap of lack of material. What caused the loss of the war, as everyone now knows, was not the failure of democracy in Spain but its failure abroad. I well remember waiting, as I read the novel, for some hint of "non-intervention," some evidence of aid to Franco from the Axis and lack of aid to the government from the foreign democracies. The only aid the Loyalists are pictured as getting is the irascible meddling of French Communists and the haughty indifferent cynicism of the Russian observers. The tremendous support of Franco by the Axis through diplomatic pressure and armed intervention plays no part in the narrative. Yet only through these was Franco's failing cause snatched from actual defeat. As a political history of the war, the novel is almost wilfully misleading.

What kept such patent facts from Hemingway's consciousness was, I think, the rationalization of his esthetic interest. He did not wish to write a political novel, but one in which political events should form the setting for a timeless story of personal tragedy. He sought to escape the notorious deficiencies of left fiction in oversimplification of motive and plot. But to put the political interest in its place does not necessitate its distortion. It might, however, distract the author from awareness of the distortion.

Nor does a timeless story require a theme that contradicts the correct political interpretation. But its contradiction may escape an author's notice in his herculean task of assembling all the purely "human" detail needed to prove his broader "human" theme. And in the process he may also lose sight of the interference with the purity of his theme by the idiosyncrasies of his own personality.

Actually Hemingway's theme obligates a wrong interpretation of political events, and is no more universal than a rationalization of the problems of the bohemian personality can be. For the "human" theme of *For Whom the Bell Tolls*, the theme of Robert Jordan's dying, is nothing more than a special instance of the conception of tragedy that has dominated romanticism in its decadence. The belief that the ideal is constantly frustrated in a wicked world is, to be sure, older than the postwar generation. It stems from the precedent of *Madame Bovary*. To say, therefore, that inefficiency wrecked the Loyalist cause would be to make a political statement that though true would be a mere corollary to a larger philosophical reflection. Virtue is everywhere inefficient, impractical, unsuccessful, like the drifting of those men in Paris after the war, believing themselves so well intentioned as they studied art or drank with their friends, and ascribing their failure to the way of the world, to the hopeless state in which the peace had left mankind. The bohemianism of the twenties may have been of good intention. It was something to have sided with democracy, whatever the inner motive. But the traits of personality in the postwar generation made these writers, against their will, unreliable as the interpreters and friends of democracy.

GEORGE HEMPHILL

Hemingway and James

1949

By way of introducing these remarks on the value of *In Our Time* I want to make a broad and somewhat crude observation which I hope will fix the reader's attention on my present focus of interest. I think of Hemingway as the writer to whom everything happens. And fortunately for us he has had sufficient skill to write up the stories of the people to whom everything happens. He is genially candid on this point: "I would like to live long enough to write three more novels and twenty-five more stories. I know some pretty good ones." Now if this is a fair view of Hemingway, it might be no less fair to compare him in this respect to Henry James. Hemingway is the writer everything happens to and should therefore end up as a non-writer, except that he has a complex sense of duty. ("Now it is necessary to get to the grindstone again.") And vulgarly speaking, Henry James is the man to whom *nothing* ever happens. Things could be worse for a writer. (One recalls James's peevish-

From *The Kenyon Review*, Winter, 1949, Vol. XI, No. 1. Reprinted by permission of the author.

ness at having his sacred mornings for work interrupted by high-minded ladies in New York.) I suggest there is a broad rift in the possibilities of fiction today and that Hemingway and James are representative of the factions. James extended magnificently the possibilities of fiction in the direction of poetic drama, ignoring the kind of social, economic, and historic verisimilitude that Edmund Wilson requires from fiction; Hemingway, with his journalistic training, his wide and not shallow experience, and his gift for colloquial language, rendered for his contemporaries the life of their own times. Put more philosophically, the distinction is this: It takes more of an act of will to put pictorial effect into a novel (and to receive it) than to put it on the stage—it's there already. Hence the novelist and the playwright are two different varieties of Nietzsche's *Augenmensch*—the playwright has more of the *Ohrenmensch* in him. James put his poetic dramas into the form of novels and sacrificed thereby much of the moral persuasive force possible in prose narrative; Hemingway, as purer, appetitive *Augenmensch*, writes moral tracts for our times. I may be dead wrong, but I feel, the world being what it is nowadays, that the novelist needs more of the *Augenmensch* in him and less of the *Ohrenmensch*.

In Our Time has its share of crudities, which would no doubt disgust a sensibility nurtured on James. But consider the harassed sensibility of the man who, within a week, reads or rereads in sequence *In Our Time*, *The Ambassadors*, *Antony and Cleopatra*, and *Lycidas*. Would he finish each work with a measured sense of disgust at the limitations of its predecessor? He should not, of course: he should reflect, Here are four reputable craftsmen working in different mediums and unto different ends—the ends seem legitimate.

I could have chosen a better work of Hemingway's for my discussion—either *The Sun Also Rises* or *A Farewell to Arms*—except that I believe *In Our Time* shows more plainly than these novels the excellences and limitations of Hemingway's non-Jamesian moral vision. The faults of *In Our Time* are glaring, but they throw the good parts into high relief. The book is of anomalous form; one hesitates as much to call it a novel as a collection of short stories. Even in the Modern Library Edition of *The Fifth Column and the First Forty-Nine Stories*, although the title is left out, the chapter numberings and the epigraphs printed in italics are retained. I think we can find evidence that the book should be judged neither as a novel nor as a collection of short stories, but as something halfway between; and the limitations of this peculiar form—if it can be called a form at all—are not the same as the limitations of *In Our Time*. I feel, for example, that if all the stories about Nick Adams were collected and entitled "In Our Time" they would not have the structure which *In Our Time* does have. "The Killers" and "Now I Lay Me" might fit, but "Fathers and Sons" and "A Way You'll Never Be" would not.

The unifying principle of *In Our Time* is the author's thematic obsession; if we fail to discover this obsession we see only the ghost or parody of a structure; i.e., alternating epigraphs and stories concerned with random cruelty abroad in the contemporary landscape. James, of course, would insist upon a more formal structure, one which would stand up whether he had any obsessions or not. (We can be sure he had.) But this is not to say that thematic unity is necessarily inferior to any formal sort of unity. On the contrary, I often feel that thematic structure is best suited to the medium of prose fiction, and that formal structure is what we expect in poetic drama. It was probably this thematic principle of unity which Edmund Wilson was trying to uncover in his Preface to *In Our Time*:

> Life is fine: the woods are enjoyable; fishing is enjoyable; being with one's friends is enjoyable; even the War is enjoyable. But the brutality of life is always there, and it is somehow bound up with the enjoyment. Bullfights are especially enjoyable. Even Nick's fishing-trip, when he is away by himself happy and free in the woods, has aspects which must make it unique among the fishing-trips of literature—for through all Nick's tranquil exhilaration we are made conscious in a curious way of the

> cruelty involved for the fish—and not only this, but even of the martyrdom of the grasshoppers used for bait. The condition of life is still pain—and every calm or contented surface still vibrates with its pangs.

Mr. Wilson concludes his paraphase by saying that "the resolution of that discord in art makes the beauty of Hemingway's stories"; but we will have to be less general.

The raw materials of *In Our Time* seem to be of two sorts: the autobiographical, and the socio-historic. I may seem to be making a naive and unrewarding observation—since all writers' raw materials are probably their own lives and the life of their times—but in Hemingway's case the observation is necessary; it bears on our problem of evaluation. You have to know more about Hemingway the man than James the man. This does not make Hemingway necessarily inferior, but simply more prosaic. I suppose that the scale from anonymity to its opposite is roughly the same as the scale from poetry to prose, but it is not the same (as I once fondly believed) as the scale from good to bad. We have in each case to examine the quality of what is anonymous and what is onymous. This means digging into the given text.

The stories in *In Our Time* are variations on a single theme. We can say that the stories are good in proportion as they seem to be fit correlative objects for that theme. This is not a subtle kind of question-begging—saying first, Here is the theme ordained and then, This is bad because it does not fit the theme—so long as we can be sure, by finding evidence in the text, that Hemingway knew sometimes what his theme was and sometimes was only groping for it. When he is groping he seems to be giving us raw material out of his own life or out of the social history of his times. Thus "A Very Short Story" is a very bad story, I think, because it is only the raw material which Hemingway later worked up as *A Farewell to Arms*. In the early story the only reason given for the breakup of the wartime love affair is quite an accident, excessively naturalistic, dramatically inert, and more cynical than it need be under the circumstances:

> He went to America on a boat from Genoa. Luz went back to Pordonone to open a hospital. It was lonely and rainy there, and there was a battalion of arditi quartered in the town. Living in the muddy, rainy town in the winter, the major of the battalion made love to Luz, and she had never known Italians before, and finally wrote to the States that theirs had been only a boy and girl affair.

In transforming this "scenario," as Edmund Wilson calls it, into *A Farewell to Arms*, Hemingway makes a meaningless accident into a social tragedy; he builds up the scene and opposes the lovers to it, achieving the sort of drama you find in *The Duchess of Malfi* and *The Wild Palms*. Another story, "The End of Something," fails because no necessary connection (other than biographical, perhaps) between the end of the boy and girl affair between Nick and Marjorie and the end of the old lumbering days in Michigan is suggested. The failure is somewhat mitigated, however, by the comic relief of the sequel to the story, "The Three-Day Blow." There is a story possible in the material of "The End of Something," but Hemingway has not written it up, and I dare say it would not be his kind of story if it were written up. A little Agrarian sentiment injected into the story would make it a fine little tract with the message: The wages of acquisitiveness is death. Just as the lumber kings of Michigan at the end of the last century denuded the pine forests by overcutting, the young lovers killed their love by going ahead with it too fast. But in "The Three-Day Blow" we find out it had been the girl's mother who ruined the affair. This is dramatically extraneous and absurd.

I have said that *In Our Time* lacks formal structure; but once we discover the thematic structure we shall see that this is not wholly true. The first half of the book is concerned with what has been called an "enveloping situation"; that is, we are made aware, in various ways, of the conditions of heroism. Life is cruel, some people stand up to it, others do not, and the reasons why some people cannot stand up are sometimes good, sometimes bad, often contingent. When Hemingway is able to dramatize for us the conditions of heroism he is getting above his autobiographical and socio-historic material. He is being scenically persuasive. The second half of the book, except probably "Big Two-Hearted River," is concerned with Insiders and Outsiders, those who are aware of the "enveloping situation," the conditions of heroism, and those who are outside it. Hemingway's writing is slightly offensive when we find that we must take him personally, and probably Nick too, as an Insider; it is highly moral in so far as we can take Nick Adams as a bewildered and attractive projection of Hemingway and not Hemingway himself. The last section of the book, the two parts of "Big Two-Hearted River," puts, quite neatly in our terms, the Insider Outside, speculating on how far Outside he may dare go:

> He wished he had brought something to read. He felt like reading. He did not feel like going on into the swamp. He looked down the river. A big cedar slanted all the way across the stream. Beyond that the river went into the swamp.
>
> Nick did not want to go in there. He felt a reaction against deep wading with the water deepening up under his armpits, to hook big trouts in places impossible to land them. In the swamp the banks were bare, and big cedars came together overhead, the sun did not come through, except in patches; in the fast deep water, in the half light, the fishing would be tragic. In the swamp fishing was a tragic adventure. Nick did not want it. He did not want to go down the stream any further today. . . .
>
> Nick stood up on the log, holding his rod, the landing net hanging heavy, then stepped into the water and splashed ashore. He climbed the bank and cut up into the woods, toward the high ground. He was going back to camp. He looked back. The river just showed through the trees. There were plenty of days coming when he could fish the swamp.

In the parts of *In Our Time* that I can return to with interest, a local detail always gives a contingent reason for a character's inability to stand up to the ordinary cruelty of 20th Century life. In this respect I find the epigraph to Chapter V at the thematic center of the book:

> They shot the six cabinet ministers at half-past six in the morning against the wall of a hospital. There were pools of water in the courtyard. There were wet dead leaves on the paving of the courtyard. It rained hard. All the shutters of the hospital were nailed shut. One of the ministers was sick with typhoid. Two soldiers carried him downstairs and out into the rain. They tried to hold him up against the wall but he sat down in a puddle of water. The other five stood very quietly against the wall. Finally the officer told the soldiers it was no good trying to make him stand up. When they fired the first volley he was sitting down in the water with his head on his knees.

In this passage each descriptive detail—the pools of water, the wet dead leaves, etc.—contributes, if rather indirectly, to the rough notion which seems to be Hemingway's obsession: that Life is cruel just as War is cruel. But Hemingway never speaks so generally: he selects and records certain details of speech, dress, custom, action, and landscape. The cabinet ministers were shot when it was raining. Rain water is cold, wet, and nasty. Hemingway wants us to know how Nick knew that Life is cruel so that we will know that Life is cruel. The passage is scenically persuasive. But at the same time, something more important is put before us, and it is put narratively and dramatically. Although there were six cabinet ministers who were to be shot, one was unfortunate enough to be sick with typhoid. It is an historical accident that cabinet ministers must be shot, but the accident that gives one of the ministers typhoid makes the incident dramatic. Typhoid is the contingency which prevents the one cabinet minister from dying heroically. He is neither an Insider nor an Outsider; it is impossible to jeer at him or feel sorry for him or, of course, to praise him. He is a representative Hemingway figure. He is closely akin to the Indian in "Indian Camp" who cuts his throat while his wife suffers and lives through a caesarean section. In this case also the cause of his trouble is accidental:

> "You see, Nick, babies are supposed to be born head first but sometimes they're not. When they are not they make a lot of trouble for everyone. Maybe I'll have to operate on this lady."

Unsympathetic readers of Hemingway call this sort of accident, and the unpleasantness that results, "random brutality." But this criticism involves one in extra-literary discussion: whether in the exhibit of random brutality we see the hand of Social Forces, God, whatnot, or Hemingway. Skirting this problem, we should only remark that Hemingway's choice of violent subject matter has its dangers, and that when he is not at his best his accidents *are* arbitrary, giving Hemingway a chance to pose, and leading to effects which are sentimental or precious. The death of Catherine Barkley does not call forth these effects, I think, but the death of Robert Jordan does. It is hard to tell how long the Hemingway writings will outlast the sort of world they report.

Cases of the ambiguously heroic and non-heroic stature of their main characters are always coming up in these stories. These characters tend to show the famous tight-lipped vision-of-evil Hemingway visage. Thus in "The Doctor and the Doctor's Wife" a siege of pneumonia is the accidental reason for the unpleasant situation Nick's father has to face. The Indian Dick Boulton owes Doctor Adams "a lot of money for pulling his squaw through pneumonia" and "wanted to start a row so he wouldn't have to take it out in work." Dick is a big man, and it would have been foolhardy rather than courageous for Nick's father to fight with him; but Doctor Adams feels ignominy just the same, and furthermore, poor man, cannot explain the matter to his wife, who is a Christian Scientist.

> "Dear, I don't think, I really don't think that anyone would do a thing like that."
> "No?" the doctor said.
> "No. I can't really believe that anyone would do that sort of thing intentionally."

Mrs. Adams has the last word here (her attitude toward evil resembles that of some of Hemingway's early audience) but the story ends on the flat stoical note (is there an exclamation mark anywhere in Hemingway?):

> "I know where there's black squirrels, Daddy," Nick said.
> "All right," said his father, "let's go there."

Doctor Adams is clearly the spiritual father of all the good people in Hemingway—the Insiders afraid of the Outside but above it. The most concise picture of this sort of figure is given in the epigraph of Chapter XIII:

> I heard the drums coming down the street and then the fifes and the pipes and then they came around the corner, all dancing. The streets were full of them. Maera saw him and then I saw him. When they stopped the music for the crouch he hunched down in the street with them all and when they started it again he jumped up and went dancing down the street with them. He was drunk all right.
>
> You go down after him, said Maera, he hates me.
>
> So I went down and caught up with them and grabbed him while he was crouched down waiting for the music to break loose and said, Come on Luis. For Christ's sake you've got bulls this afternoon. He didn't listen to me, he was listening so hard for the music to start.
>
> I said, Don't be a damn fool Luis. Come on back to the hotel.
>
> Then the music started up again and he jumped up and twisted away from me and started dancing. I grabbed his arm and he pulled loose and said, Oh leave me alone. You're not my father.
>
> I went back to the hotel and Maera was on the balcony looking out to see if I'd be bringing him back. He went inside when he saw me and came downstairs disgusted.
>
> Well, I said, after all he's just an ignorant Mexican savage.
>
> Yes, Maera said, and who will kill his bulls after he gets a *cogida*?
>
> We, I suppose, I said.
>
> Yes, we, said Maera. We kills the savages' bulls, and the drunkards' bulls, and the *riau-riau* dancers' bulls. Yes. We *kill* them. We *kill* them all right. Yes. Yes. Yes.

Maera dies, however, in the sequel, and is one of the authentic Hemingway tragic heroes. It should not bother us much that he is just a bullfighter ("Who were these bullfighters anyway?" the substitute bullfight critic of a Madrid newspaper asks: "Kids and bums") and not a king or a cultivated sensibility. The tragedy of situation rather than that of character is so common in modern literature that it has to be judged each time in its own terms.

Maera discovers what the son of the jockey in "My Old Man" discovers: that the race is not always to the swift.

The really unpleasant stories in *In Our Time* are concerned with the absurdity of Outsiders. Hemingway's scorn for those who seem to be unaware of moral uncertainty in our times, and the need for heroic discipline, is at times almost masochistic. The scorn at any rate produces some cheap satire. Mr. and Mrs. Elliot, who keep trying to have a baby, Mr. Elliot meanwhile writing "very long poems very rapidly," and Mrs. Elliot meanwhile finding a girl friend to sleep with and have many a good cry with, are not worth Hemingway's attention or anybody else's. Nor are the rich Americans in "Out of Season" who do not take the local customs seriously. These people are contrasted too patly with the Insiders (they can ski well) Nick and George, and Villalta (who can kill a bull handsomely).

Robert Penn Warren has observed that Hemingway cannot create a large variety of characters. In this important respect, Mr. Warren feels, Hemingway is clearly inferior to William Faulkner, and also to Henry James. Whenever Hemingway tries to write about the Elliots of this world, or the rich people in *To Have and Have Not*, he does not give them half a chance. James too had his Insiders—and as Hemingway's Insiders are remarkably like Hemingway himself, James's Insiders also resemble James—but he treated his Outsiders as flat characters necessary for his structure, and never was scornful in any ungentlemanly way toward them. Mr. Warren has put his finger on the main limitation Hemingway's books have, and he goes on to justify this limitation: The community of people fit for being either an audience or a subject for reputable fiction has greatly shrunk since the beginning of the present century. The shrinkage must have been always in the back of Henry James's mind as he proceeded to write more and more fully about smaller and smaller actions, as his "central intelligence" became more and more a refined and sensitive gentleman, as fewer people read him, and as more and more businessmen looked down from their office windows, as he remarks in *The American Scene*, on the spire of Trinity Church. Hemingway at his best meets this shrinkage. Nick Adams has a sense of the past and what is lost, and does the best he can.

The writings of James will probably outlast those of Hemingway, but I feel that the James vision is not to be rehad, while the Hemingway vision should be examined and, if possible, clarified. After all, Hemingway was not thinking of Henry James, whom he admired, when he wrote

> that while decorum is an excellent thing some must be indecorous if the race is to be carried on since the position prescribed for procreation is indecorous, highly indecorous, and it occurred to me that perhaps that is what these people [the Humanists] are, or were: the children of decorous cohabitation. But regardless of how they started I hope to see the finish of a few, and speculate how worms will try that long preserved sterility; with their quaint pamphlets gone to dust and into footnotes all their lust.

This passage shows as much the strength and weakness of our time as it shows the strength and the weakness—heavy and bitter and not quite adult irony—of Hemingway. The Humanists are no more a worthy opponent of Hemingway's insiders than are the Elliot people. They are too much the straw men Hemingway himself sets up to knock down: the "story" in which the passage occurs is more nearly persuasive prose than fiction; i.e., even less anonymous than fiction.

The formula "HJ + EH" will probably not go; but this is no reason for despair. There can never again be a Henry James world, and meanwhile it is good to have a Hemingway around.

THEODORE BARDACKE

Hemingway's Women

1950

Hemingway is known to millions of readers as an author primarily concerned with violence and sex. His realistic treatment of this part of life has created a series of spectacular short stories and four major novels built around strong and arresting protagonists. Many critics have discussed the heroic proportions of his heroes. Little, however, has been said of his heroines beyond an acknowledgment of an antagonism towards women that is especially noticeable in his later short stories. But heroines should not be ignored, for often an author's whole attitude towards sex and love is revealed as much through his conception of the partner as through his dilineation of the hero. This is especially true in Hemingway's writings, where heterosexual intercourse symbolizes love in the same manner that war and bull fights symbolize violence and death.

His objective treatment of his heroines creates a pattern of attitudes and symbols that are more completely crystallized and revealing than his more complicated subjective treatment of his protagonists. Only in the chaotic novel *To Have and Have Not* are the women treated subjectively. While Brett in *The Sun Also Rises* is revealed by Jake, Catherine in *A Farewell to Arms* by Lieutenant Henry, and Maria and Pilar in *For Whom the Bell Tolls* by Robert Jordan, Marie Morgan and Dorothy Hollis are allowed some reflections, if only upon that part of their lives that are immediately concerned with their men.

The frequent occurrence of sex in Hemingway's work is neither accidental nor mere literary fashion; nor can it be simplified as a Freudian compulsion in Hemingway's personality. Virility or its absence is an important symbol for the author, a strong, direct and primitive symbol, as virility has always been symbolically interlaced with man's acceptance of life. Hemingway, in spite of his insistence upon objective method and realistic tone, depends strongly upon a background of associations and symbols for the depth and mood of his stories. Even his natural settings become meaningful; consciously or not, he endows them with specific emotional values. His mountains, rivers and woods are often symbols of nostalgia. Rain and snow repeated over and over again in both his novels and short stories, suggest various aspects of death and disillusion. It is just this underlying use of associations and emotional suggestion through objectively reported details that gives to Hemingway's stories the fourth and fifth dimensions that he writes of in the *Green Hills of Africa.*

As a writer Hemingway has been fighting constantly against a modern world that has lost its ideals. From his first volume of short stories, *In Our Time*, it is obvious that the upheaval of an age, World War I, coincided and became integrated with his breaking away from a youthful world of ideals to one of disillusioning reality. The theme is also the core of one of Hemingway's last stories, "The Capital of the World." Since one of the most important of his lost ideals is love, he has often expressed his frustrations and desires of the modern world with sexual symbols. For Hemingway, the complete relationship that unites sex and love has been lost, divorced into either love without sex, as in Jake, or sex without love as in Brett and her friends. Sex, therefore, is not merely an intriguing part of a good story but a symbol of the protagonist's relation to life. Jake's castration by a war injury is a symbol of the post World War I generation and Harry Morgan's satisfying relation with his wife are a measure of his affirmative strength and an adjustment to the world.

In Hemingway's earlier stories and novels the complete and satisfying relationship, even when attained, is antagonistic to the modern world, and is destroyed at the first opportunity. As a result, the lovers are left doubly wounded, because their love has made them more vulnerable. It is only after 1935, when Hemingway discovers an affirmative political view, that love becomes a force that can transcend the immediate moment and even death. At her husband's death Marie Morgan is lost but still strong, and Maria carries away the memory and spirit that He has bequeathed to her.

Second only to death, love is an important center of Hemingway's work. In his novel of World War I, this love is doomed. It is frustrated, spiritually meaningless, or sexually perverted in his novel and stories of the postwar world. It re-emerges as an affirmative force only after the author's political conversion in the middle Thirties. Women are traditionally an important part of the love relationship and in Hemingway's changing conception of them with their deficiencies or attributes it is possible to trace many of his attitudes toward sex.

In Hemingway's first important novel, *The Sun Also Rises*, Brett is the dominating character. She is the embodiment of what the author conceived as the postwar woman. Although not possessive and honorless like Cohn's mistress, Frances, she has been emotionally stunted by a shallow world without spiritual meaning, and has become a woman devoid of womanhood. She has experienced two loveless marriages; the first with a man who died of dysentery during the war, and the second with an officer in the British Navy who returned from the war suffering from shock. Her love life, a kind of war casualty in itself, has decayed into alcoholism and a series of casual sex relations. She is "engaged to marry" Mike who is bankrupt economically and spiritually. The sexual level of their relationship is indicated by the hotel-brothel where they stay in Paris.

Jake, who is genuinely in love with Brett, is kept from her by an impotency that is the result of a war accident rather than any deficiency in his personality. While it mars his life and frustrates his love, the wound establishes Jake as a sympathetic observer of Brett's search for sexual meaning. As a result of her loss of womanliness and in spite of her promiscuity, Brett has become desexed. She is introduced in the novel with a group of homosexuals and "she was very much with them." This company, her clothes, her mannish felt hat and bobbed hair, all are indications of the loss of her true sexuality. Jake wonders if even her love for him isn't merely a longing for the unattainable. He doubts her very capacity to love as a woman.

However, during the fiesta in Spain when reality is tempered by ritual and celebration and the "fear of consequences" has disappeared, Brett falls in love with the matador Romero. Neither Cohn, who is a shallow sentimentalist, nor Mike understands the importance of Brett's emotional experience. Jake does, though, and is willing to face the anger of his friends, the scorn of the hotel owner, whose respect was hard won, and the possible destruction of the young bullfighter, to arrange Brett's meeting with Romero.

After Brett's union with Romero, Hemingway pictures her as a changed woman. Later, she goes with Jake to church and for the first time tries to pray, but her attempt fails. Just as her praying was unsuccessful because it came too late, Brett finds her relationship with Romero is doomed. She realizes that she is too old, too much the person that the modern world has made her; it is too late to change. Although Romero offers her a relatively pure body, a complete and satisfying relationship of love and sexual fulfillment, and marriage, she cannot accept because it is too late for her to respond completely. This impossible change back to womanliness is symbolized by Romero's wanting her to let her hair grow. Knowing that to remain with her lover would only destroy him, Brett leaves and in so doing preserves the only thing left to her, her self-respect. She becomes heroic in her sacrifice and returns to Mike and his world of shallowness and alcohol because that is, after all, her world too. "He's so damned nice and he's so awful. He's my sort of thing."

The lack of womanhood that is Brett's tragedy had been expressed by Hemingway in an earlier short story, "A Cat in the Rain." In this story, the author suggests the womanly longings of the modern wife, who is aware of a basic loss but not conscious of its meaning. Looking at herself in the mirror and pondering her emotions, frustrations and bobbed hair, she asks her husband if she should let her hair grow long again. "I get so tired of looking like a boy." When her husband remains insensitive to her meaning, she adds, "And I want to eat at a table with my own silver and I want candles. And I want it to be spring and I want to brush my hair out in front of a mirror and I want a kitty and I want some new clothes." Silverware, spring, long hair and the feminine vanity of new clothes are all the longings of a frustrated new woman and are the symbols for the more abstract loss of her true sexual role. This longing is suddenly crystallized for the woman when she sees a cat in the rain from the window of a strange hotel in postwar Europe.

This first volume of Hemingway's short stories, *In Our Time*, reads almost like an autobiographical novel of maturation and deals with the gradual loss of illusions as man grows out of childhood into the reality of war, violence and tragedy. The love theme occurs in seven of the fifteen stories. In "The End of Something" and "Three-Day Blow," Hemingway treats the death of first love with a mastery of understatement. In both of these stories the author is concerned with the boy Nick, rather than the girl. It is a tragedy of adolescence when he discovers that love dies with no more violence or lingering than a seasonal storm at the end of summer, when "The fruit had been picked and the fall wind blew through the bare trees." This theme of disillusionment in love develops as irony in "Mr. and Mrs. Elliot," as confusion and complication in "Soldier's Home," as a feeling of having been let down and trapped in "Cross Country Snow," and as complete bitterness in "A Very Short Story." This last story grimly foreshadows *A Farewell to Arms* in the love affair of a wounded soldier and a nurse, but it ends with a denouement of decay and disease, not with the more romantic climax of the novel.

Hemingway's second volume of short stories, *Men Without Women*, is not actually a collection of short stories that excludes women. The volume, rather, presents men in various situations of defeat in a world that can no longer produce a deep relationship between men and women. The one satisfying relationship is told in a short story interestingly enough titled "In Another Country" and, besides, the wife is dead. The most important story in relation to Hemingway's belief in the frustration of modern woman, however, is "Hills Like White Elephants." In this story an American and his girl try to fight a growing tension and antagonism that are created by an impending abortion. The girl is convinced that the operation will not restore their former happiness but will prove instead a serious and irrevocable step toward their gradual loss of meaning in life.

It is in Hemingway's next novel, *A Farewell to Arms*, that his first relatively affirmative mate appears. This novel, which begins and ends before the end of the first World War, is historically situated before *The Sun Also Rises*. Malcolm Cowley points out that, "*A Farewell to Arms* helps to explain the background of Jake Barnes and Lady Brett in *The Sun Also Rises*." It is in this war novel that Lieutenant Henry experiences the disillusionment that is an accepted fact in the earlier written novel, *The Sun Also Rises*. Catherine Barkley, the heroine of *A Farewell to Arms*, is Hemingway's ideal woman, and she is certainly more old-fashioned than she is new. Essentially a womanly woman, Catherine is passionate but never dominating, submissive and fulfilled in love. The effect of love on Catherine is to completely destroy her as a separate personality, "I want what you want. There isn't any me any more. Just what you want." And this complete subjection is the core of Hemingway's conception of the ideal woman. Catherine's hair, in contrast to Brett's, is extremely long, and this abundance of long blonde hair is symbolic of her womanhood. In speaking of her first love during her first conversation with Lieutenant Henry, Catherine tells him that after the news of her fiancé's death she had wanted to cut off her long hair. Evidently the love-loss was not shocking enough, for Catherine keeps her tresses and is still capable of falling deeply and completely in love with Frederick Henry. At first, their love skirmishes are merely a game, but after he is wounded, the Lieutenant discovers that he is really in love. This love, in spite of Catherine's submissive role, surrounds, envelops and isolates him and at the end of the book becomes his tragedy. When Frederick Henry describes Catherine's hair, some of this feeling is projected.

On the Italian front Frederick Henry discovers the intellectual deception of war and the unheroics of retreat. He declares his separate and individual peace as Nick had done in "Chapter VI" of *In Our Time*. In turning from war, Lieutenant Henry escapes to the one affirmative thing he has found, his love for Catherine, and together they retreat into the never-never land of a neutral zone. There they live completely within each other, awaiting the birth of their child. The world catches up with them, however; Catherine dies in childbirth leaving Frederick Henry in a meaningless world of irrational rules whose only end is death. Thus, through Catherine's death, even this very affirmative love relationship has ended in tragedy. Although his ideal of love has not been proven false, Lieutenant Henry is nevertheless hurt by it for its past completeness has left the world only more empty and more meaningless. Catherine's death is the romantic basis of Hemingway's novel. Had she not died, their intensely isolating love might have disintegrated as in "A Very Short Story." Even by the end of their short sojourn in Switzerland, they have feared each other's restlessness. Catherine has already threatened to cut her hair after the child's birth to become a "fine, new and different girl for you." Without Catherine's death, the shorn Catherine and Lieutenant Henry, both finally disillusioned in love as well as in war, might very well have become the hero and heroine of Hemingway's *The Sun Also Rises.*

In Hemingway's third volume of short stories, *Winner Take Nothing*, the defeat of man in the modern world has become even more violent. Suicide, castration, shell shock and homosexuality are all of them the effect of modern reality upon man. In one of the stories, "The Gambler, the Nun and the Radio," everything, even the basic fact of bread, becomes an illusion and an opiate.

The first story, "After the Storm," sets the mood for the whole volume. Certainly, this story of a sea-scavenger who finds a wreck but cannot break it open for its treasures, is the example of a winner who gets nothing as his prize. Here again one of the most interesting things about the story is the author's use of the woman. After a night of violence in a café, the protagonist escapes in his boat out into the storm-wracked Gulf of Mexico. There he finds the wreck of a pleasure cruiser and tries to loot it. While trying to break into a porthole, he sees the body of a beautiful woman with long, flowing hair. He is, however, never able to break into the porthole although he tries several times. Considering the woman, the physical properties of a porthole, and the violent exhaustion after each attempt, it is not difficult to interpret this story on a level of sexual frustration, an inability to reach the true female partner.

In relation to the problem, another story "The Sea Change" is even more revealing. Here a modern woman, tweed-suited, hair bobbed and living in postwar Paris, wants permission from the man who loves her to leave him for a lesbian affair (an obvious indication of her loss of womanliness). When the man gives his permission and accepts the fact that he will take her back afterwards, he too becomes changed, "as he looked in the glass, he saw he was really quite a different looking man. The other two at the bar moved down to make room for him." The sea change is the modern world which has remolded the woman, and through her the man, into something different from what they were intended to be.

In contrast with the rest of the stories of the book, the last one expresses a search for new roots. To do this, Hemingway returns to Nick Adams whose autobiographical associations are unmistakable. Nick, traveling through the United States by car with his son, thinks back on his old relationship with his father and to the one satisfying sexual relationship of the volume. This is an adolescent union with a little Indian girl who is submissive and devoid of any real individual personality.

Hemingway's preoccupation with disillusion and tragedy has made him one of the most important spokesmen for the Lost Generation. However, by the middle Thirties, the Lost Generation was a thing of the past. Those who had not destroyed themselves or turned to the Church, had discovered politics. They had anchored themselves to the class struggle and were growing vicarious roots in the proletariat. With his novel *To Have and Have Not*, Hemingway officially joined the class struggle. In this novel, it is the rich alone who are impotent and perverted. Dorothy Hollis is the female crystallization of the sexual decay and meaninglessness of the rich. Her sleep depends on drugs and her sexual satisfaction on masturbation. For Hemingway she is the result of a way of life rather than a vicious personality, and in her soliloquy at the end of the novel she finds she can blame neither herself nor the men who love her for the frustration of her life: "I suppose we all end up as bitches but whose fault is it."

Marie Morgan, Harry Morgan's wife in *To Have and Have Not*, is of the real proletariat, although flagrantly misinterpreted by Richard Gordon, a writer in the novel, who writes of a stereotyped class struggle and toadies to the rich. Marie and her husband experience a real and complete relationship. There is between them a loyalty, respect, and virility that to a certain extent remains with Marie even after the death of her husband, who has learned his lesson of brotherhood too late. Marie, although socially a completely different woman from Brett, is not as far removed from the heroine of *The Sun Also Rises* as she seems at first glance. She has bobbed hair which she has dyed blonde. She wears a mannish felt hat and is approximately the age that Brett would have been by the middle Thirties. Marie has found in her husband a complete man and for him she has given up a former life of promiscuity. At one point in the book, she has started to let her hair grow, but Harry persuades her that it is not necessary.

Hemingway's next expression of this political conversion and its sexual levels is in his play *The Fifth Column*, published in 1938. This is the account of Philip Rawlings, who, although ostensibly a gay, uninvolved onlooker in Spain, is, by night, an active, dedicated and hunted comrade. The play centers about a love affair with Dorothy, a vain, empty and useless daughter of the American middle class, whom Philip finally renounces for a Moorish tart as more in keeping with his political convictions. This renunciation gains added meaning from Hemingway's statement in the preface that Dorothy's name "might also have been nostalgia." It is evident from this characterization of Dorothy that Hemingway, in *The Fifth Column*, has begun to symbolize the enemy class by wealthy and unsatisfied American women as he previously ascribed all sexual perversions and incapacities to the rich in *To Have and Have Not.*

In two of the short stories that were published at the same time as *The Fifth Column*, the same associations are made. In *The Short Happy Life of Francis Macomber*, Mrs. Macomber in her "American female cruelty" is secure if unhappy with a coward for a husband. Their relation is one of antagonistic convenience rather than love. At the end of the story, when Macomber regains his courage (and manliness), Mrs. Macomber shoots him rather than lose her dominating role. In "The Snows of Kilimanjaro" a dying writer, regretting his still unwritten works, reflects on his past life to try to discover where it lost its purpose and fulfillment. He is married to a wife who is sexually satisfying, but whom he does not love. The story searches back into the writer's life for understanding and meaning and becomes nostalgic for former days, days of comradeship in poverty. Although he blames his own desires and his loss of touch with the world for his present empty state, he cannot hide a growing antagonism toward his wealthy wife, in spite of her consideration and comfort. A "kindly caretaker" of his body, she has nevertheless become for him a symbol of the destruction of his talent.

Finally in *For Whom the Bell Tolls,* Hemingway has recreated Catherine Barkley in the form of Maria, with one important difference—her political convictions. Maria is submissive and without individual personality; altogether, as Edmund Wilson pointed out, an "amoebic" creature. But Hemingway has no antagonism toward her, actually she is his first wholly affirmative heroine. This is possible only because in ascribing negativeness to a certain type of wealthy dominating woman, Hemingway is able to destroy an ambivalent attitude that existed in both *A Farewell to Arms* and *The Sun Also Rises.* Catherine, for all her womanliness, was the ultimate ruin of Lieutenant Henry through her isolating love. Brett, essentially a desexed and destructive force, was nevertheless a tragic and honorable woman. Maria, as a daughter of the proletariat instead of the destructive rich, is allowed a complete affirmativeness. The love relationship between Maria and Robert Jordan is not only completely satisfying but strengthening, as it is of the social conflict rather than in opposition to it. Catherine's love in *A Farewell to Arms* lived as a thing apart from the war and when Lieutenant Henry turned his back on society and isolated himself in Catherine's arms, he decided his own tragedy. Maria, in contrast, strengthens and inspires her lover for his social service and at the conclusion of the novel neither his love nor his convictions are betrayed.

Pilar is a problem of courage rather than sex, but even she is a symbol of emotional and instinctive courage rather than intellectual bravery.

Hemingway, with his treatment of women as wholly sexual beings, would conceive of the female components of courage in such anti-intellectual terms. Maria is symbolically the daughter of Pilar, who had rescued the girl and nursed her back to health. Maria is, however, also Pilar's vicarious youth, almost as if Pilar, who has become desexed with age, had recreated her sexual youth by identification with the young girl.

Robert Jordan follows the pattern of the author's virile heroes, disdaining even what Kinsey would call normal variations. Although considered by a Russian friend to be of "slight political development," he is convinced of the need to unify for battle and the importance of the Spanish struggle in the future world. Falling in love with Maria while on an assignment for the Loyalists behind the Fascist lines is not Jordan's first affair; but it is his first complete sexual and spiritual relationship, as all others have ended "meaningless." Only with an entirely affirmative mate is this possible.

Maria, as the author's third major heroine, has completed a cycle of womanhood. Catherine, who was a long-haired and affirmative woman, died. Brett who bobbed her hair lost her womanhood. Maria's hair, however, was shaved by the Fascists (as much a violation as her rape) and she was already letting her hair grow long again before she met Jordan.

With the Hemingway heroine returned to a womanly role and intricately related to affirmative political convictions as well, *For Whom the Bell Tolls* can and does become an affirmative book. Thus, if his women and his sexual symbols are at all valid criteria, Ernest Hemingway has, within the frame of the two world wars, turned from love to emptiness and back again to love.

But the final love, for a sexually affirmative woman and buttressed by a social consciousness, is no longer made vulnerable or nullified by its isolation and antagonism toward society.

The Works of Ernest Hemingway

1923: THREE STORIES AND TEN POEMS. Limited edition of 300 copies, bound in wrappers. (Dijon)

1924: IN OUR TIME. Published in Paris. Enlarged edition published in New York, 1925. An additional story is contained in the 1930 edition published in New York.

1926: THE TORRENTS OF SPRING.

1926: TODAY IS FRIDAY. Limited edition of 300 copies, bound in wrappers. (Englewood, N. J.)

1926: THE SUN ALSO RISES.

1927: MEN WITHOUT WOMEN.

1929: A FAREWELL TO ARMS.

1932: DEATH IN THE AFTERNOON.

1933: GOD REST YOU MERRY GENTLEMEN. Limited edition of 300 copies.

1933: WINNER TAKE NOTHING.

1935: GREEN HILLS OF AFRICA.

1937: TO HAVE AND HAVE NOT.

1938: THE SPANISH EARTH.

1938: THE FIFTH COLUMN AND THE FIRST FORTY-NINE STORIES.

1940: FOR WHOM THE BELL TOLLS.

1942: MEN AT WAR. Edited by Ernest Hemingway.

1950: ACROSS THE RIVER AND INTO THE TREES.

Reprint Editions: THE SUN ALSO RISES (Novels of Distinction and Modern Library); A FAREWELL TO ARMS (Charles Scribner's Sons, Modern Library, Novels of Distinction); MEN WITHOUT WOMEN (The Living Library); SHORT STORIES (Modern Library Giant); THE PORTABLE HEMINGWAY, Edited by Malcolm Cowley, Viking Press); TO HAVE AND HAVE NOT (Novels of Distinction).